Liquid and Dry Measure Equivalents

a pinch = slightly less than ¼ teaspoon

a dash = a few drops

3 teaspoons = 1 tablespoon

2 tablespoons = 1 ounce

1 jigger = 3 tablespoons

8 tablespoons = ½ cup = 4 ounces

2 cups = 1 pint = 1 pound*

4 cups = 32 ounces = 2 pints = 1 quart

4 quarts = 1 gallon

8 quarts (dry) = 1 peck

4 pecks (dry) = 1 bushel

Dry ingredients measured in cups will vary in weight.

Flour (unsifted)

Spoons and cups	Ounces
1 tablespoon	¼ ounce
¼ cup (4 tablespoons)	1¼ ounces
⅓ cup (5 tablespoons)	1½ ounces
½ cup	2½ ounces
⅔ cup	3¼ ounces
¾ cup	3½ ounces
1 cup	5 ounces
1½ cups	7½ ounces
2 cups	10 ounces
3½ cups	16 ounces (1 pound)

Note: 1 cup sifted flour = 1 cup unsifted flour minus 1½ tablespoons.

Granulated Sugar

Spoons and cups	Ounces
1 teaspoon	⅙ ounce
1 tablespoon	½ ounce
¼ cup (4 tablespoons)	1¾ ounces
⅓ cup (5 tablespoons)	2¼ ounces
½ cup	3½ ounces
⅔ cup	4½ ounces
¾ cup	5 ounces
1 cup	7 ounces (6¾ ounces)
1½ cups	9¾ ounces
2 cups	13½ ounces

ALSO BY MARION CUNNINGHAM

The Fannie Farmer Cookbook
(twelfth edition)

The Breakfast Book

The Fannie Farmer Baking Book

The Fannie Farmer Cookbook
(thirteenth edition)

The Supper Book

Cooking with Children

Learning to Cook with Marion Cunningham

Learning to Cook with Marion Cunningham

with photographs by Christopher Hirsheimer

ALFRED A. KNOPF   NEW YORK   1999

THIS IS A BORZOI BOOK
PUBLISHED BY ALFRED A. KNOPF, INC.

Copyright © 1999 by Marion Cunningham
Photographs © 1999 by Christopher Hirsheimer

www.randomhouse.com

Knopf, Borzoi Books, and the colophon are registered trademarks
of Random House, Inc.

Library of Congress Cataloging-in-Publication Data
Cunningham, Marion.
Learning to cook with Marion Cunningham / by Marion Cunningham ;
with photographs by Christopher Hirsheimer.
p.   cm.
Includes index.
ISBN 0-375-40118-0
1. Cookery.   I. Title.
TX651.C86   1999
641.5—dc21   98-31102
CIP

Manufactured in the United States of America
First Edition

This book is dedicated to my beginning cooks,
Julie Scharmer, Pat Teabeau, David Laudenat, Jamie Jobb,
and Summer Dawn. They taught me how a newcomer
feels about tackling the rudiments of cooking,
and what made it easy and what made it hard to learn.
Without their input I couldn't have written this book.
Even though they have graduated—with honors—
I hope we will continue to cook together
and share our efforts at the table.

Contents

Acknowledgments

My lasting appreciation to the following friends who have given their time and talent so generously to this book.

Bill Hughes, who worked tirelessly to correct and complete this book.

Betsy Feitchmeir, who went over every page and made corrections.

Doe Coover, my literary agent, who brought good ideas to the book.

Thank you to those who helped with the writing: Bill Staggs, Katie Morford, and John Hudspeth for his generous efforts.

And to all the students who took classes here every Saturday.

A special thank-you to Bill Coulis for pointing out to me that there was a great need for a cookbook that could be understood by beginners.

It was a joy to work with Christopher Hirsheimer on the photographs for this book. Her keen eye and her understanding of the simplicity of home cooking are expressed in all the pictures she took.

Last, a deep appreciation to my editor, Judith Jones, who has given the book so much time and effort.

WITH ALL THE HUNDREDS OF cookbooks flooding the market and the procession of cooking shows available to us, you might well ask: "Why is there a need for a book on learning to cook?"

I have become increasingly aware in recent years of the fact that very few people are really cooking at home. There are all kinds of reasons given—lack of time, other demands at the family dinner hour, anxiety about wasting ingredients not eaten up, the ease of eating in a restaurant, the lure of take-out foods. But the main reason nobody's in the kitchen, I began to suspect, was that people today are uneasy about cooking. They don't enjoy it, and many actually fear it. And that is very troubling to me, because I feel they are missing one of the greatest pleasures in life.

Only a few years ago I did a book called *Cooking with Children* because I sensed there was a genuine need for a cookbook that took children seriously, a book that taught them through doing—lesson by lesson—the basics of good home cooking. So few young people have a mother or aunt or grandmother bustling around the kitchen, so they aren't learning by osmosis, by watching and smelling and tasting, as most of my generation did. In preparation for writing that book, I spent many hours giving classes to youngsters from about age six to eleven, so that I could observe them at work and find out just what they needed to know. It was such a rewarding experience, watching those youngsters throw themselves fearlessly into mixing, measuring, kneading, and beating, and they loved every minute of it.

But teaching children is vastly different from teaching adults, I soon learned. As we grow up, we accumulate a lot of baggage, and we become apprehensive about learning new skills. I realized that in myself when I bought a laptop computer, hoping to join the modern world, but I was so thrown by all the new terminology that I quickly went back to the comfort of my old typewriter.

Just after the children's book was out, I had a chance encounter with a doctor I met at a resort. We started talking about cooking, which—not surprisingly—is my favorite subject, and he told me he wanted to learn to cook. He had bought several cookbooks to get started, but he quickly became discouraged, because the recipe directions assumed he knew much more than he did. What did "dredge," "sear," and "blanch" mean? And how are you supposed to "fold" flimsy egg whites into a "batter"? When he finally asked me if I could write a recipe that he could understand, I felt challenged.

So I gathered together a group of adult students, people from their early twenties to retirement age who didn't know the first thing about cooking, and we started to meet every Saturday in my home kitchen. I would give them one of my recipes that I thought was written in simple language, and together we would work out what they understood and what they didn't. Many of their questions were basic: how do you hold an onion when you are trying to cut it up, how high is "medium heat," how to tell when an expensive piece of fish, which you don't want to ruin, is properly cooked, or how to have all the elements of a meal—meat, potatoes, vegetables—come out on time.

At that same time, I learned from them what their anxieties were, what the feelings were that had scared them away from cooking, or were drawing them to it. I remember one middle-aged man who had joined our group because he felt his wife was having all the fun cooking, and he wanted to get in the kitchen for a change. He couldn't believe how simple it had been to roast a chicken with the potatoes and carrots and onions in the same pan so that everything was ready at once (and only one pan to clean up). When we sat down to lunch after the class and he took his first bite of each ingredient, he was so thrilled with the result that he said he couldn't wait to go home that night and make the very same meal for his wife.

As I cooked with these eager but anxious learners, they talked about the difficulties of shopping, finding their way around a supermarket and buying the right products. One student told me how a recipe she was doing called for "soft butter," and how she searched in vain in the dairy section for it. Another assumed that because green onions are called just that, she should use only the green part and throw away the white. They all worried about how much to buy for each meal, what would keep and what wouldn't. They wanted to learn ways to make cooking work for them, to learn how to think—as home cooks always have—about cooking for the week ahead, about deliberately cooking enough to have leftovers on hand so that they could be used again for simple, good meals. When we talked about roasting two chickens at once, one for the evening dinner and one for other dishes later in the week, everyone had that same "Why didn't I think of that?" reaction.

It is now two years since I started those Saturday classes, and this book has taken shape as a result of the experience. I have tried to put together recipes that I have proved will answer the needs of the beginning adult cook, dishes that I know can be done without any experience in the kitchen, and that will turn out well and taste good. I believe they are written in language that the troubled doctor I met will understand, and throughout there are references to basic techniques, so that if you are not familiar with them you can check back and get all the help you need. Most important, there are lots of recipes that will just give you pleasure to master—the kinds of things that make a meal. There is nothing, for instance, like having a good Baking Powder Biscuit fresh from the oven at suppertime. I remember seeing the delight on my students' faces when they first looked into the oven window and saw the golden puffy biscuits they had made from blobs of dough just ten minutes before. They were every bit as fascinated, and as pleased with their efforts, as the children in my earlier classes had been looking at their first biscuits through that very window.

Every time we cooked, we sat down around my dining-room table and looked at the results of our lessons. Cooking in my kitchen, then enjoying each other's company over a home-cooked meal, helped introduce (or re-introduce) these adult beginners to the social pleasures of cooking and eating together, pleasures that are often missing in busy lives. They tell me how they learned that going home at the end of the day, after busy work pressures, to a quiet time of cooking can be the best kind of therapy. That feeling is one of the best gifts that cooking at home can give us, and I hope that all of you using these recipes and sitting down to enjoy a meal with your friends, family, or even alone will find the same kind of satisfaction.

◆

Learning to Cook with
Marion Cunningham

◆

Five Simple Truths About Home Cooking

◆

IF IT IS REALLY SO DIFFICULT to learn to cook, how did all those early pioneer women manage to cross the country in rugged covered wagons and feed troops of people from one big pot hung over an open fire? Today it's so easy to equip a kitchen and turn out a simple meal. You *can* learn to cook! And, believe it or not, you'll probably come to enjoy it.

Here are some simple truths that will help you along the way:

1. Always read through a recipe and check to see that you have all the ingredients you need before you begin. For some reason people don't like to do this, but it will save you time and energy and anxiety if you have all your ingredients at hand before you start.

2. Decide what you are going to make for the complete meal and see if there is anything you can do ahead, such as preparing your dessert, or making the salad dressing and washing the greens. Then figure out what parts of the dinner are going to take longest and determine when you should start the preparations. If there are unfamiliar techniques involved in a recipe, read the introductory material and the instructions carefully, so that you'll understand every step. In the case of this book, read any relevant sidebars that give fuller explanations of techniques, such as how to cut up an onion or separate an egg.

3. The most important habit you can develop (and somehow most home cooks don't do it) is to taste as you are preparing something. Take a sample and taste it critically at different stages of the cooking, then "correct the seasonings," as recipe instructions often put it. What you want to achieve is a balance of flavors. Haven't you often tasted something you are prepared to enjoy and found it disappointingly flat? Then suddenly a shake of the salt cellar makes it come alive.

Actually, there are only four tastes: sweet, sour, salty, and bitter. You won't encounter them necessarily all at once, but if your food seems lacking you'll know that it needs heightening and balancing out in one of those directions. Think of making a glass of lemonade, where the balance between sour (acid lemon juice) and sweet (sugar) is critical. If you get it right, the drink is pleasing.

The only way to learn this all-important aspect of cooking is to keep tasting and figure out just what's needed. It will make the difference between a mediocre and a delectable dish.

4. I often hear this complaint from home cooks: "I don't mind cooking but I hate the mess afterwards." But that's just a result of poor planning—of leaving everything to the end, letting the mess pile up, and allowing food to harden on your utensils so that everything is difficult to get clean.

When I was teaching children how to cook, the first lesson they learned was: "Wash your hands and fill a big friendly bowl with sudsy hot water." Well, the lesson wasn't just for children. I wouldn't be without that bowl of sudsy water in my sink.

It's so simple. As you are going along, just drop every utensil and pot you've used into that bowl. Then, when everything has soaked a few minutes, wash it up, rinse, and let drain while you continue your cooking.

Train yourself to practice this habit and you'll end up with a clean kitchen.

5. It is hard to know how much food can comfortably serve how many people. If your friends and family members are over forty-five years old, they will probably eat about half of what teenagers can put away.

My rule of thumb is, when in doubt, cook more than you think you may need. One of the joys of home cooking anyway is having leftovers for the nights when you come home tired and want to fix something quick and simple. Home cooks don't think of one recipe at a time but of what may be needed throughout the week, and those treasures in the refrigerator can provide inspiration for another meal.

Beginners' Essential Kitchen Tools

◆

THE FOLLOWING LIST of kitchen equipment will serve your basic needs in preparing, cooking, and baking all the recipes in this book. As you graduate into cooking more and varying your repertoire, you will slowly add to this beginning list.

I have not included fairly expensive electric equipment, such as a food processor, a blender, or a standing mixer. But you might want to invest in a mini–food processor and a hand-held electric mixer just to make chopping, mixing, and whipping quicker and easier.

2-cup saucepan with lid

2-quart saucepan with lid

6-quart saucepan with lid

8-inch frying pan with lid

10- or 12-inch sauté pan with lid
(A sauté pan is a straight-sided heavy-bottomed pan about 2½ to 3 inches deep. See box, page 105, for definition of sautéing.)

12-by-17-inch roasting pan
(You need a good-size one for cooking vegetables alongside a roast.)

8-cup ovenproof casserole

Paring knife

7-to-8-inch chef's knife

Bread knife with serrated edge

Plastic or wooden chopping board

2 rubber spatulas: one small and one standard-size

Metal spatula

Wooden spoon

Large metal spoon

Stainless-steel slotted spoon

2 wire-mesh strainers: one 3-inch round, one 7-inch round

Colander

Flat hand-grater

Citrus juicer

Soup ladle

Potato masher

Tweezers (great for removing small fish bones)

Roasting thermometer (The one with the large face that you insert in the meat before cooking. The smaller instant-read thermometers, which you insert in different parts of the meat at the end of cooking for a quick reading, are very accurate, but too often beginners have been known to leave them in the oven and they melt. So play it safe.)

Bottle opener

Can opener

Set of measuring spoons:
1 tablespoon, 1 teaspoon, ½ teaspoon, ¼ teaspoon

1- and 2-cup measuring cups with spout

1- and 2-cup jars with screw-on lids

8-inch wire whisk

For baking:

1-quart mixing bowl (in stainless steel, ceramic, or glass)

3-quart mixing bowl (I prefer Pyrex, because you can see through it and it is inexpensive and sturdy.)

8 small Pyrex cups (generally useful but particularly handy if you make popovers)

12-cup muffin pan

8-inch round cake pan

9-inch round cake pan

8-by-8-by-2-inch (deep) cake or baking dish

9-by-13-by-2-inch (deep) baking dish

2 baking sheets with rims

Waffle iron (if you plan to make waffles)

Set of dry measuring cups:
¼ cup, ⅓ cup, ½ cup, and 1 cup (usually metal with level tops, so you can level off dry inredients to measure accurately)

Large wooden rolling pin (a heavy one will do a much better job—about 17 inches long, with ball bearings, and weighing about 5 pounds)

Eggbeater

2 wire cake racks

2-inch cookie cutter

Toothpicks (for testing doneness of baked goods)

◆

Appetizers/Odds & Ends

◆

INTRODUCTION

———

APPETIZERS OFTEN USED to be fancy, and home cooks would spend more time creating artistic finger food than preparing the dinner. Thank goodness those days are gone. My motto is, keep your appetizers simple. They are only little bites to enjoy while having a drink, waiting for dinner. And if you are rushed and have no time to fix anything, serve salted nuts and/or olives. They are always welcome. Make use of leftover sauces such as the Creamy Garlic Dressing (page 237) or Green Sauce (page 223) by serving them with carrots, zucchini, and/or celery sticks as a dip.

But here I do offer for special occasions a few simple recipes, which always seem to make a hit.

RECIPES

———

SMOKED SALMON TOASTS

ONION SANDWICHES

STUFFED CHERRY TOMATOES

TINY RED ROASTED POTATOES WITH ROSEMARY

DEVILED EGGS

Smoked Salmon Toasts

MOKED SALMON HAS a wonderful flavor, and is often served around the holidays as a special treat. Even though it is much more expensive than fresh salmon, a little goes such a long way that it probably balances out. Smoked Salmon Toasts are an example of an easy party food; these finger-size pieces are delicious served with drinks.

6 slices rye bread

1 8-ounce package cream cheese

1 teaspoon fresh or 1 teaspoon dried dill

8 ounces smoked salmon, thinly sliced

1 lemon

Making the Salmon Toasts

- Trim the crust off the bread.
- Toast the bread. Spread each slice of toasted rye bread with about 3 tablespoons of cream cheese. If using fresh dill, remove the feathery green leaves from the stem and chop them into small pieces. If using dried dill, crumble it into tiny bits.
- Sprinkle the dill over the cream cheese. Place the thin slices of smoked salmon over the cream cheese and dill.
- Cut the lemon into quarters, and squeeze a few drops of lemon juice over each toast. Cut each slice of toast lengthwise into 4 pieces and serve.

24 FINGER-SIZE PIECES

◆

USING DRIED HERBS

Dried herbs often have a stronger flavor than fresh herbs, but not always. Dried herbs age in their jars and with time their flavor fades. The best way to find out if a dried herb is still flavorful is to taste it. Hold a little of the herb on your tongue for a few seconds so the warm moisture of your mouth brings out the flavor, and if it seems like sawdust, throw it out.

◆

■ USING AND STORING FRESH HERBS ■

Fresh herbs are readily available in most markets these days, and they are always nice to use. But they can be expensive, and they have a short life span. Moreover, you have to buy a good-size bunch when your recipe may call for just a few sprigs. So it is important to store fresh herbs carefully and use them up (they always add something special to eggs or a salad).

To clean, gently rinse the bunch of fresh herbs under cold water. Shake to get rid of excess water, or put into a salad spinner, if you have one, and spin dry. To store, take a paper towel, dampen it lightly with cold water, and loosely wrap the herbs in the dampened towel, then put it into a plastic bag. Don't squeeze all the air out—the herbs need to breathe to stay fresh. Refrigerate.

Onion Sandwiches

THESE LITTLE ROUND SANDWICHES with their parsley-green edges will amaze you. They taste just as good as they look. The best part is that they are made with ordinary white bread, yellow onion, mayonnaise, and parsley. They are perfect to serve for the winter holidays, stacked on a pretty platter, or just serve them any time with drinks.

10 thin slices white bread	¾ cup mayonnaise
1 large yellow onion	¼ teaspoon salt
½ bunch parsley	

Cutting the Bread

- Trim off the crust with a knife.
- Using a 2-inch round cookie cutter, cut out 2 circles of bread from each slice.

Making the Sandwiches

- Peel the onion and slice it very thin (for full details, see opposite).
- Cut the sliced onion with the cookie cutter, making onion rounds the same size as the bread.
- Rinse the parsley and pat dry.
- Remove and discard the stems from the parsley and finely chop the leaves (for details, see box). You should have about ½ cup.
- Spread each round of bread generously with mayonnaise. On half the rounds, place a very thin slice of onion round and sprinkle it lightly with salt.
- Set another round of bread on top of the onion—making a bread-onion-bread sandwich.
- Put the remaining mayonnaise on one small plate and the chopped parsley on another.
- Roll the edges of the sandwiches first in mayonnaise and then in parsley, so you will have a charming little white round sandwich with bright-green parsley edges.
- Arrange the little rounds on a platter and serve.

◆

HOW TO CHOP PARSLEY

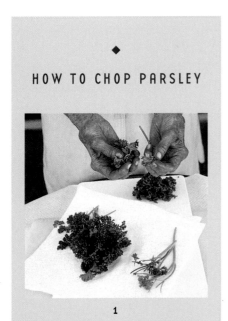

1

After rinsing and drying the parsley, 1) remove the leaves and discard the stems. 2) Make a dense little pile of the leaves, holding them together with your fingers, and chop the parsley with a large sharp knife. Continue to chop until the parsley is cut into tiny pieces.

2

HOW TO PEEL, SLICE, AND CHOP AN ONION

2

TO PEEL: Using a paring knife, slice off the fuzzy brownish root end and the stem top of the onion and discard. 1) Peel off the papery outer brownish-yellow skin of the onion with your fingers or a paring knife, and discard.

TO SLICE AN ONION:
2) Cut the onion in half from stem top to root end. Put the onion halves cut side down on a cutting board. 3) Cut slices crosswise from each half. The thickness will depend on how you plan to use it, but ⅛ inch thick is usually about right. As you slice, curl under the ends of the fingers of your hand holding the onion, so that you don't cut yourself; move your hand back on the onion after each slice.

TO CHOP AN ONION: Slice the onion in half from the stem top through the root end. Place each half flat side down on a cutting board. Holding a half firmly with one hand, make about 7 vertical slices into the onion, from the end to the root end, but don't slice completely through the root end (this will make it easier to slice). 4) Next, slice crosswise, letting the little pieces fall. Repeat with the remaining half of the onion.

1

4

3

Stuffed Cherry Tomatoes

16 TO 20 APPETIZERS

THESE ARE TINY COUSINS of the BLT sandwich—minus the bread. You can put them together in no time at all, and they disappear just as quickly at a party. They hold up well even if you prepare them a day ahead of time. If you make these ahead and refrigerate them, let them warm to room temperature before serving.

4 strips bacon	½ cup mayonnaise
1 pound cherry tomatoes	

Cooking the Bacon

- Separate the bacon slices and put them side by side in a skillet, not overlapping. Turn the heat to medium.
- When the bacon fat (the white part) begins to brown, turn the slices over with a fork. When the white fat becomes completely brown on the second side, the bacon is cooked.
- Remove the bacon from the pan with a fork and put it on a paper towel. Using a second paper towel, pat the top of the bacon to mop up any excess fat. Set aside.

Assembling the Appetizer

- Rinse the tomatoes and pat dry.
- Using a sharp knife, cut off the top quarter of each tomato, including the stem, and discard. With a small spoon scoop out and discard a little of the tomato, leaving a small, rounded cavity to fill.
- Crumble the cooked bacon into a bowl with your fingers—you want small bits, about the size of Rice Krispies.
- Add mayonnaise and stir with a spoon until well mixed.
- Scoop up about a teaspoon of the mayonnaise and bacon and fill the cavity of each tomato.
- Arrange the tomatoes on a plate or small platter. If you make these in advance, cover with plastic wrap and refrigerate until serving time.

Tiny Red Roasted Potatoes with Rosemary

THIS IS A TERRIFIC SMALL TREAT to pass at parties with drinks, or to serve with a roast chicken or roast pork for dinner. As a party food, it is easy for guests standing up to eat them without spilling. The potatoes also make good picnic fare. If you make them ahead and refrigerate them, bring them up to room temperature before serving.

4 pounds tiny red potatoes (about 60), about 1 inch in diameter, unpeeled

4 tablespoons fresh rosemary leaves, or 2 tablespoons

crumbled dried rosemary leaves; plus rosemary branches for garnish

¼ cup olive oil

1 tablespoon kosher salt

Preheat oven to 375°F.

Preparing and Roasting the Potatoes

- Rinse the potatoes in a colander and allow to dry, or pat dry with paper towels.
- If using fresh rosemary, remove the needlelike leaves from the fresh rosemary branches, and chop them very fine.
- Put the potatoes in a roasting pan and add the olive oil, salt, and chopped rosemary or crumbled dried rosemary. Using your hands, roll the potatoes in the olive oil, salt, and rosemary so they are all well coated, and spread them out in a single layer.
- Bake in the oven for 30 minutes. Check to see if the potatoes are done; when a fork easily pierces the center of a potato, they are ready. If not, bake 5 or 10 minutes longer and test again.
- Serve warm or at room temperature on a platter, surrounded by fresh rosemary branches, if you have them.

◆

KOSHER SALT

Kosher salt is a coarse-grain salt. It is favored by many cooks who like the coarseness and the taste better than the finer-grained table salt. On these potatoes, it adds a little crunch, which is pleasing.

◆

Deviled Eggs

LESS IS BEST with Deviled Eggs. Some people add all kinds of flavors to the mashed yolks, but they taste best with just mayonnaise and mustard. It's surprising how good deviled eggs are served with drinks.

4 large eggs	¼ teaspoon salt
3 tablespoons mayonnaise	¼ teaspoon black pepper
1 teaspoon Dijon mustard	

Preparing the Filling
- Hard-boil the eggs and remove the shells.
- Slice the eggs in half lengthwise. Scoop the yolks out into a small bowl, and mash with a fork until smooth like a paste.
- Add the mayonnaise, mustard, salt, and pepper and stir until blended and creamy.

Stuffing the Egg Whites
- Spoon equal amounts of the yolk filling into the hollows of the egg whites.
- Serve on a platter.

■

HOW TO HARD-BOIL EGGS

Put the number of eggs you want to hard-boil in a saucepan and pour in enough water to cover them by about 2 inches. Set the saucepan over high heat, and when the water comes to a boil, turn the heat to simmer and cook the eggs 20 minutes. Remove the pan from the stove, take it to the sink, and tilt it to pour off the hot water, then run cold water over the eggs for a few seconds. Pour all the water off and let the eggs cool until you can handle them. To shell the eggs, lightly tap each one gently all over to crack the shell, then peel it off.

Hard-boiled eggs can quell hunger pangs. Boil several extra for a quick snack. They keep for 2 weeks in their shell and refrigerated.

■

◆

Soup for Supper

◆

INTRODUCTION

LEARN TO THINK of soup for supper as the main dish. Soup is easy to make, which is why the early settlers served it most of the time for dinner, often tossing in old chunks of leftover bread to give it heft. Look carefully in your refrigerator for any leftovers. We often have the makings of good soup and don't even know it. The other day I chopped up 3 raw strips of hickory-smoked bacon, added some canned beans, a chopped onion, and a bay leaf to a pot, and simmered these rather ordinary ingredients together in water for 20 minutes. And what a good soup it was. So use the recipes in this chapter as a guide and add your own improvisations. You often have treasures you don't recognize.

RECECIPES

RECIPES

SIMPLE VEGETABLE SOUP

GOOD OL' CHICKEN SOUP

LEEK AND POTATO SOUP

QUICK TOMATO STEW

SPLIT PEA SOUP

TUNA AND CORN CHOWDER

BEST BLACK BEAN SOUP

MEXICAN LENTIL SOUP

MEXICAN CORN SOUP

OVEN ONION SOUP

Simple Vegetable Soup

8 CUPS

THIS SOUP IS like a painter's canvas. You can be creative, trying different vegetables that you may have on hand. Make this soup the first time just as the recipe reads. Then try using parsnips and/or turnips and/or leeks or whatever. As long as you chop the pieces of vegetable small, the soup will still cook in 20 minutes.

1 medium-size yellow onion	½ bunch spinach (about 2 cups leaves)
2 carrots	2 tablespoons butter
2 stalks celery (see box, page 23)	8 cups chicken broth, canned or homemade, or 8 cups water
2 medium tomatoes	Salt
2 zucchini	Ground pepper
1 handful of green beans	

Preparing the Vegetables

- Peel and finely chop the onion (for full details, see page 13).
- Peel the carrots; cut off and discard ¼ inch of the rounded stem end. Cut the carrots in half lengthwise, then cut into slices ¼ inch thick.
- Cut off and discard about ½ inch from the root end of the celery stalks. Cut the stalks in half lengthwise, then slice the stalks into ¼-inch slices.
- Chop the tomatoes (for full details, see page 27).
- Cut off and discard about ¼ inch from each end of the zucchini, cut them in half lengthwise, and slice crosswise into ¼-inch pieces.
- Cut off the pointy tips and ends of the green beans and cut them crosswise into 1-inch pieces.
- Rinse the spinach (for full details, see box, page 47). Tear the stems off the leaves, and discard the stems.

Making the Soup

- Melt the butter in a medium-size pot over medium heat, then add the onion, carrots, and celery. Cook, stirring often, for about 5 minutes.
- Add the broth and tomatoes, and simmer for another 10 minutes, then stir in the zucchini and beans and cook for 2 minutes.
- Add the spinach and cook 1 minute more.
- Season with salt and pepper to taste. Serve hot.

◆

SEASONING WITH SALT AND PEPPER

You have probably always known how much salt and pepper you like to add to the food you are eating at the table. It's the same when you're the one doing the cooking. Just remember to add seasonings a bit at a time and taste to avoid overdoing it.

When you are making soups, stews, beans, or any preparation that is cooked a long time in liquid, add less salt to start with than you would normally use, because as liquid cooks it evaporates, so that the salt flavor is intensified as the liquid reduces. At the end of cooking, taste and then add if necessary a little more salt to please your palate.

◆

Good Ol' Chicken Soup

YOUR OWN CHICKEN BROTH will always taste better than the flavor of canned broth, so it is definitely worth making. But there are times when it helps to have canned chicken broth on hand. When you make your own, you have the bonus of cooked pieces of chicken for sandwiches and salads.

1 whole chicken, about 3 to 4 pounds (the larger the chicken, the richer the broth)	3 stalks celery, with leaves (see box, opposite)
	2 bay leaves
8 cups cold water, maybe more	6 peppercorns, or 1 teaspoon ground black pepper
1 onion	2 teaspoons dried thyme
2 carrots	1½ teaspoons salt

Preparing the Chicken

• Remove the giblets from the chicken cavity (see roast chicken recipe on page 96 for details on giblets).

• Rinse the chicken inside and out under cold running water.

Adding Water and Aromatic Vegetables to the Chicken Pot

• Put the chicken in a large pot and add the cold water.

• Peel the papery outer skin from the onion, cut the onion in half, and add it to the pot.

• Rinse the carrots and trim off the stem tops and the end tips. Cut the carrots into 1-inch chunks and add to the pot.

• Cut the celery stalks in half, and add to the pot.

• Tear the bay leaves in half and add to the pot, along with the peppercorns or pepper, plus the dried thyme. Don't add the salt yet.

Cooking the Broth

• Bring the broth to a boil over high heat, then reduce the heat to low so the liquid will just simmer ("simmer" is a word for gentle bubbling). A frothy gray scum will begin to form as the broth cooks.

• Using a large spoon, skim the frothy gray scum off the top of the broth 2 or 3 times and discard during the first 30 minutes of cooking. Clearing away the froth will give you a clean, clear broth.

• Simmer for 1½ hours, then remove the pot from the heat.

■

REMOVING THE COOKED CHICKEN SKIN AND MEAT FROM THE CARCASS

Pull the chicken skin away from the carcass and discard. Using your hands, remove the meat from the bones. The meat should come away easily.

If you are not going to use the chicken meat in the soup right away, put the pieces in a container with a lid and store in the refrigerator for sandwiches or salads. If you don't plan to use the meat within 3 days, wrap it tightly in plastic wrap, then put it in an airtight container and freeze.

■

Finishing the Broth

- Insert a large fork into the chicken cavity and lift the bird up, then tilt it so all the broth runs back into the pot. Put the chicken on a platter to cool a little.
- Set a large bowl in the sink, and place a colander over the bowl. Line the colander with a double layer of paper towels, and pour the broth through the colander into the bowl. Discard the paper towels and vegetables from the colander, and move the bowl from the sink to the counter.
- Add the salt and taste the broth; add more if you like.

Serving the Broth

- Ladle the broth into serving bowls and serve hot.
- If you want a simple supper, cut one half of the breast meat into small pieces and stir them into the broth to be heated through for a minute. Wrap the remaining chicken pieces and refrigerate. They will provide a dandy sandwich or salad, or filling for a taco, or serve cold with Sour Cream Caper Sauce (page 227) and a baked potato.

◆   **STORING CHICKEN BROTH**   ◆

Chicken broth will keep well in the refrigerator in a covered container for 3 days. If you won't be using it in that time, freeze it in a container with a tight-fitting lid. You can also freeze it in small containers so you can have 1 or 2 cups available when you need it. After a few months in the freezer, a broth, like most foods, will lose some of its flavor. As with all soups and broths, you can also bring your 2-day-old refrigerated soup to a boil for a few seconds. That preserves the broth, and you can then refrigerate for another 2 days.

■

CELERY

You always have to buy a full head of celery even though you may need only a few stalks for your recipe. But celery keeps well if loosely wrapped in plastic and stored in the refrigerator. And you can use it all week in salads, soups, and sandwiches, or just have some crisp stalks as a snack before dinner.

To prepare, break off the number of stalks you need and trim off ¼ inch from the bottom. The stalks toward the center—the heart of the celery—are the tenderest for salads or for nibbling, and the outside stalks are fine for soup.

■

Leek and Potato Soup

SERVES FOUR TO SIX

THICK AND CREAMY Leek and Potato Soup can lift drooping spirits. Leeks are part of the onion family. They look like giant scallions and they can vary in size. The recipe makes enough for four people as a main dish, or enough to serve six if accompanied by a sandwich or hearty salad.

2 or 3 leeks (1 pound)
1½ pounds medium-size russet
   potatoes (about 5 potatoes)
4 tablespoons butter
   (½ stick)

6 cups chicken broth, canned or
   homemade (if you don't have
   quite enough, make up the
   difference with water)
Salt to taste

Preparing the Vegetables

- Cut the tops off the leeks where the color begins to turn from very light green to darker green. Cut off the root ends and discard along with the tops.
- Cut the leeks in half lengthwise. Leeks often have dirt lodged in between the layers of the stalks. Separate the layers with your fingers and rinse under cold running water to remove all the dirt.
- Put the leeks on the cutting board and cut crosswise into ¼-inch pieces. You should have about 4 cups—the exact amount is not crucial.
- Peel and rinse the potatoes and cut in half lengthwise. Put halves cut side down on a cutting board and slice crosswise into ¼-inch-thick pieces. You should have about 4 cups.

Making the Soup

- Melt the butter in a heavy-bottomed pot (5-quart capacity, or larger, with a lid) over medium heat, stirring regularly. Tilt the pot from side to side so the butter covers the bottom.
- Add the leeks and potatoes and use a large spoon to distribute the vegetables over the bottom of the pot. Cook for about 5 minutes, stirring occasionally. If the leeks begin to brown, turn the heat down.
- Pour in the chicken broth, adding a little water to make 6 cups if you don't have enough broth, stir, and turn the heat to high. When the liquid boils, turn the heat to low, cover with a lid, and cook for 30 minutes.

• After 30 minutes, check to see if the soup is done by scooping up a piece of potato with a spoon. Let it cool a moment and bite into it. If the potato is soft it is done, so remove the soup from the heat. If it is still a bit firm, continue to cook for another 5 minutes and test again by tasting.

Finishing the Soup

• To make this soup smoother and creamier, mash the pieces of potato. If you have a potato masher, use it to mash until they are almost smooth but handle it gently in the hot broth. Or use a fork, pressing the potatoes against the sides and bottom of the pot until the soup is smooth. As the mashed potatoes mix with the soup, it will become creamy.

• Return the soup to the burner over medium heat. Add salt, about ½ teaspoon at a time, tasting all the while, until it tastes good to you. Serve hot.

■

MANAGING HEAT

The heat on the burners of different stoves can vary. Medium heat on an electric range can be just right for the initial cooking of vegetables in butter and/or oil, for example. But a gas stove is more variable, and you often have to adjust the heat. It is essential to watch what you are cooking and if the vegetables start to brown (unless that is specifically called for), turn the heat down. It is particularly easy to cook finely chopped garlic too quickly, so that it turns brown and takes on a bitter flavor.

■

Quick Tomato Stew

SERVES FOUR THIS IS A CROSS between a soup and a stew that you can make in no time from the pantry. It's the simplest of dishes, and a soothing tonic when life gets the better of you.

3 strips smoky-style bacon
1 medium-size red onion
1 28-ounce can stewed
    tomatoes (3½ cups)
1 5½-ounce can tomato juice
    (⅔ cup)

1½ teaspoons sugar
¾ teaspoon salt
Pepper to taste
2 slices white bread, torn into
    bite-size pieces

Preparing the Bacon and Onion

◆ Stack the 3 strips of bacon, and cut lengthwise into 3 or 4 slices. Cut the long slices crosswise into pieces about ¼ inch square.

◆ Peel the papery skin from the onion and chop (see page 13 for full details).

Cooking the Stew

◆ Put the bacon in a heavy-bottomed pot and set over medium-high heat. Separate the pieces of bacon with a fork, and cook, stirring occasionally, until the bacon is slightly browned. Add the onion, turn the heat to medium-low, and spread the onion over the bottom of the pot. Cook until the onion is soft, about 3 to 5 minutes.

◆ Add the tomatoes (including all the juices in the can), tomato juice, sugar, salt, and pepper, and stir. If the chunks of tomato are large, mash them with a fork as they cook. Cook for another minute or two.

Thickening the Stew

◆ Add the pieces of bread and cook for another 2 or 3 minutes, using a fork to mash the bread into the juices. The bread will absorb lots of juice, and that's what makes this soup so delicious. If it seems too thick, add a little more tomato juice or water—until the consistency is right.

◆ Serve hot, although this dish is also good cold.

HOW TO CHOP A TOMATO ◆

Cut off the stem top and discard.
1) Cut the tomato on a chopping board into about 6 slices.

3) Cut into bite-size pieces. A very ripe tomato can be difficult to cut, so be sure to use a sharp knife or a good serrated-edge knife.

1

2

2) Stack the slices in 2 or 3 piles

3

Split Pea Soup

SPLIT PEA SOUP IS a real comfort food. It is a thick, creamy, light-green soup that tastes nourishing and satisfying. Split peas are peas that have been split in half and dried. If you soak them a few hours before cooking, it will soften them and shorten the cooking time. If you forget to do this, it will take the peas about 1½ hours to simmer and become creamy. If you have some smoked bacon in your freezer, you can use several slices of it, chopped, as the flavoring meat rather than a ham bone or ham shank. Serve this soup with warm rye bread and a baked apple for dessert.

2 medium-size yellow onions	bone with some meat
3 stalks celery, with leaves	attached
(see box, page 23)	2 quarts (8 cups) water
1 pound (2 cups) split green peas	1 teaspoon salt
1½ pounds smoked ham shanks	Freshly ground pepper to taste
or hocks, or a leftover ham	

Preparing the Vegetables

• Peel and chop the onions (for full details, see page 13).

• Break 3 stalks off the celery, rinse, trim the stem ends, and cut the stalks crosswise into 1-inch pieces.

Starting the Soup

• Put the split peas, ham shanks, onions, and celery into a large heavy-bottomed pot, add the water, and set over high heat. Bring to a boil, reduce the heat to low, and add the salt. You want this soup just to simmer.

• Simmer the soup for 1 to 1½ hours, stirring occasionally, then check for doneness. The soup is done when the peas are soft and mushy. Taste, add more salt if needed, and add freshly ground pepper to taste.

Serving the Soup

• Let cool until you can handle the meat, then carefully remove the ham hocks or ham bone from the soup. Discard the bones and any skin, cut the meat into bite-size pieces, and put them back into the soup. Serve very hot in warm soup bowls, and have plenty of freshly ground pepper on the table.

Tuna and Corn Chowder

THIS IS THE PERFECT ANSWER for a satisfying supper when you come home late and tired. Just reach into your "first aid cupboard" and refrigerator, then stir these ingredients together. You will have a delicious chowder in 10 minutes.

8 CUPS

1 12-ounce can white tuna packed in water (found in all supermarkets)	2 cups milk
	2 cups canned creamed corn
	½ teaspoon salt
3 tablespoons butter	Pepper to taste
2 cups chicken broth, canned or homemade	Several sprigs parsley

Making the Soup

♦ Drain the liquid from the tuna and discard.

♦ Put a 3- or 4-quart pot on the stove and add the butter. Turn the heat to medium, and when the butter melts, tilt and turn the pot so the butter completely covers the bottom. Add the drained tuna and, using a fork, break the large chunks of tuna into small pieces. Stir and move the tuna around for about 2 minutes, until all the pieces have absorbed the butter.

♦ Stir in the chicken broth, milk, creamed corn, salt, and pepper, and turn the heat to low. Let the chowder cook about 5 minutes, just enough to get good and hot. Taste, and correct the seasoning, if necessary.

Serving the Soup

♦ Rinse the parsley and pat dry on paper towels. Remove the stems and discard. Finely chop enough parsley to make about 3 tablespoons.

♦ Ladle the chowder into bowls, sprinkle a little parsley over, and serve hot.

Best Black Bean Soup

BLACK BEANS HAVE A rich flavor, and their dramatic color looks striking with white rice or sour cream, red onion or lemon slices. Remember to start soaking the beans the night before you plan to cook them.

1 pound dried black beans (about 2 cups)	3 cloves garlic
	½ cup olive oil
2 to 3 quarts (8 to 12 cups) water	1¼ teaspoons dried oregano
	½ teaspoon black pepper
1½ teaspoons salt	1 small red onion
1 large yellow onion	1 cup sour cream
1 large green bell pepper	

Soaking the Beans and Starting the Cooking

◆ Rinse the dried beans and put them in a large heavy-bottomed pot. Add the water, enough to cover the beans by about 2½ inches. Soak overnight, or for at least 8 hours. This step shortens the cooking time dramatically and makes for tender beans.

◆ Use the same water to cook the beans. The water level will have gone down, so add 2 or 3 cups more, enough to bring the water level to 2½ inches above the beans.

◆ Add 1½ teaspoons salt, and set the pot on a burner turned to high; bring to a boil. When the water boils, turn the heat to medium-low and simmer the beans uncovered for 45 minutes stirring every so often.

Preparing the Vegetables While the Beans Are Cooking

◆ Peel and chop the onion (for full details, see page 13).

◆ Chop the bell pepper into ¼-inch pieces (see box, opposite).

◆ Peel and chop the garlic (see box, page 33).

◆ Heat the olive oil in a large heavy-bottomed skillet over medium heat. Add the onion, green pepper, and garlic. Turn the heat to low—stirring occasionally—cook until tender, about 3 minutes.

◆ Add the vegetables to the beans, then add the oregano and black pepper. Simmer for 1 hour on medium-low heat.

◆ Just before the beans are finished cooking, peel and finely chop the red onion.

Serving the Soup

◆ After the beans and vegetables have simmered for 1 hour, taste for seasoning and add more salt if needed.

◆ To serve, ladle the soup into bowls, put about a tablespoon of sour cream in the middle of the bowl, and sprinkle on some finely chopped red onion.

◆ PREPARING BELL PEPPER ◆

1

1) Slice the stem top and the root bottom off the pepper.

2

2) Cut the pepper in half.

3

3) Open each side up into one long rectangular piece. Remove the seeds and veins with a paring knife and discard.

4

TO SLICE: 4) Stack the rectangles and cut the pepper into strips ¼-inch wide.

TO CHOP: Line the strips up, side by side; then, holding them in a bunch, chop them crosswise into little pieces.

Mexican Lentil Soup

8 CUPS

ONE OF THE CHARMS of lentils is that they need no overnight soaking to tenderize them, as do other dried beans—or legumes, as they are called. Lively and filling, the soup can be ready to eat in just about an hour. And you don't have to watch the pot constantly. Serve it with tortillas you have warmed up by wrapping them snugly in foil and putting them into a 350°F oven for about 15 minutes.

3 cloves garlic	1½ cups dried lentils
1 large yellow onion	1 teaspoon ground cumin seed
2 carrots	1½ teaspoons salt
2 tablespoons olive oil	2 cups store-bought red
6 cups water	tomato Mexican salsa*

Preparing the Vegetables

♦ Peel and mince the garlic (see box, opposite, for full details on chopping garlic).

♦ Peel and chop the onion (see page 13 for full details on cutting up onions).

♦ Peel the carrots, cut them in half lengthwise, and then cut crosswise into ¼-inch-thick pieces.

Cooking the Soup

♦ Put the olive oil into a 4-to-5-quart soup pot and tilt it from side to side so the oil covers the bottom.

♦ Set the pot over medium heat and add the chopped garlic, onion, and carrots. Stir with a spoon to coat the vegetables with oil.

♦ Turn the heat to low and cook the vegetables, stirring occasionally, until they soften (about 5 minutes). Don't let them brown.

♦ Add the water, lentils, cumin, 1 teaspoon of the salt, and the salsa to the pot, and stir. Taste the liquid to see if it has enough salt. If not, add the remaining ½ teaspoon of salt.

♦ Turn the heat to high and bring the soup to a boil. Immediately reduce the heat and simmer the soup, uncovered (see box, page 119, for details on simmering).

♦ Cook for 45 minutes, checking on the soup now and then to make sure it is gently simmering, not boiling. Give the soup a stir.

♦ At the end of 45 minutes, taste a few lentils to see if they are done.

* The fresh salsa sold in the refrigerated section of the supermarket is best.

They should be soft and tender. If so, remove the pot from heat. If the lentils are still a bit firm, continue to cook for another 10 minutes and taste again.

◆ Serve hot.

TO PEEL: 1) First, separate the cloves from a head of garlic. You may need to pound the top of the head with your fist or the flat of a big knife to loosen the cloves.

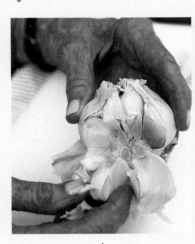

1

2) Using a paring knife, peel the papery skin off each clove.

2

3) TO SLICE: Hold the tip of the garlic clove and with a sharp knife cut it into about 5 slices lengthwise.

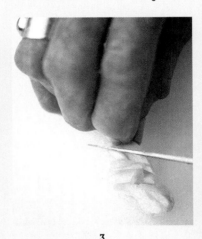

3

4) TO CHOP: Make a pile of the slices and cut through them first horizontally, then vertically.

4

If you sprinkle ½ teaspoon salt on garlic and then finely chop, the salt brings out the juices and the resulting minced pieces will be more readily absorbed as a seasoning. You can also puree the garlic, after you have salted and minced it, by mashing the pieces (*puree* means *mash*) with the flat blade of your knife.

◆ ABOUT CILANTRO ◆

Cilantro (on the right side of the cutting board in the picture below), also called Chinese parsley, is actually the leaves of the coriander plant. It is a favorite flavoring in many Mexican dishes. The taste of cilantro is very different from parsley, which it resembles, and sometimes it takes getting accustomed to before you appreciate it. It is sold in bunches that are usually larger than your needs, so store it as you would parsley (see box on storing herbs, page 11) and use it in guacamole or in a tortilla with sliced avocado, or sprinkle some over sliced tomatoes. It is also chopped the same way as parsley (see box, page 12).

■ ABOUT MASA HARINA

Masa harina is a corn flour made from cooked dried corn that is used in Mexico to make tortillas. It is added to Mexican Corn Soup to give flavor and to thicken the soup. Quaker Oats makes a masa harina that can be found in most supermarkets. Buy the package labeled "Masa Harina" . . . not "Instant Masa Harina." Store it in the refrigerator or freezer.

■

Mexican Corn Soup

THIS IS A SOUP that makes a whole meal. Top it with sour cream, chopped green chilies, and cilantro. Serve it with corn tortillas that you have wrapped in foil and warmed 15 minutes in a 350°F oven.

4 cups fresh corn kernels (about 6 ears), or frozen corn kernels	½ cup water
	½ cup sour cream
	4 to 6 teaspoons chopped green chilies (from a 4-ounce can)
4½ cups milk	
½ teaspoon salt, or to taste	A few sprigs cilantro
2½ tablespoons masa harina	Freshly ground pepper

Preparing Fresh Corn

◆ If using fresh corn, first cut the kernels from the cob with a sharp knife. The best way is to stand the cob upright on a cutting board, with one hand securing the upper end. Using a large sharp knife, cut downward, slicing the kernels from the cob. You'll be surprised how easy this is.

Making the Soup

◆ Put the corn—fresh or frozen—into a heavy-bottomed pot with the milk and salt and set over medium heat. Bring to a boil, reduce to a simmer, and cook gently for 15 minutes.

◆ In a pint (2-cup) jar with a lid, vigorously shake together the masa harina and the water. Add the mixture to the soup, stirring to blend in well and heat through, about 4 to 5 minutes. The masa harina will thicken the soup as well as flavor it.

Serving the Soup

◆ Ladle soup into warm bowls. Drop a tablespoon of sour cream in the center of each bowl, add a healthy teaspoon of chopped green chilies, and finish with some cilantro leaves and a sprinkle of freshly ground pepper.

Oven Onion Soup

IF YOU HAVE NEVER thought of the oven as your friend, this onion soup will convince you. Slide the bowl into the oven, and after 30 minutes, stir for a moment, cover, and ignore it for 2½ hours. The oven quietly does the work. The last step will take about 6 minutes, and you will have the best onion soup you have ever tasted.

5 medium-size yellow onions	4 cups milk
5 tablespoons butter (½ stick plus 1 tablespoon)	3 tablespoons flour
	1½ teaspoons salt
1½ cups plus ½ cup water	Pepper to taste (optional)

Preheat oven to 275°F.

Peeling and Chopping the Onions

- Cut the onions into slices ⅛ inch thick (for full details, see page 13).
- Put the onions into a 3-quart casserole with a lid. Or you can use a Pyrex bowl, covering the top snugly with aluminum foil during cooking.

Adding the Butter and Water

- Cut the butter into small bits and dot it over the onions. Put the lid on the casserole, or crimp aluminum foil snugly on top of the mixing bowl. Put the casserole or bowl into the oven and bake for 30 minutes. Now remove the cover and stir the onions so the butter coats all the onion. Cover again, return the dish to the oven, and bake for 2½ hours.
- After 2½ hours, add the 1½ cups of water, stir, cover again, and bake for another 45 minutes.

The Last Step

- Just before the onions finish baking, put the milk into a good-size pot and turn the heat to medium-high.
- Put the flour and the ½ cup of water into a jar with a lid, screw on the lid, and shake vigorously until the flour and water are well mixed.
- Stay right by the stove and watch the milk. Heat it just short of boiling, called scalding. It's ready when you see a ring of tiny bubbles form around the edge. At that point, pour the flour and water into the milk and stir briskly until blended smoothly together. Add the salt, and cook, stirring, for 4 or 5 minutes, until the flour blends and thickens the milk. This will give your soup a pleasing texture, like heavy cream.
- Remove the casserole from the oven, set it on a heatproof counter, and pour the milk over the onions. Stir to mix. Taste for salt and add if needed. Stir again and serve hot.

A Bowlful of Salad

INTRODUCTION

LIKE A GOOD SOUP, a good salad can be the main dish for lunch or supper. You will be surprised at how many salad possibilities you have in your refrigerator—those leftovers that are the bonuses of home cooking. A salad can be made with any good cooked cold ingredient. For instance, beans, potatoes, or other vegetables, little pieces of cooked roasts, chops, chicken, or even fish can make a welcome salad supper.

But first I have included here some lighter salads that serve as simple accompaniments to a meal.

RECIPES

GREEN SALAD

PARSLEY SALAD

WATERCRESS SALAD

SPINACH SALAD WITH CHUTNEY DRESSING

CAESAR SALAD

CHILLED ASPARAGUS SALAD

GREEN BEANS WITH MUSTARD SHALLOT DRESSING

RED AND GREEN COLE SLAW

CELERY VICTOR

ORANGE AND RED ONION SALAD

AVOCADO AND BACON SALAD

SHRIMP AND PAPAYA SALAD

WHITE BEAN AND TUNA SALAD

HEARTY SALAD OF POTATOES, EGGS, AND GREEN BEANS

THE POTATO SALAD

CHICKEN SALAD

BEEF SALAD

1. Look over your salad greens and discard any yellowed, discolored, limp, or wilted leaves.

2. All fresh, raw ingredients should be rinsed under cold running water before using.

3. Rinsed greens must be dried; salad dressings can't adhere to wet greens. Use either paper or cloth towels to pat dry, or use a salad spinner, which is a handy piece of kitchen equipment. If you decide to buy a salad spinner, be sure to get the type that is spun by pulling a cord. Don't pack the greens in too tight, and pull on the cord sharply about 10 times to get rid of all the water. Pour out the collected water at the bottom of the spinner bowl and spin another batch of greens.

4. The best way to store the greens is to put them in a plastic bag after they have been rinsed, and leave some head space before closing with a baggie tie.

5. You can vary your salads by using different greens, either by themselves or in combination. Try romaine, iceberg, Boston lettuce; try small spinach leaves, or watercress; and red oakleaf for color. Add fresh herbs, too, such as basil and tarragon. Chicory and endive lend a nice bitter accent to salads.

6. If you are using an oil dressing, 1 tablespoon will coat 2 cups of salad greens.

7. Don't put the dressing on the greens until you are ready to serve or they will wilt. However, if you are making a salad of cooked ingredients, toss the ingredients with the dressing an hour or more before serving, so they can become nicely flavored.

Clockwise from the upper left: watercress, Boston lettuce, red oakleaf lettuce, and romaine

8. When you add the dressing to the greens, gently using your hands, go to the bottom of the bowl and scoop up, then toss the greens so that you move them around, coating all leaves with dressing. Add only enough dressing to give a shiny coating to the salad greens.

Green Salad

ABOUT 6 CUPS

MORE OFTEN THAN NOT a green salad is very ho-hum, just plain dull. But since we eat salad almost as often as bread, it should be fresh and lively, and tossed with a good salad dressing. Add just enough dressing and toss well, so the leaves shine and don't wind up salad soup.

THE SALAD

1 large head romaine lettuce, or mix with iceberg or Boston lettuce (see suggestions in Salad Sense, on page 41)

THE DRESSING

1 tablespoon wine vinegar, red or white

1 tablespoon cold water

¼ teaspoon salt

5 tablespoons olive oil

Rinsing and Drying the Lettuce

• Tear off and discard the coarse outer leaves, as well as any leaves that have brown spots or look wilted. Cut off the stem end, discard, and separate the leaves.

• Put the lettuce leaves in a colander and rinse them for a minute or so under cold running water, moving the leaves around with your hands to remove any grit. Shake the colander well to remove the excess water.

• It's essential to dry the leaves well before making the salad, since any remaining water will keep the dressing from sticking to the leaves. See Salad Sense for two good ways to dry the lettuce.

Making the Salad Dressing

• Put the vinegar, water, and salt in a jar with a lid. Screw the lid on and shake vigorously to dissolve the salt. Remove the lid and add the oil. Put the lid back on and shake vigorously a few seconds, until the dressing looks cloudy and thicker. The dressing will quickly separate, but remember always to shake or stir it just before you use it so it is well blended.

Putting the Salad Together

- Toss the lettuce into a salad bowl, stir the dressing to blend it well, and drizzle the dressing over the lettuce. Hold back a little of the dressing until you have tossed and coated all the pieces of lettuce. You want only to coat the leaves, not to add so much dressing that there is some sitting in the bottom of the bowl and the leaves become too wet. Be sure to reach down to the bottom of the bowl so all the lettuce can be coated with dressing.

- Dress the salad just before serving, so the leaves are crisp and fresh-looking.

- Serve immediately.

■

SALAD DRESSING

Make double or triple the amount of dressing. It keeps very well in the jar with the lid on in the refrigerator. If you like, you can add a couple of teaspoons of chopped garlic to give more flavor; you can also use the dressing as a sauce over pasta and/or chicken. Think creatively for other uses, and test and taste on a little bite before adding more if you aren't sure it will taste right.

■

Parsley Salad

SERVES FOUR TO SIX

THERE IS SOMETHING UNEXPECTED about Parsley Salad. It is like a fresh relish, and it enhances lots of dishes. Don't think of this as a typical salad; it should be served in portions of ½ to ¾ cup per serving. Try it with steak, or James Beard's Roasted Spare-ribs (page 129), or add it to spaghetti. The salad will keep refrigerated for about a week.

THE DRESSING

2 cloves garlic

6 tablespoons olive oil

1 ½ tablespoons red-wine vinegar

½ teaspoon salt

¼ teaspoon freshly ground pepper

THE SALAD

2 or 3 bunches parsley, the curly-leaf kind (enough to yield 4 cups chopped)

⅓ cup freshly grated Parmesan cheese

Making the Dressing

- Remove the papery skin from the garlic cloves.

- If you are using a food processor or blender, put the oil and the peeled garlic cloves into the bowl of the processor and blend until the garlic is smoothly incorporated into the oil. Add the vinegar, salt, and pepper, and blend.

- If you're not using a food processor, crush the garlic cloves by setting them on a cutting board and smashing them under the broadest flat surface of a large knife—the part nearest the handle. Sprinkle the salt over the smashed garlic and use the same knife to chop the cloves finely. The garlic juices melt the salt and help spread the garlic flavor through the salad.

- Using the flat side of your knife, scrape up the garlic-and-salt mash and put it into a small jar with a lid. Add the olive oil, vinegar, and pepper, screw the lid on the jar, and shake well.

Preparing the Parsley

◆ Rinse the parsley under cold water and shake to get rid of excess water. Pat dry with paper towels, or spin dry in a salad spinner. Pinch or cut off the stems and discard. Separate the little clusters of parsley leaves (see illustration, page 12). The curly leaves make a fluffy pile of green.

Making and Serving the Salad

◆ Put the parsley in a bowl, pour the dressing over it, and sprinkle on the grated Parmesan cheese. Using your hands or a large spoon, mix well so the dressing and cheese coat the parsley evenly.

◆ Serve small portions, about ½ cup per person.

◆

MAKING PASTA WITH PARSLEY SALAD

For one generous serving:

Boil 4 ounces of spaghetti (this is ¼ pound, which when cooked makes 2 cups) for each serving. Add 1 cup of parsley salad to each serving and toss to mix well.

◆

Watercress Salad

SERVES FOUR

WATERCRESS MIXED WITH the delicate, tender Boston lettuce adds lots of contrast to a meal. The small dark-green watercress leaves give a peppery sparkle to the salad. Use the stems of the watercress if they are tender, but taste first and discard them if they are coarse and tough.

The Salad

1 head butter or Boston lettuce   1 bunch watercress

Watercress Dressing (about ¾ cup)

2 tablespoons white-wine vinegar

1 tablespoon water

½ teaspoon salt

½ cup olive oil

2 green onions or scallions, chopped

½ cup watercress leaves (from above bunch; see procedure)

Preparing the Greens

- Cut the core out of the butter lettuce and discard. Separate the leaves, rinse, and pat dry.
- Remove the leaves from the stems of the watercress, discarding the stems. Rinse and dry the leaves.
- Chop half of the watercress leaves—about ½ cup—and set aside.
- Put the remaining watercress and the lettuce greens into a large bowl. Cover the greens with a damp paper towel and refrigerate them while you make the Watercress Dressing.

Making the Watercress Dressing

- Put the vinegar, water, and salt in a jar. Screw on the lid and shake until well blended.
- Add the olive oil, chopped green onions, and watercress leaves.
- Put the lid on again, and shake well to blend and mix. The dressing will look cloudy after shaking, which means it is thoroughly mixed.

Finishing the Salad

- Pour half the dressing over the bowl of greens.
- Toss the leaves gently, preferably with your hands, going to the bottom and sides of the bowl to coat all the leaves.
- Taste a leaf, and if it needs more salt, lightly sprinkle some over and toss the greens again.
- Serve cold.

■

OPEN-FACED SANDWICHES

WATERCRESS: Spread some cream cheese over slices of good bread and cover the cheese with watercress leaves. It makes a fine combination.

MELTED CHEESE: Cover the bottom of a baking sheet or cookie sheet with aluminum foil and arrange however many slices of bread you want on top. Make a layer of Monterey Jack or cheddar cheese—any kind you favor—on each slice of bread. Place the oven rack anywhere from 3 to 5 inches under the broiler and turn the broiler on. Stand by and watch because broilers get very hot and the cheese will melt quickly. As soon as it melts—it shouldn't take more than a minute or two—remove the molten slices with a spatula and serve with the Watercress or Spinach Salad or with just a green salad.

■

Spinach Salad with Chutney Dressing

THIS SALAD—delicious, healthy, and easy to make—could be the main attraction for a supper. Muscat raisins are larger than most, and are chewy and sweet. Serve the salad with an open-faced sandwich with sharp cheddar cheese (see box, opposite).

THE SALAD

2 bunches (about 1½ pounds) young, small-leaf spinach

2 Red Delicious apples (or any firm, sweet apples)

4 or 5 green onions or scallions (to make ½ cup chopped)

1 cup pecan halves

½ cup muscat raisins

CHUTNEY DRESSING

1 or 2 lemons

½ cup vegetable oil

4 tablespoons Fresh Pineapple Chutney (see page 232)

1 teaspoon curry powder

1 teaspoon dry mustard

½ teaspoon salt

Preparing the Spinach, Apples, and Onions

◆ Wash the spinach thoroughly (see box), then dry it in a salad spinner, or place the spinach leaves between layers of paper towel, loosely roll up the paper towels, and refrigerate to cool and crisp.

◆ Slice the apples in half from top to bottom, then cut each half in half again. Remove the seeds and tougher bits of the core. Cut the apples into thin slices.

◆ Chop the green onions (for full details, see page 51).

◆ Put the spinach, apples, pecans, raisins, and scallions in a large salad bowl and toss to mix.

Making the Dressing

◆ Use a citrus juicer to juice 1 or 2 lemons; you need 2 tablespoons. Strain the juice.

◆ Put the oil, chutney, curry powder, dry mustard, salt, and lemon juice in a small bowl and stir well. Or you can put all the dressing ingredients in a pint jar with a lid and shake vigorously.

◆ Pour the dressing over the salad and toss gently to coat all the ingredients.

◆ Serve immediately.

◆

ABOUT SPINACH

Choose crisp-looking bunches of spinach, with dark, fresh-looking leaves. Young spinach with small leaves will be best for this salad, if you can find it. But the larger leaves are fine, cut in bite-size pieces.

Spinach is gritty, with bits of sand and dirt clinging to the leaves, so plunge the leaves into a bowl of cold water, swish around, and the dirt will sink to the bottom and the leaves float to the top of the bowl. Rinse in several changes of cold water, if necessary, until the water in the bottom of the bowl is clear. Dry well in a salad spinner and store in a plastic bag in the refrigerator.

◆

Caesar Salad

SERVES FOUR

CAESAR SALAD HAS BEEN as popular as the most famous movie star for almost a century, and it is still on restaurant menus across the country. Anchovies, which were called for in the original recipe, have a strong flavor that many people don't like, but you might try mashing one anchovy and see if you like it. An important ingredient in this classic salad is Parmesan cheese—which can be quite expensive. So, rather than just omit it, try other cheeses (see box, opposite). Caesar Salad makes a satisfying main dish by itself. Add strips of sliced chicken breast, leftover pork roast, or seafood to the salad and—voilà! you have another wonderful meal. Try having Mexican Lentil Soup (page 32) with this Caesar Salad. Serve an icy lemon sorbet with a biscotti for dessert. (You can buy both the sorbet and biscotti cookies in most markets.)

3 heads romaine lettuce

2 slices white bread

For the dressing, see recipe for
A Caesar Dressing, page 236

⅓ cup grated Parmesan cheese

Rinsing the Lettuce

♦ Pull the lettuce leaves from the firm white core of the head of lettuce, and discard any limp, coarse, or discolored leaves. They are unusable. Put the leaves in a colander and rinse under cold water, turning them to rinse them clean of dirt. Shake the colander to eliminate the water, and pat the leaves dry with a paper towel or dish towel. Or dry in a salad spinner. It is important to dry the lettuce well, because salad dressing won't adhere to wet leaves. Wrap lettuce loosely in a towel or paper towels, and place in the refrigerator.

Preparing the Croutons

♦ Preheat the oven to 350°F. Trim the crusts off the bread slices, cut the bread into ½-inch cubes, and place on a cookie sheet so the pieces are not touching. Put the cookie sheet in the oven for 10 to 15 minutes, or until the bread slices are firm and dry and lightly golden.

Tossing the Salad

◆ Cut or tear the lettuce leaves into large bite-size pieces, and put them in a large bowl.

◆ Shake the jar of dressing well, and pour about ⅓ cup over the greens. Use your hands to toss the salad, reaching down to the bottom of the bowl and scooping up the lettuce. Repeat this several times, until each piece of lettuce is dressed. If the lettuce doesn't have enough dressing, add another ¼ cup and continue to toss until well coated. Refrigerate leftover dressing to use another time. Sprinkle Parmesan cheese and the croutons over the salad and toss again to distribute. Serve at once.

◆

PARMIGIANO REGGIANO

Parmigiano Reggiano cheese is a fine, aged imported grating cheese that is used on pastas and salads. The bad news is that it is quite expensive, but a little bit goes a long way, and the flavor is splendid. Wrapped well and refrigerated, it keeps indefinitely. It also keeps well in a jar with a lid in the refrigerator. But if your budget is limited, try grating cheeses that are reasonably priced and also very good: Monterey Jack, or Asiago, or Romano. It is best to grate cheese shortly before using it, but if you have some left over, store it in the refrigerator in a jar with a tight cover.

◆

Chilled Asparagus Salad

SERVES FOUR

I**T'S ALWAYS A CHEERFUL SIGN** to see the first asparagus. Although it's delicious cooked until just tender with nothing more than butter, salt, and pepper to season it, this salad can be a light supper served with hard-boiled eggs.

THE SALAD

2 quarts (8 cups water)   2 pounds asparagus

2 teaspoons salt   1 head butter lettuce

THE DRESSING

2 green onions or scallions   ¼ teaspoon salt

A few sprigs parsley   Pepper to taste

2 tablespoons white-wine   6 tablespoons vegetable oil
   vinegar   ¼ teaspoon sesame seed oil*

1½ teaspoons Dijon mustard

Preparing the Asparagus

• Put the water in a wide pot or skillet, add the salt, and place on a burner set to high. Bring to a boil.

• Rinse the asparagus and cut off the tough, woody bottoms of the stalks.

ABOUT ASPARAGUS

It is personal taste whether you like your asparagus pencil-thin or thick as your thumb—both are equally good. Look for firm stalks that don't feel or look limp. If you don't eat it right away, stand the stalks upright in a jar or measuring cup with about 1 inch water in the bottom and refrigerate. My favorite dip for asparagus is ½ cup mayonnaise mixed well with ½ teaspoon sesame seed oil. Serve a dozen or so lightly cooked fat spears (more if they are thin) on a platter with a little bowl of sauce on the side so everyone can dip a piece in. You won't believe how good this is.

* Found in the Asian-food section of the supermarket.

- Lay the spears in the boiling water, turn the heat down a little, and boil gently until they are just tender when pierced near the base with a knife. Begin testing after 3 minutes if the stalks are thin, the size of a pencil, or after 5 minutes for the fatter spears. The asparagus should be firm yet tender.
- When done, lift the spears out of the water with a large spoon and put them into a bowl of cold water to stop the cooking process; hot food continues to cook while cooling down.
- Put the asparagus on a plate, cover with plastic wrap, and chill.

Preparing the Dressing
- 1) Trim the roots off the white ends and peel off any coarse outer leaves of the green onions or scallions.
- 2) Remove the coarse green tops of the scallions, leaving about 2 inches of green tops, then slice them fine.
- Rinse the parsley, pat dry; remove and discard the stems. Finely chop the leaves.
- Put the vinegar, mustard, salt, pepper, green onion, and parsley in a jar with a lid. Put on the lid and vigorously shake the jar to mix and blend. Remove the lid and add the vegetable oil and the sesame oil. Again, put on the lid and shake for a few seconds. Set the dressing aside until needed.

Preparing the Lettuce Leaves
- Separate enough lettuce leaves from the head to make a nice cup-like bed for the asparagus. Rinse the leaves, pat or spin them dry, and put them in a plastic bag in the refrigerator to chill.

Serving the Asparagus
- When ready to serve, make a bed of the lettuce leaves on a serving platter or individual plates, and arrange the asparagus spears on top. Spoon the vinaigrette over and serve cold.

1

2

Green Beans with Mustard Shallot Dressing

THESE TENDER BUT SLIGHTLY CRUNCHY green beans are tossed with a snappy mustard dressing. If you serve them with a hot baked potato (see page 182) with butter, salt, and pepper, you have a good supper. The Mustard Shallot Dressing is also good on spinach, broccoli, and brown rice. If you don't want such a large salad, cook just the amount of green beans you need—count on about ¼ pound per person—and use a proportionate amount of dressing, reserving the rest for another salad (it keeps well).

THE SALAD
- 1½ pounds green beans
- 1 tablespoon salt

MUSTARD SHALLOT DRESSING
- 1 shallot, about 2 tablespoons chopped
- 2 large garlic cloves
- A few sprigs parsley (to make about ½ cup chopped)
- 2 teaspoons Dijon mustard (be sure the label says Dijon mustard)
- 2½ tablespoons red-wine vinegar
- ¾ teaspoon salt
- Pepper
- ⅔ cup vegetable oil

Preparing the Beans

- Using a small paring knife, trim about ¼ inch off both ends of the beans. You can also snap the ends off easily with your fingers. Discard the ends and leave the beans whole.
- Fill a large pot (quart-size) about ⅔ full of water, place on a burner, and turn the heat to high. When the water boils, sprinkle in 1 tablespoon of salt and drop the whole beans into the boiling water.
- Let the beans cook for 4 or 5 minutes only. Scoop up a bean from the pot after 4 minutes, run under cold water, and bite into it to test for doneness. It should be tender but still crisp—not limp.
- Put a colander in the sink, take the pot to the sink, and pour the beans and the water into the colander. When the water has drained away, turn on the cold water and let it run over the beans for a few seconds to cool them. The cool water stops the cooking process so the beans stay crunchy.

- Let the beans drain thoroughly; you can give the colander a few shakes to make sure all the water has fallen through.
- Put the beans on one large platter in a neat pile, or divide them onto serving plates.

Making the Dressing

- Finely chop the shallot (see box).
- Peel and finely chop the garlic.
- Remove the stems from the parsley and discard. Finely chop the leaves. You should have ½ cup.
- Put the chopped shallot, garlic, and the parsley, the prepared mustard, vinegar, salt, and pepper in a jar with a lid. Screw the lid on and shake vigorously for a few seconds. Uncover and add the oil. Cover and shake the jar a few more seconds, until the mixture is well blended. The dressing should be opaque and creamy. Set it aside until ready to serve the beans. Refrigerate the dressing if it's going to be a while, but take it out of the refrigerator about 30 minutes before serving to let the dressing warm to room temperature.
- If you prepare the beans ahead of time, wrap them snugly in plastic wrap. Refrigerate until needed. Remove them from the refrigerator about 30 minutes before serving to let them warm to room temperature.
- To serve, shake the dressing again to mix it up and spoon it over the beans. Serve at room temperature.

■

HOW TO CHOP SHALLOTS

Shallots are a member of the onion family, though much smaller and milder in flavor, and they have reddish skins. Cut off the root end and remove the papery skin. Set the shallot on a cutting board on its flattest side, so it is stable. Then proceed to chop as you would an onion (page 13) skipping the step of cutting it in half first.

■

Red and Green Cole Slaw

SERVES SIX

THIS IS A SALAD that tastes as good as it looks. It is an ideal choice for the holidays and winter menus—thin strips of red and green cabbage combined with dried cranberries, and finished with a peppy celery-seed dressing. Dried cranberries are usually available in the supermarket alongside the raisins and currants, or among the bulk bins where other dried fruits and nuts are kept in most health-food stores. This is a very easy recipe to double for a party of a dozen or so or for a holiday buffet. But if you do make it for only six, check the index for good ways to use up the extra red and green cabbage you'll be storing in the refrigerator.

The Salad

1 head green cabbage	1 medium-size red onion
1 head red cabbage	1 cup dried cranberries

The Dressing

3 tablespoons apple-cider vinegar	3 tablespoons sugar
	1 teaspoon celery seed
3 tablespoons vegetable oil	¾ teaspoon salt

Cutting the Cabbage and Onion

◆ 1) Cut the green cabbage in half from the top down to the core end. Wrap and refrigerate one half for another use. Cut the other half down the center again. Cut the solid white core out of each piece of cabbage and discard. 2) Put the 2 pieces of cabbage—flat side down—on a cutting board, and cut down into thin strips no more than ⅛ inch wide. Use your hands to separate the strips of cabbage, and be sure to throw away any coarse white pieces from the core. Measure out 3 cups of cabbage strips and put in a large salad bowl.

◆ Cut the head of red cabbage just as you did the green cabbage, and thinly slice enough to make 3 cups. Add to the bowl.

◆ Peel and cut the onion in half, down from the stem top. Wrap and store one half for future use. Set the remaining half flat side down on a cutting board and cut down in thin slices. Separate the onion layers and add to the cabbage.

◆ Put the dried cranberries in the bowl and toss all the above ingredients together so they are well mixed.

1   2

Making the Dressing and Mixing the Cole Slaw

◆ Put the vinegar, oil, sugar, celery seed, and salt in a small jar with a lid. Screw on the lid and shake vigorously for about 5 seconds. If you don't have a jar, mix the dressing ingredients briskly in a small bowl with a fork or whisk.

◆ Pour the dressing over the salad, and with a large fork and spoon, or your hands, toss the ingredients until the dressing evenly coats the cabbage.

◆ If you are not going to serve the slaw immediately, cover and refrigerate until serving time. It will keep in the refrigerator for 3 days.

Celery Victor

MORE OFTEN THAN NOT, celery is a background flavor in other dishes, such as chicken or tuna-fish or shrimp salad. But in this recipe, the staple vegetable is the star of the show. Moreover, because it is cooked, the celery here is more refined than when it is served raw and goes particularly well with chicken or other roasts. Note that Celery Victor must be prepared several hours ahead so that it has time to chill before serving.

THE SALAD

3 celery hearts (the tender, interior part of the celery bunch)	1 bay leaf
	½ teaspoon salt
	Pepper to taste
3 cups chicken broth, canned or homemade	

THE DRESSING

1 tablespoon Dijon mustard	½ cup mayonnaise

Preparing the Celery

◆ Using a large knife, cut each celery heart in half lengthwise. Cut off the root end—about ¼ inch or so—and remove any tough or discolored outer stalks. Save a handful of celery leaves to use later.

◆ Arrange the celery hearts in a skillet large enough to hold them all in a single row. Pour the chicken broth into the pan, and add the bay leaf, half the celery leaves, salt, and pepper. The broth should just cover the celery. Add a little water if it doesn't.

◆ Place the skillet on a burner and turn the heat to high. Bring to a boil and then reduce the heat to medium-low. Simmer for 8 minutes, covered. To test for doneness, pierce one of the hearts with a sharp knife. If the knife goes in easily, it is cooked; if not, simmer for another 3 or 4 minutes, then test again. You want the celery to be tender, but it should not be so cooked that it becomes limp.

◆ Remove the skillet from the heat, transfer the celery to a bowl, and pour the broth over it. Place the bowl in the refrigerator and chill for 3 or 4 hours or overnight.

Making the Dressing

- When you are ready to serve, remove the chilled celery from the refrigerator and drain. Arrange on individual serving plates.

- Stir together the mustard and mayonnaise in a small bowl. Add 2 tablespoons of the chilled celery broth and mix well to give the dressing a creamy consistency.

- Spoon the dressing over the celery and garnish with remaining celery leaves.

■

ABOUT CELERY

Celery usually comes in big bunches with some of the leaves attached. Often you can find in the super-market only the hearts of celery packaged—2 or 3 to the package—which is what you need for this Celery Victor recipe. But that is an expensive way to buy celery. And if you buy the big bunches instead, you can easily trim away the darker green, more coarse stalks to get to the pale, tender hearts. You'll find lots of uses for the larger stalks—chopped in salads and sandwiches (such as tuna fish, turkey, and chicken), simmered in soups, or just as something to munch on, particularly when you have a delicious dip. The outer ribs may need some trimming into more manageable pieces and sometimes there will be strings on the outer ribs, which are easy to scrape away. Having celery in the veg-etable bin is a real asset and it keeps well, wrapped loosely in plastic wrap or waxed paper.

■

Orange and Red Onion Salad

SERVES FOUR

ORANGE AND RED ONION SALAD IS not only very good by itself, it refreshes and lends balance to rich dishes. Try to use oranges that are sweet. Served with fish, or with cold meats or chicken, this colorful combination adds the same fresh lightness that lemon provides. It is a particularly good match for Poached Halibut with Fennel (page 84).

THE DRESSING

2 tablespoons white-wine vinegar	Freshly ground black pepper
½ teaspoon salt, plus a pinch more	6 tablespoons olive oil
	1 teaspoon lemon juice (from ½ lemon or less)

THE SALAD

2 medium-size red onions	1 teaspoon sugar (maybe more)
3 large navel oranges	

Making the Dressing

◆ Put the vinegar and ½ teaspoon of salt in a medium-size bowl and mix thoroughly with a whisk. Add the pepper, olive oil, and lemon juice, and beat until the ingredients are well mixed. (You can also put all the ingredients into a small jar with a lid and shake vigorously to mix.)

Preparing the Onions and Oranges

◆ Peel the papery skin off the onions and discard. Cut the onions in half, using a large sharp knife—such as a chef's knife or a large serrated knife—and slice them very thin (for full details, see page 13). Add the onions to the bowl containing the vinaigrette.

◆ 1) Still using the same knife, cut off and discard the top and bottom of the oranges—just enough to reveal the orange interior, maybe ¼ inch. The amount you cut off will vary, depending on the thickness of the peel.

◆ 2) Hold the orange firmly in one hand on a cutting board and, with a sharp knife, cut down from the top of the fruit to the board, following the curve of the orange. Remove the peel. Trim off any pith (the white part) still clinging to the orange. Navel oranges have no seeds, or very few, so you won't have to deal with removing seeds.

◆ Cut the peeled orange crosswise into slices about ¼ inch thick, then cut the slices in half. Add the orange slices to the bowl.

◆ Using two large spoons, or your hands, mix the onions and oranges into the vinaigrette. Taste. If the oranges are not naturally sweet, sprinkle on a teaspoon of sugar—or more if the oranges are still too tart. A pinch of salt can also add a bright note to the salad.

◆ Serve the salad in the same bowl you used for mixing or on small individual plates. Make sure each portion has a good balance of onions and oranges.

1

2

Avocado and Bacon Salad

SERVES FOUR

THIS SIMPLE, SATISFYING SALAD can become a supper sandwich if you pile it on toasted, buttered whole-wheat bread or other bread with good texture and flavor. Serve it with a bowl of soup, such as tomato soup.

The Dressing

1½ teaspoons lemon juice (from ½ lemon or less)	¼ cup sour cream
	½ cup mayonnaise

The Salad

8 slices bacon (about ½ pound)	2 ripe avocados
1 bunch green onions or scallions	1 head iceberg lettuce
	Salt and pepper to taste

Making the Dressing

◆ Mix together the lemon juice, sour cream, and mayonnaise in a small bowl. Stir until smooth and chill until needed.

Preparing the Bacon

◆ Separate the slices and place in a single layer in a heavy-bottomed skillet. Fry the slices over medium-high heat until they start to turn brown. This should only take 3 or 4 minutes, so stand by the stove and move the bacon pieces around with a fork, turning them over as one side becomes brown, until they are done. Remove the bacon from the pan, place on a paper towel, then pat both sides to remove the fat. Set aside.

Preparing the Salad Ingredients

◆ Cut off and discard the root end (about ¼ inch) and the coarse green tops of the green onions or scallions, then cut the remaining white and green crosswise into very thin slices, no more than ⅛ inch (for details, see page 51).

◆ Peel and seed the avocados (for details, see box, opposite), and cut lengthwise into slices about ¼ inch thick.

◆ Rinse the head of lettuce, discard any discolored leaves, and remove and set aside four good leaves. Cut the head of lettuce in half from top to bottom, remove the core, then slice the lettuce into bite-size pieces (for full details, see illustration of cabbage, page 59).

◆

SCALLIONS OR GREEN ONIONS

Scallions or green onions are immature onions. They have a white undeveloped root end, and long, straight green leaves. Usually when they are called for in a recipe, you use the trimmed white part and some of the tender green, either sliced thin or chopped fine (see illustrations, page 51). Store in a plastic bag in the refrigerator. They last about a week, and sometimes a little longer.

◆

Assembling and Serving the Salad

♦ Put a whole lettuce leaf on each serving plate and about a cup of the chopped lettuce on each lettuce leaf. Distribute the avocado slices evenly on top of the lettuce, lightly salt and pepper the slices, and sprinkle the bacon pieces over the avocado. Spoon the dressing over all, and finish by sprinkling the sliced green onion on top.

■ ABOUT AVOCADOS ■

The avocado is one of the fruits that will ripen on the kitchen counter, so you can choose ones that are still a bit firm if you aren't planning to use them right away. They may take several days to ripen. The small, dark-green Hass variety—the ones with the pebbly skin—have the flavor. Don't buy overly soft or bruised avocados.

The skin of an avocado is thick and easy to pull away. First, cut into the avocado as though cutting it in half lengthwise; the pit will prevent the knife from going all the way through, so continue the cut around the pit. 1) Now hold the avocado in both hands and twist the halves.

1

2

2) Open up the two halves.

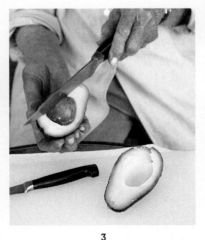

3

3) Hold the other half, with the pit, in one hand (pit up), and gently but forcefully strike the pit with the blade of a knife until it is stuck in

the pit. Gently twist the knife and your hand in opposite directions to free the pit. 4) Using your fingers, slip the skin away from the pale green flesh. Cut away and discard any browned areas of avocados.

4

Dark spots or shadings start to appear quickly when avocado is cut and exposed to the air. Brush or rub the halves of the avocados with lemon juice to keep this from happening.

If you are going to refrigerate an unused portion of an avocado for later use, leave it unpeeled, with the pit back in place, rub the exposed flesh with a cut lemon, and wrap tightly in plastic wrap. The cut surface may darken a little but you can just scrape that away.

Shrimp and Papaya Salad

SERVES FOUR

THIS SUMMER SALAD can make a light but satisfying lunch or supper. You buy the shrimp already cooked. Serve the salad with a small bowl of broth and some buttered warm crackers. For something sweet to finish this light meal, I love to get a good thick bar of chocolate, break it into chunks, and serve it with iced coffee topped with whipped cream.

1½ pounds cooked bay shrimp	A few sprigs parsley
1 papaya	2 tablespoons milk
1 head butter or Boston lettuce	½ cup mayonnaise
	Salt

Preparing the Shrimp

◆ Rinse the cooked shrimp under cold running water, pat dry with paper towels, cover with plastic wrap, and refrigerate.

Preparing the Papaya

◆ Cut the papaya in half lengthwise, and 1) use a spoon to scoop out and discard the seeds. Peel off the skin with a paring knife and discard, then place the papaya cut side down on a cutting board. 2) Use a sharp knife to cut the fruit lengthwise into slices ½ inch wide, then slice those

1

2

pieces crosswise into ½-inch chunks. Remember that a ripe papaya is fragile, and will turn to mush if harshly handled.

Finishing the Salad

- Rinse the lettuce leaves and pat dry with paper towels.
- Rinse the parsley and pat dry; remove the stems and discard. Finely chop the leaves (for full details, see box, page 12).
- Arrange 2 or 3 lettuce leaves on each serving plate, making them into a bed for the salad.
- Stir the milk into the mayonnaise to thin it.
- Distribute the shrimp and papaya onto the 4 plates. Sprinkle on salt, drizzle the dressing over each serving, and scatter some chopped parsley on top. Serve.

■

ABOUT PAPAYA

When you buy a papaya, look for one that has some yellow coloring and no bruises or dark spots, and gives a little when you press the skin. It should also have a fruity aroma. A ripe papaya will last about 2 days in the refrigerator.

If you can't buy a ripe papaya, an unripe papaya will ripen in 2 to 3 days.

■

White Bean and Tuna Salad

SERVES FOUR

THIS IS A SALAD with substance. It makes a meal, because it's more filling than the term "salad" implies. Remember to soak the beans the night before you prepare the salad. Or you can use canned beans if this is a last-minute choice for supper; just dump them into a strainer and run cold water over them to rinse away the thick canning liquid. Canned beans are a good product to keep in the cupboard, "a friend in need." You could also add a small Green Salad (see page 42) to the plate.

THE SALAD

1½ cups dried cannellini beans (or any other white beans)

About 8 cups water

2 teaspoons salt, plus more to taste

A few sprigs fresh basil

6 sprigs parsley

1 large white or red onion

1 12-ounce can solid white tuna

Pepper to taste

THE DRESSING

2 tablespoons red-wine vinegar

6 tablespoons olive oil

Soaking the Beans a Day Ahead

◆ Put the beans in a colander and rinse them under cool running water. Pick through them to remove any shriveled beans, pebbles, or other foreign matter. Put the beans in a 3-quart pot, add the water and the 2 teaspoons salt, and allow to soak overnight.

◆ Cook the beans in the same pot you've used to soak them—the beans will have absorbed some water, so add enough water to again cover them by about 2 inches. You don't need to discard the soaking water.

◆ Bring to a boil over high heat. Reduce the heat to medium-low or low, cover, and simmer 1 hour, or until the beans are tender. Make sure the beans remain completely covered with water while they're cooking. Check now and then, give them a good stir, and add just a cup or two more water if necessary.

Preparing the Basil, Parsley, Onion, and Tuna While the Beans Cook

◆ Pick a few leaves from sprigs of fresh basil and chop enough to yield about 3 tablespoons.

◆ Finely chop the leaves from several sprigs of parsley, enough to yield ½ cup. Reserve a few sprigs, if you have any remaining, for garnish.

◆ Peel and finely chop the onion (for full details, see page 13).

◆ Open the can of tuna; drain off and discard the liquid. Break the fish into bite-size flakes.

Making the Dressing and Finishing the Salad

◆ When the beans are tender, drain off the liquid through a strainer or colander and allow the beans to cool. Put the beans in a large serving bowl, season with salt and pepper, stir to mix well, and taste again to check the salt, adding a little more if it tastes flat and dull.

◆ In a small bowl, stir together the vinegar and olive oil, or shake in a small lidded jar. Pour over the beans, and toss until well mixed.

◆ Sprinkle the basil and parsley over the beans, add the onion and tuna, and mix well. Garnish with sprigs of parsley. Taste and add salt if necessary.

◆

SERVING SUGGESTION

A good accompaniment to this salad is toasted English muffins topped with chopped tomato, drizzled with olive oil, and sprinkled with salt and pepper. The muffins come out looking like little pizzas.

◆

Hearty Salad of Potatoes, Eggs, and Green Beans

SERVES FOUR

THIS IS A FILLING LUNCH or supper salad that tastes just as good as it looks—even when you make it a day ahead. Serve whole-wheat or another nourishing bread with it, and perhaps the Seattle Crisp for dessert (see page 286). The Caesar Dressing is measured and mixed in a jar and can be prepared ahead. It's a snap to put together and does wonders for the vegetables and eggs. The small red potatoes don't need to be peeled. Their skin is very thin, and the color makes the salad look appealing.

1½ pounds small red potatoes, about 1½ inches in diameter (about 10 to 12 potatoes)

8 large eggs

1 tablespoon plus 1 teaspoon salt

½ pound green beans

Caesar Dressing (page 236)

Preparing the Potatoes, Eggs, and Green Beans

• Put the potatoes in a large pot, then carefully place the whole, unshelled eggs on top of the potatoes (this way the eggshells are less likely to crack during cooking). Add enough water to cover the potatoes and eggs by 2 or 3 inches, and sprinkle in the 1 tablespoon salt. Turn the heat to high and bring to a boil.

• When the water boils, reduce the heat to medium or medium-high, just enough to maintain a gentle boil. Cook uncovered for 20 minutes.

• Meanwhile, rinse the green beans, and cut off the very tips (about ¼ inch) at both ends.

• After 20 minutes, test a potato for doneness by piercing its center with a small sharp knife. If the blade slides easily into the potato, it is done and so are the eggs.

• Remove the potatoes and eggs from the water with a slotted spoon. Turn the heat under the pot of water to high so it will return to a boil for cooking the beans.

• Drop the beans into the same water you cooked the potatoes and eggs in. Cook the beans for 4–5 minutes, until they are tender but still have some snap. You don't want them limp.

◆ To test the beans, spear one with a fork, break it in two, and taste it. It should snap and have a cooked, not raw-bean flavor. Empty into a colander or strainer set in the sink.

Finishing the Dish

◆ Cut the potatoes into bite-size chunks, and peel the shells from the eggs (for details on shelling eggs, see box, page 16). Cut the eggs into quarters lengthwise and set aside. While the potatoes and eggs are still warm, put them and the green beans into a large bowl and sprinkle on the remaining teaspoon of salt.

◆ Shake the jar of Caesar Dressing, and pour about ½ cup onto the salad. Mix gently with a large spoon to coat the ingredients thoroughly. Add another ¼ cup if the salad seems too dry. Don't worry if the eggs break apart.

◆ Serve the remaining dressing in a small bowl to pass at the table.

■

ABOUT POTATOES

Russets and Idahos are considered good for baking and making French fries because of their mealy texture.

"Tiny" or "small" red potatoes are immature potatoes that have been harvested before they are fully grown. When a recipe in this book calls for tiny or small red potatoes, look for potatoes 1½ to 2 inches in diameter. If this size is not available, just buy larger potatoes and cut them into chunks about that size.

A red potato is a waxy variety and is best for boiling and in recipes such as The Potato Salad (page 68).

If a potato is beginning to sprout but is still firm, just rub off the sprouts and use it. If you see patches of green on the potato, don't use the potato.

■

The Potato Salad

8 CUPS, SERVING 8

POTATO SALAD MAKES a wonderful supper served with lots of hard-cooked eggs and a platter of lettuce and tomatoes. The secret to making this good potato salad is to toss the potatoes while they are still hot with the lemon juice and olive oil.

THE SALAD

2 pounds red potatoes	1½ teaspoons salt, plus more
¼ cup lemon juice	to taste
3 stalks celery	

THE DRESSING

¼ cup olive oil	Pepper to taste
1¼ cups mayonnaise	

Cooking the Potatoes

◆ Rinse the potatoes, cut them into bite-size pieces, and put them in a 4-quart pot. Add enough water to cover the potatoes by 2 inches. Boil the potatoes over high heat until tender—about 8 to 10 minutes. You can tell if the potatoes are ready by piercing one with a sharp knife. If the knife goes in easily, they are done. Don't leave the potatoes in the water too long after they are done, because potatoes continue to cook after they have been removed from the heat.

Squeezing the Lemons, Preparing the Celery

◆ While the potatoes are cooking, cut a lemon in half crosswise, and squeeze the juice using a citrus juicer. The juiciness of lemons varies greatly, so squeeze one, then juice a second, if you need to, to fill ¼ cup.

◆ Trim off the leaves and stem ends of the celery stalks. Cut the stalks lengthwise into strips about ¼ inch wide, then cut the long strips crosswise into ¼-inch dice.

Finishing the Salad

◆ Drain the potatoes in a colander set in the sink.

◆ While the potatoes are still hot, put them into a large bowl, sprinkle the 1½ teaspoons salt all over them, and toss to coat all sides. Put the lemon juice and olive oil in a small jar. Screw on a lid and shake well, then pour over the potatoes and toss.

◆ Add the celery and mayonnaise, season with salt and pepper to your taste, and toss until the ingredients are well mixed.

◆ Serve at room temperature or chilled.

Chicken Salad

T HIS CHICKEN SALAD HAS everything going for it—a crisp, crunchy texture and a sweet, tangy taste. I like to serve it with Yellow Cornbread (see page 246) warm from the oven. Together they make a fine supper.

THE SALAD

1 small red or green apple
⅓ cup shelled walnuts
1 head iceberg lettuce
2 cups bite-size pieces of light
    and dark chicken meat

(left over from recipes on
    pages 22 or 97)
1 teaspoon salt

THE DRESSING

1 lemon (to squeeze 2
    teaspoons lemon juice)
½ cup mayonnaise)

2 tablespoons yogurt, plain
1 ½ teaspoons honey

Preparing the Salad Ingredients

- Peel the apple and cut it into small pieces.
- Chop the walnuts into pieces about the size of peanuts.
- Cut the core out of the lettuce. Cut the head of lettuce in half from the core end to the rounded top. Wrap and store one half for another use. Cut the remaining half lengthwise into 1½-inch thick strips. Then cut these strips across so they measure about 1½ inches long. You should have about 4 cups of lettuce.
- Put the lettuce pieces, apple, walnuts, and chicken in a large bowl. Sprinkle the salad with the salt and toss a few times with 2 forks or your hands.

Making the Dressing

- Measure the lemon juice, mayonnaise, yogurt, and honey into a small bowl. Using a fork or small whisk, mix the ingredients until the dressing is very smooth.

Serving the Salad

- Pour the dressing over the salad and use your hands or 2 forks to toss it and distribute the dressing evenly over the ingredients. If you don't want to eat right away, cover the bowl with plastic wrap and refrigerate until serving time.
- Distribute the salad evenly onto 2 or 3 individual plates and serve.

Beef Salad

SERVES FOUR

THIS SALAD IS very good made with any leftover cooked beef, pork, lamb, or chicken. The amount of meat in this recipe can vary; if you don't have enough to make 2 cups, just add what you have. Reheating meats sometimes makes it lose some of its good flavor, so this is a dandy way to preserve their taste and enjoy your leftovers. Serve a plate of sliced tomatoes and cucumbers, and the Garlic Rolls on page 242, to make a very satisfying supper.

THE SALAD

4 medium potatoes
3 hard-boiled eggs (see box, page 16)
1 teaspoon salt
About 2 cups (when sliced) leftover cooked beef
(about ½ pound), or other leftover meat
1 bunch green onions or scallions
4 stalks celery
2 dill pickles

THE DRESSING

1 clove garlic
¾ teaspoon salt
2 tablespoons Dijon mustard
½ cup olive oil
½ teaspoon freshly ground pepper
2 tablespoons red-wine vinegar
2 tablespoons cold water
2 tablespoons capers

Cooking the Potatoes

◆ Put the unpeeled potatoes and the eggs in a medium-size pot with water to cover them by 1½ inches. Add the teaspoon of salt and set over high heat. Bring to a boil, and boil for 20 minutes. Check for doneness by piercing a potato with a paring knife. If it slides in easily, the potatoes are done. If the potatoes are not tender, cook, after removing the eggs, for another 5 or 10 minutes and test again. When they are done, remove the pan from the heat, drain through a colander, and set the warm potatoes aside.

◆ When the potatoes are cool enough to handle, peel the skins from them with a paring knife. Cut them in half lengthwise, and cut each half into 3 or 4 long slices. Cut the slices crosswise into ½-inch chunks and set aside.

Preparing Other Ingredients

◆ Remove the shells from the hard-cooked eggs and separate the whites and the yolks. Set the yolks aside for the dressing. Chop the whites coarsely and put in a large glass or ceramic mixing bowl.

◆ Slice the cooked roast beef very thin—about ⅛ inch thick. Stack a few slices at a time, cut into ½-inch strips, and cut the strips crosswise into 2-inch pieces. Add to the bowl.

◆ Slice the green onions or scallions (for full details, see page 51). Add to the bowl.

◆ Coarsely chop the celery. Add to the bowl.

◆ Cut the pickles in half lengthwise, and cut the halves in half again. Cut the lengths crosswise into ¼-inch pieces. Add to the bowl.

Making the Dressing

◆ Peel and finely chop the garlic (for full details, see box, page 33). Sprinkle the ¾ teaspoon of salt on the garlic and mash with the flat of your knife, then chop them together to release the oils in the garlic.

◆ Use a fork to mash the reserved egg yolks in a small bowl. Stir in the mustard, olive oil, the garlic and salt, pepper, vinegar, water, and capers. Blend well. Taste, and add salt and pepper if necessary.

Finishing the Salad

◆ Pour the dressing over the beef salad and toss.

◆

Easy Fish

◆

INTRODUCTION

MANY BEGINNING COOKS are uneasy about buying and cooking fish because they are not confident that they can cook it properly. But in fact, it is fast and easy to cook. Not only does fresh fish taste good, it is a healthful addition to your diet.

It's important to know which cooking technique you should use for the type of fish you buy, and these recipes will tell you. Some preparations require that you stand right by the stove, checking on how the fish is cooking, but there are others that call for popping the fish in the oven so you can do other supper preparations in a leisurely way.

After buying fish, as soon as you get into your car, open the package and smell the fish. If it smells fishy or unpleasant, go back into the market and get your money back. Don't wait until you get home to check on it.

Fish is more perishable than meat. Although you can never know when the fish was caught or the meat slaughtered, you want to take precautions to keep your fish or meat fresh until you cook it. When you get home, put the fish in the refrigerator right away. Wrap it first or put it in a plastic ziplock bag, then place it in a pan with ice on the bottom and ice covering the wrapped fish. You can also use those handy freezer packs used on picnics to keep food and drinks cold, instead of ice.

RECIPES

———

BAKED SALMON STEAKS

BAKED RED SNAPPER WITH VEGETABLES

PARCHMENT-WRAPPED FISH FILLETS

TROUT WITH CELERY ROOT

POACHED HALIBUT WITH FENNEL

POACHED SALMON WITH CUCUMBER AND CAPER SAUCE

SHRIMP CURRY

SMALL SHELL PASTA WITH TUNA AND CAPERS

ORZO WITH SMOKED SALMON

Baked Salmon Steaks

COOKING SALMON THIS WAY could not be easier than this. The oven does all the work, leaving you free to prepare a sauce for the salmon, or a vegetable. If it is asparagus season, make the Brown Butter Sauce (see box, page 79), which is magic on both salmon and asparagus. If asparagus is not on the scene, make the Green Sauce (page 223) and use it on spinach or zucchini as well as the salmon.

4 salmon steaks, about
½ pound each
(1 to 1¼ inch thick)

2 tablespoons olive oil
Salt and pepper to taste

Preheat oven to 450°F.

Preparing and Cooking the Fish

- Rinse the salmon steaks with cold water and pat dry.
- Brush both sides of the steaks with the olive oil, and sprinkle with salt and pepper.
- Arrange the steaks in a baking dish large enough to hold them in one layer, cover snugly with foil, and put in the hot oven. After 20 minutes, lift the foil and check for doneness. The salmon should have turned from a deep orange-pink to a dull, pale-pink color. Test by cutting into a piece: if it still has any of the deep translucent color, bake for another 5 minutes and check again.
- To serve, lift the steaks carefully onto serving plates with a spatula. Their shape makes it easy for them to fall apart, so ease the spatula under each one, using a second spatula, if necessary, to lift the steak out whole.

Baked Red Snapper with Vegetables

SERVES FOUR

RED SNAPPER IS A fine-flavored, firm, white-fleshed fish, which is delicious and can be cooked using just about any method. But this combination of snapper, cabbage, celery, carrots, and fresh lemon juice is a winner. Round out the meal with steamed buttered red potatoes (see box), include warm Yellow Cornbread (page 246), with Baked Apples (page 288) for dessert. This is a perfect meal.

¼ head cabbage (about 3 cups chopped; see procedure)	2½ tablespoons butter at room temperature
3 stalks celery	1 pound fillet of red snapper or other white fish (4 fillets)
2 carrots	Salt and pepper to taste
1 or 2 lemons (to make 1½ tablespoons lemon juice)	

Preheat oven to 450°F.

Preparing the Vegetables

◆ Cut a head of green cabbage in half, then cut one of the halves in half again. You will use only one quarter here, so save the other three quarters for another use. Check the index for suggestions.

◆ Place the quarter head of cabbage flat side down on a cutting board, and use a sharp knife to cut it into slices about ½ inch thick. Cut the slices crosswise into ½-inch pieces.

◆ Trim the stem and leaf ends from three stalks of celery. Cut the stalks lengthwise into strips about ½ inch wide, then cut the long strips crosswise into pieces ½ inch square.

◆ Peel the carrots. Trim the tip and stem ends, then rub carrots up and down against the large holes of a metal grater to shred them.

◆ Squeeze the juice from 1 or 2 lemons to obtain 1½ tablespoons juice.

Making a Bed for the Fish

◆ Melt the butter in a small pot over medium heat. With your fingers smear the melted butter over the bottom and sides of a 9-inch square baking dish.

◆ Layer the cabbage in the baking dish, then spread the celery and carrots on top of the cabbage.

◆ Rinse the fillets with cold water and pat dry. Put the fish fillets on top of the vegetables in a single layer. Sprinkle with salt and pepper to taste and drizzle the lemon juice over.

◆

STEAMED POTATOES

Start the potatoes cooking just before you put the fish in the oven. For 4 people, wash 2 pounds of small red potatoes and put them on a steaming basket (you can buy these steaming baskets—they are made of metal or plastic—in hardware and cookware stores for very little money) set over a pot of water. The bottom of the basket should sit above the water level. Sprinkle with salt and pepper. Turn the heat to high and put a lid on the pan. When the water begins to boil, turn the heat to medium-low and let the potatoes steam about 15 minutes. Check for doneness by piercing a potato with the tip of a paring knife. If it feels tender, they are done. Remove them to a warm bowl, add about 2 tablespoons butter (preferably at room temperature), and toss until the butter melts.

◆

• Cover the dish with foil and place in the oven. Bake for 15 minutes, then test for doneness. The fish is done when the fillets have turned opaque at the thickest part. If the fillets are still translucent, cook for another 5 minutes and test again. The exact cooking time will vary according to the thickness of the fish.

Serving the Fish and Vegetables

• Remove the pan from the oven and serve immediately, lifting out plenty of the vegetables with each portion of fish. Spoon any pan juices over the fish.

■

BROWN BUTTER SAUCE

This is the most overlooked sauce, but I find it one of the most flavorful. Try it with fish, asparagus, green beans, zucchini, baked winter squash (use the honey brown butter variation on the baked squash, page 197, it is also wonderful), on carrots, and with all varieties of potato, rice, pasta, and more. Use salted butter to make this sauce if you wish to save some in the refrigerator, because it will keep longer than unsalted butter. Just reheat and serve.

Cut 1 stick butter (½ cup) into 5 or 6 pieces, kind of like pats of butter.

Use a small saucepan (not a black, nonstick-lined skillet or pan, because you can't see the browning process). Put the butter in the pan, turn the heat to medium-high, and let the butter melt. In about 1 minute it will be melted, and then it will begin to foam. Stay by the stove. Now, holding the handle, move the pan around so the butter swirls in the pan. In a minute or two, you will see the butter turning a light-caramel color. Let it cook, continuing to move the pan for about 5 more seconds, then remove from the stove and stir once or twice. Let cool.

If you are saving your Brown Butter Sauce for later use, let it cool for about ten minutes, then pour it into a small jar, cover, and refrigerate until needed. When you are ready to use it, just run hot water around the jar and the butter will slide out. Heat in a little pan.

Variation: With Honey

To make honey brown butter, add 2 tablespoons honey to the melted butter after you have browned it and cooled it for a minute, and serve it over Roast Zucchini (page 191) or Baked Butternut Squash (page 197).

■

Parchment-Wrapped Fish Fillets

Serves four

PARCHMENT-WRAPPED FISH FILLETS ARE easy to prepare and quick to cook. The fillets are wrapped with a dash of Chinese sauce in parchment paper, making a neat, tidy package (see illustration on page 74). The steam created inside the packet cooks the fish gently and quickly, keeping it moist and holding in all the good flavors. Parchment paper comes in a roll and can be found in most supermarkets, but if you can't locate any, aluminum foil works well, too. Fish fillets are boned pieces of fish, although you need to check for bones in each piece by running your index finger over it to feel if any bones have been left in. If so, the easiest way to remove them is to use eyebrow tweezers to grip the bones and pull them out. (The Chinese ingredients can all be found in supermarkets and they keep indefinitely.) This is an exciting way to present fish. When you open each packet at the table the fresh, fragrant aroma of the Chinese sauce and fish is quite wonderful.

1

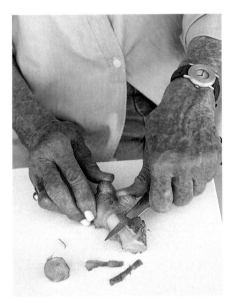

2

A chunk of gingerroot, about 1½ inches long
2 cloves garlic
2 tablespoons light soy sauce
2 tablespoons sesame oil
2 tablespoons rice-wine vinegar
1½ tablespoons sugar
Four 4-to-5-ounce fish fillets such as red snapper or cod
4 pieces of parchment paper, 12 by 18 inches
Vegetable oil or butter for the paper
Salt and pepper to taste

Preheat oven to 425°F.

Preparing the Sauce

◆ 1) Peel the outer skin off 1½ inches of ginger with a sharp paring knife. Slice the chunk into thin rounds or "coins." 2) Stack the coins and cut them into sticks, then cut the sticks crosswise into tiny dice. You should have about 1½ tablespoons.

◆ Peel the papery skin off the garlic, and cut the cloves into tiny dice (see box, page 33, for full details).

◆ Mix the soy sauce, sesame oil, rice-wine vinegar, and sugar in a small bowl, stirring well to dissolve the sugar. Add the ginger and garlic.

Preparing the Fish

◆ Rinse the fish with cold water and pat dry.

◆ Fold the long side of each piece of parchment in half, then open it up and lay it out flat. Using your fingers, rub a little butter or oil on the entire inside surface of the parchment. Place one fillet on one half of each piece of parchment, and sprinkle the fish with salt and pepper.

◆ Spoon 1½ tablespoons of the sauce over each piece of fish, making sure you include bits of garlic and ginger in each spoonful.

◆ Cover each fillet by folding the empty half of the parchment over the fish. Seal the packets by rolling up the edges of each packet tightly and pinching them together. Turn the packets over and place them on a large baking sheet.

Baking the Fish

◆ Be sure your oven has reached the temperature of 425°F when you put the baking sheet into the oven with the packets.

◆ Set the baking sheet on the middle rack of the oven and bake for 12 minutes. Unwrap one packet to check for doneness. Cut a little slit in the center of the fillet. If the inside looks like the outside—dull rather than shiny—it is done. If it is shiny—i.e., not opaque—and not firm, leave the packets in the oven for 3 to 5 minutes longer.

◆ Turn each packet onto a serving plate, folded side up, and let everyone open his own at the table. There's an appealing aroma when you open the package.

ABOUT GINGER

Fresh gingerroot (found in the produce section of the super-market) is much more lively and spicy than ground dried ginger. The dried is used in baking and the fresh is used more often in savory, not sweet, preparations. Fresh gingerroot becomes more tame when cooked.

◆ SERVING SUGGESTION: ORZO ◆

With your packages of fish, try serving the small pasta called orzo, tossed with a little butter and salt and some fresh chopped cilantro (see box, page 34). Orzo, which looks like grains of rice, takes about 10 minutes to cook in a pot of boiling water. One and one-third cups of dry orzo yield 3 cups when cooked. Mix ¼ cup of cilantro leaves into every cupful of cooked orzo.

Trout with Celery Root

SERVES FOUR

GIVE THIS RECIPE a try and you won't be disappointed. Trout is a fine, inexpensive fish with tender, clean white flesh. As for celery root, it is mostly overlooked, probably because it is a big, misshapen, dirty-looking round root. But once you peel off the ugly outer skin you will discover a treasure. The peeled root is delicately flavored and very good with fish, salads, soups, and stews. In this recipe the celery root is coarsely grated to make a bed for the trout and both are baked together. You could serve this with rice or Steamed Potatoes (box, page 78) and Parslied Small Red Potatoes (page 186) and for dessert the Lemon Pudding Cake (page 266), which can be made ahead.

1 celery root (about 1 pound)	8 to 10 sprigs parsley
2 tablespoons butter	½ cup cream
4 whole trout, cleaned and boned	4 teaspoons Dijon mustard
	Salt to taste

Preheat oven to 400°F.

Preparing the Celery Root

♦ Using a large sharp knife, slice off and discard the root end and the green stalks of the celery root if there are any. Cut off the brownish, gnarled sides, revealing the fragrant white interior. The outside is not as tough as it looks.

♦ Grate the celery root, using the larger (¼-inch) holes of either a flat or the box variety of grater.

♦ Smear butter on the sides and bottom of a 9-by-13-by-2-inch baking dish, and spread the grated celery root over the bottom of the dish.

Preparing the Trout

♦ Rinse the fish with cool water and pat dry. If the trout still have their heads and tails, cut them off and discard, if they offend you.

♦ Using your hands, open up and flatten out the trout. Feel to see if there are any stray bones that weren't removed when the fish were cleaned. Cut the bones out with a sharp knife or pull them out with tweezers.

♦ Place the opened-up trout in the baking dish, skin side down, on top of the grated celery root.

♦ Rinse and pat dry the parsley sprigs, and finely chop the leaves (you want about 3 tablespoons).

• In a small bowl, mix together the cream and mustard and spread it all over the fish. Sprinkle on 2 tablespoons of the chopped parsley and a little salt, cover the dish with foil, and put in the oven.

• Bake for 20 minutes, then test for doneness. The trout are ready when the flesh has turned opaque and lifts easily from the skin. If not quite cooked, bake for another 5 minutes.

Serving the Trout

• Using a broad metal spatula, lift the trout—along with the portion of celery root under each fish—onto serving plates. Spoon any pan juices over the top, and sprinkle on the chopped parsley.

◆ COOKING RICE ◆

Be sure to buy long-grain white rice for ordinary purposes—not converted or instant or short-grained rice. One cup will yield 3 cups when cooked, and you will need ½ to ¾ cup cooked per serving, depending on appetites. It is always nice to have some rice left over, which you can fry in a little butter with some chopped onion and green pepper and perhaps some diced ham, or you can make a rice salad. So err on the side of generosity when you calculate how much to cook.

Here is the formula:

AMOUNT RICE	AMOUNT SALT	AMOUNT LIQUID	YIELD COOKED
1 cup	¾ teaspoon	2 cups cold water	3 cups
1½ cups	1 teaspoon	3 cups cold water	4½ cups
2 cups	1¼ teaspoons	4 cups cold water	6 cups

Pour the water into a heavy-bottomed pot (1-quart size for the smaller amount of rice; 1½-quarts for the larger amounts of rice). Add the salt and the rice and set over high heat. Bring to a boil, then immediately turn the heat to low, cover, and cook 15 to 20 minutes.

Check after 15 minutes to see if all the water has been absorbed and if there are holes on the surface of the rice (what Chinese cooks call the "eyes"). If so, the rice is done. If it is not ready, cook another 3 to 5 minutes. Turn off the heat and let steam, covered, for 5 minutes.

Fluff up the rice with a fork and serve hot.

Cooking Brown Rice

Cook by the same method, but brown rice will take at least double the amount of time to cook. Check after 35 minutes. If the water is all absorbed and the rice is not quite done, add a little more water and cook another 5 minutes. One cup brown rice yields only 2 cups when cooked.

Poached Halibut with Fennel

FENNEL, which is found in the fresh-produce section of the supermarket and sometimes labeled "anise," is a rounded, slightly flat white bulb, with feathery leaves atop its stalks. It is crisp like celery, and has a very mild licorice flavor that seems to complement fish. This quick recipe takes only about 6 minutes to prepare, and you cook the vegetables and fish together in one dish. Steamed potatoes (see box, page 78) are good to round out the meal, and you should put them on to steam about 15 minutes before you prepare the fish dish.

1-pound fennel bulb with feathery green tops	¾ cup water
3 tablespoons butter	1½ pounds halibut steaks (4 pieces)
1½ teaspoons salt	2 lemons
Pepper to taste	

Preparing and Cooking the Fennel

◆ Cut the stalks with the feathery green tops off the round bulb and set aside. Trim any brown, discolored spots off the bulb and discard. Slice off the tough bottom or root end—about ½ inch—and discard.

◆ Slice the bulb crosswise, making 5 half-inch slices of fennel.

◆ Put a 10- or 12-inch sauté pan or skillet (one with a lid) on the stove, turn the heat to medium, and add the butter. When the butter has melted, tilt the pan around so the butter coats the bottom. Using a spatula, put the fennel slices in one layer in the pan, salt and pepper them, and cook for about 3 minutes.

Cooking the Halibut

◆ Rinse the halibut with cold water under the tap and pat dry.

◆ Lightly salt and pepper both sides of the halibut. Place a halibut slice on top of each fennel slice, add ¾ cup of water to the pan, bring to a boil, then turn the heat down to medium-low, and put the lid on. The halibut will cook very quickly, in about 3 to 5 minutes. Check after 3 minutes; it is done when the fish looks white and dull. To be sure, cut a little slit in the center of the fish. If it is the same dull white in the middle, the fish is done. Be careful not to let the fish cook for too long. Overcooked halibut can be very dry.

Serving the Halibut

◆ Using a wide spatula or pancake turner, lift the fennel slices and halibut onto plates. Spoon 2 or 3 tablespoons of the pan juices over each serving.

◆ Cut the lemons into quarters lengthwise and remove the seeds from each wedge with the point of the knife. Squeeze a little lemon juice over each serving, put a wedge or two on the plate beside the halibut, and put a sprig of the feathery fennel on top of each serving. Serve hot.

■

FISH FOR POACHING

You need a sturdy cut of fish for poaching. Thin, flimsy fillets are apt to disintegrate in the poaching liquid. So I recommend a steak that is cut from larger fish, such as halibut, cod, salmon, or a good-sized bass, and you can use them interchangeably in this recipe. The steaks are cut, about ¾- to 1-inch thick, directly through the backbone, so there is a piece of fillet on each side held together by a central bone. The skin is usually left on and gives flavor as well as keeping the steak intact.

■

Poached Salmon with Cucumber and Caper Sauce

SERVES FOUR

POACHING—THAT IS, COOKING in gently boiling water—is a foolproof method for any firm piece of fish cut like a steak and leaves the fish delicate and moist. But you do need a firm fish cut like a steak; a thin fillet would dissolve. In this case, poaching the salmon takes about 4 minutes. The Cucumber and Caper Sauce adds crispness and tartness to the salmon. It is also a good, all-around sauce for any kind of fish.

CUCUMBER AND CAPER SAUCE

1 cucumber	Salt to taste
4 sprigs parsley	3 tablespoons water
3 tablespoons butter	1 tablespoon capers

THE FISH

4 salmon steaks, about ½ pound each (1 to 1¼ inches thick)	Water for poaching Salt

Making the Sauce

♦ Peel the cucumber. Cut it in half lengthwise; then, with a spoon, scrape out the seeds and discard them. Cut each half into 3 or 4 lengthwise slices, then cut those long pieces crosswise into dice.

♦ Rinse the parsley, pat dry, and remove and discard the stems. Finely chop the leaves. You should have about 2 teaspoons. Set aside.

♦ Melt the butter over low heat in a small pot. Add the diced cucumber and salt lightly. Cook for about 2 minutes, stirring constantly.

♦ Add the 3 tablespoons of water and the capers and stir to blend. Taste, and add more salt if needed. Cucumbers sometimes need a good dose of salt to bring out the flavor.

♦ Stir in the chopped parsley, and remove the sauce from the heat.

Preparing the Salmon

◆ Rinse the salmon steaks with cold water and pat dry.

◆ Four salmon steaks should fit into an 11-inch sauté pan, or any straight-sided pan about 2 to 3 inches deep, with a capacity of 2 to 3 quarts. Put about 1½ inches of water in the pan, add salt, and stir. Set the pan on a burner turned to high and bring to a boil.

◆ When the water boils, turn the heat down to low, so the water is at a low simmer, or what I like to call a lazy bubble. You want just that bare bit of motion to cook the fish gently.

◆ Put the salmon steaks in the pan, and simmer for about 4 minutes after the water resumes its gentle bubbling. Stand at the stove and spoon the simmering water over the top of the fish so the pieces cook on top as well. The salmon is done when the meat turns from a deep to a pale pink. Use a fork or the point of a knife to poke into the center of a steak; the middle, too, should be that paler pink. Remove the pan from the heat as soon as the steaks are done.

Serving the Salmon

◆ Remove the salmon steaks from the pan with a slotted spoon (leaving the poaching liquid behind) and place on serving plates. Spoon the Cucumber and Caper Sauce over the steaks, or serve the sauce separately to be passed at the table.

Shrimp Curry

SERVES SIX

THIS IS A SPLENDID DISH to serve friends, or for a special occasion. It is an easy, basic recipe, but it becomes festive when served with steamed rice (see box, page 83) and some small dishes of Fresh Pineapple Chutney (page 232) or other chutney, sliced bananas, golden raisins, peanuts, and a small bowl of finely chopped scallions or cilantro. Have fun making up your own assortment of sweet, crunchy, and fiery condiments.

1 medium-size yellow onion
4 green onions or scallions
5 tablespoons butter
5 tablespoons all-purpose white flour
2½ cups chicken broth, canned or homemade

1¼ tablespoons curry powder
½ teaspoon salt, or to taste
2 teaspoons fresh lemon juice
2 pounds cooked shrimp

Making the Curry Sauce

• Peel and finely chop the yellow onion (for full details, see page 13).

• Trim and chop the green onions or scallions (for full details, see page 51).

• Melt the butter over medium heat in a medium-size skillet, add the yellow onion, and cook until it is tender—about 4 or 5 minutes. Add the flour and stir constantly for about 2 or 3 minutes.

• Slowly add the chicken broth, curry powder, and salt, and cook over medium-low heat until the sauce thickens to the consistency of melted ice cream, stirring constantly.

• Add the lemon juice and shrimp, and heat through, for about 3 to 5 minutes.

• Serve with white rice, and sprinkle on the chopped green onion or scallion. Serve the Fresh Pineapple Chutney and other condiments alongside.

Small Shell Pasta with Tuna and Capers

YOU PROBABLY NEVER THOUGHT a little 12-ounce can of tuna could come to your rescue when you needed a quick dinner, or that it could taste so good. Canned tuna is one of our unsung pantry heroes. It also makes a hearty Tuna and Corn Chowder (see page 29).

4 quarts water	3 tablespoons butter
1 tablespoon salt	1 12-ounce can solid white
4½ cups uncooked small shell	tuna in water
pasta (about 1 pound)	1 cup chicken broth, canned
A few sprigs parsley (to make	or homemade
3 tablespoons chopped)	1½ tablespoons capers

Cooking the Pasta

◆ Put the water and salt in a large heavy-bottomed pot and place over high heat. Bring to a boil, stir in the pasta shells, and cook at a gentle boil. Start checking for doneness after 12 minutes. Extract a shell with a slotted spoon; it should be tender when you bite into it.

Preparing the Parsley and Tuna

◆ While the shells cook, rinse the parsley and pat dry. Discard the stems, and finely chop the leaves (for full details, see box, page 12)—you want 3 tablespoons chopped.

◆ Melt the butter in a small pot over medium heat. Drain the liquid from the can of tuna, discard, and add the tuna to the butter. With a fork break up the solid tuna into bite-size pieces, add the chicken broth, and simmer for 5 minutes to heat thoroughly.

Serving the Pasta

◆ When the pasta is done, drain into a colander set in the sink. Shake the colander to get rid of all the water, and dump the shells into a large warm bowl.

◆ Pour the tuna and broth over the shells, and add the chopped parsley and the capers. Toss well and serve on warm plates.

Orzo with Smoked Salmon

ORZO IS A TINY PASTA that looks like grains of rice. Quick to cook, it lends just the right background to the smoked salmon. Smoked salmon always seems celebratory, and a little goes a long way, adding flavor and color to the orzo. A small Watercress Salad (page 46) is good with this dish.

2 quarts (8 cups) water
2 teaspoons salt
2 cups orzo
4 ounces smoked salmon, or
    about ½ cup chopped,
    firmly packed into cup

3 tablespoons olive oil
Freshly ground pepper
¼ cup capers, drained

Cooking the Orzo

◆ Put the water and salt in a medium-size saucepan and bring to a boil over high heat.

◆ Slowly add the orzo to the boiling water and stir once or twice.

Finishing the Dish

◆ After about 10 minutes of cooking, scoop up a piece of orzo from the pot and taste it. If it is tender it is done. Pour the orzo into a colander in the sink to drain off the water.

◆ Cut the salmon into small pieces.

◆ Put the cooked orzo into a medium-size warm bowl and add the olive oil and the pepper. Stir well.

◆ Add the salmon and the capers (do not add the liquid from the capers). Taste and add more salt if needed. Stir again and serve warm.

◆

Thank Goodness for Chicken

◆

INTRODUCTION

———

I SAY THANK GOODNESS for chicken because it is inexpensive and versatile, it tastes good, and almost everyone likes it. Plus there are endless ways of using leftover chicken—in salads, vegetables, and pastas, and you can't beat a chicken-salad sandwich.

Roasting a chicken takes about 1 hour, but you don't need to fuss with it once it is in the oven. If you cook chicken pieces (legs and thighs), you can pan-fry them on top of the stove in about 20 to 25 minutes. The breast takes only 12 to 15 minutes. Once you have learned to handle and cook chicken, you'll find that you can prepare any kind of poultry—turkey, duck, small birds—the basics are the same.

RECIPES

———

ROAST CHICKEN WITH VEGETABLES

SMOTHERED CHICKEN WITH MUSHROOMS

PAN-FRIED CHICKEN

CHICKEN WITH FEATHER DUMPLINGS

CHICKEN VINEGAR SAUTÉ

GINGER CHICKEN BREASTS

CHICKEN PIECES ROASTED WITH VEGETABLES

Carving a chicken is a simple process that takes a little patience; it gets easier each time you do it. If your chicken truly is cooked enough, it should be easy to remove the meat. It's not a delicate process, though, so don't be shy about manhandling the chicken a bit. Wait until it has cooled just enough for you to handle it comfortably.

Set the chicken breast side up. Pull the leg and thigh back to expose the joint that attaches it to the body (have a little patience; wiggling the thigh section and pulling it away from the body with your hands helps). 1) Use a sharp paring knife to probe for the socket and cut through it, separating the leg and thigh from the carcass.

Repeat with the other leg and thigh.

1

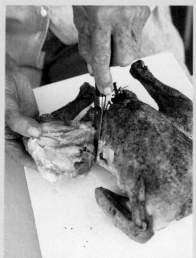

2

2) Use the knife to cut through the joint that connects the leg to the thigh.

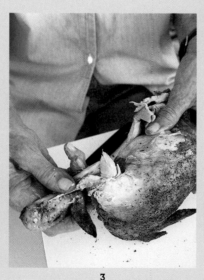

3

3) Pull off the wings by gently twisting them away from the carcass. You may need the aid of your knife to separate the wings fully.

The breastbone runs along the top center of the chicken carcass. Feel for it with your fingers. Make a 3-inch-long slit along both sides of the breastbone. 4) Dig your fingers into one of the slits and peel the entire half of the breast meat off the carcass. Do the same to remove the breast meat on the other side. Slice each half of breast meat crosswise, making 5 or 6 slices per breast half.

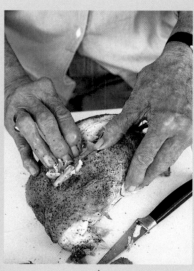

4

Pick or cut off whatever meat remains on the carcass. Arrange the legs, thighs, wings, and meat on a platter and serve.

Roast Chicken with Vegetables

SERVES FOUR

NEW COOKS ARE INTIMIDATED by the idea of roasting a chicken, but nothing could be simpler. If you roast the chicken with some vegetables in the same pan for about an hour, you will have a moist, golden bird and savory accompaniments—all ready to eat at the same time. While they cook, you can set the table, watch the news, maybe make a dessert. Sometimes it's handy to roast 2 chickens at the same time; it takes no extra effort, and you will have plenty of left-overs for salads, soups, sandwiches, or a main dish of cold chicken with Green Sauce (see page 223).

8 whole carrots	1 teaspoon black pepper
2 medium-size yellow onions	4 sprigs fresh or 1 tablespoon
8 small white or red potatoes	dried rosemary
(about 1½ inches in	1 whole chicken, about
diameter)	3½ pounds
3 teaspoons salt	

Preheat oven to 425°F.

Preparing the Vegetables

◆ Peel the carrots and cut them crosswise into 1½-inch-long pieces. Cut the thicker pieces in half lengthwise as well (for full details on preparing carrots, see box, page 201).

◆ Peel each onion and cut into quarters (for full details on cutting onions, see page 13).

◆ Wash the potatoes under cold water to get rid of any dirt. Leave them whole and unpeeled.

◆ Scatter the carrots, onions, and potatoes on the bottom of a 9-by-13-inch baking or roasting pan. Sprinkle 1½ teaspoons of the salt and ½ teaspoon of the pepper over them, and lay 2 sprigs of the rosemary on top. If you are using dried rosemary, put 1 tablespoon in the palm of your hand and crumble it over the vegetables.

Preparing the Chicken

◆ The giblets, which consist of the liver, gizzard, and heart, plus the neck, are usually in a package inside the cavity of the chicken, between the legs. Remove them and discard or refrigerate them to use later (see box, this page, Cleaning the Chicken).

◆

CLEANING THE CHICKEN

The first step in preparing a whole chicken for roasting is to reach inside the chicken cavity and remove the giblets (liver, gizzard, heart) and the neck. Sometimes they are in a little bag, sometimes loose, and sometimes they are not included. The liver can be chopped and quickly cooked in a little butter or oil in a skillet, then added to an omelet, or just cooked and eaten as a treat. The remaining giblets can be used in a soup; or, if you don't care to use them, cook them for the dog.

◆

- If there is a pale-yellow chunk of fat on either side of the cavity, pull or cut it off and discard.
- Hold the chicken under cold running water and rinse it inside and out. Shake off excess water and pat dry with paper towels.
- Sprinkle the remaining 1½ teaspoons of salt and ½ teaspoon of pepper over the outside of the chicken, rubbing them all over the skin.
- Set the chicken, the breast side facing up, on top of some of the vegetables, with the remaining ones surrounding the bird.
- Insert a dial-type (not instant-read) thermometer into the breast, taking care that the rod of the thermometer does not touch any bones.

Roasting the Chicken
- Put the chicken in the center of the oven and set the timer for 30 minutes.
- When the timer rings, remove the pan from the oven and, using a large spoon, turn over the vegetables that surround the chicken. Don't bother with the vegetables under the chicken.
- Return the pan to the oven and set the timer for 30 more minutes.
- After 30 minutes, take the chicken out of the oven to check for doneness. Insert the tip of a small paring knife into the meat of the thigh where it attaches to the body. If the juices that run out are pink, the chicken needs to continue cooking for another 10 to 15 minutes. If the juices are clear, it is done. The meat thermometer should show a temperature of 170°F to 180°F when the chicken is done.

Carving the Chicken
- Carve the chicken according to the instructions on the preceding page.
- Scoop the vegetables out of the roasting pan and onto a serving platter. Remove the fat from the pan juices (see box, this page).
- Arrange the cut chicken pieces on top of vegetables, spoon some pan juices over the chicken and vegetables, scatter the 2 remaining rosemary sprigs on top, and bring the dish to the table for serving.

■

REMOVING THE FAT FROM A ROASTING PAN

Remove your roast and vegetables to a serving platter. Tilt the pan they were cooked in and spoon off and discard some of the shiny, clear fat floating on the surface; you can also use a bulb baster to suck it up. You won't get every bit of fat off, but don't worry about it. Now pour all the good pan juices onto the chicken and vegetables.

■

Smothered Chicken with Mushrooms

THIS IS ONE of those dishes that everyone seems to like. The flavors are captured in the simple sauce that brings together the delicate chicken flavor and the earthy mushrooms.

4 chicken half breasts (with their ribs and skin)	4 tablespoons all-purpose white flour
2 medium-size yellow onions	½ pound mushrooms
Salt and pepper	½ bunch parsley
4 tablespoons vegetable oil	4 slices bread
1½ cups chicken broth, canned or homemade	2 tablespoons butter

Preheat oven to 350°F.

Starting the Chicken

◆ Rinse the chicken pieces under cold running water and pat dry with paper towels.

◆ Peel and chop the onions (for full details, see page 13).

◆ Lightly salt and pepper the chicken pieces.

◆ Put the oil in a large skillet and set it over medium-high heat. Hold your hand about an inch above the bottom of the pan, and if it feels hot it's ready.

◆ When the oil is hot, place the chicken, skin side down, in the hot oil. After 1 or 2 minutes, spear a piece with a fork and inspect the underside to see if it's turning brown. If so, turn it over and cook for another 2 minutes; if not, cook another minute or two before turning. When all the pieces are browned, put them into a casserole (one with a lid).

◆ Put the onions in the same skillet you cooked the chicken in, and stir them around to brown just slightly. This takes about 2 or 3 minutes. Put ½ cup chicken broth and the flour in a jar with a lid. Tighten the lid and shake the jar vigorously for a minute, until well mixed and without any flour lumps. Pour into the skillet with the heat still at medium-high, and keep stirring continuously for about a minute as the sauce thickens. Slowly add the remaining cup of chicken broth and constantly stir all around the sides and bottom of the skillet. You can use a whisk to help break up any small lumps. Keep stirring—the sauce will thicken in a minute. When it is smooth and the consistency of thick soup, remove from the stove.

◆ Pour the sauce over the chicken in the casserole, put the lid on, and place in the oven.

◆ While the chicken is cooking, wipe the mushrooms clean with a paper towel and cut them into quarters (for full details, see box, page 169).

◆ After 20 minutes, remove the lid from the casserole, add the mushrooms, cover again, and continue to cook for another 10 minutes.

Preparing the Parsley and the Bread
◆ While the chicken is in the oven, finely chop enough parsley to make about ½ cup.

◆ Just before the chicken is done, toast 4 slices of bread and butter generously.

Serving the Chicken
◆ Remove the casserole from the oven, and taste the sauce. Add salt and pepper to taste.

◆ Put the slices of toast on 4 plates, place a chicken breast on each toast, and spoon the mushrooms and sauce over the top. Sprinkle the parsley generously over the chicken and mushrooms and serve hot.

Pan-Fried Chicken

SERVES FOUR

PAN-FRYING CHICKEN MEANS cooking it in a very small amount of fat, in this case vegetable oil. The nice things that go with chicken are Mashed Potatoes (page 184), Baking Powder Biscuits (page 238) with honey, Green Peas (see box, opposite), and Chocolate Pudding for dessert (page 271). It wouldn't hurt to pan-fry more chicken pieces than you need for one meal. Cold fried chicken is just as good—if not better—the next day. The potatoes and biscuits you would probably want to prepare just before you start frying the chicken, which requires close attention. For the peas, put them on during the last few minutes of the chicken cooking (see box, opposite).

1 cut-up chicken (8 pieces), 2½ to 3 pounds (see box, page 102)	1 teaspoon salt
	½ teaspoon freshly ground pepper
½ cup flour	3 tablespoons vegetable oil

Preparing and Cooking the Chicken

• Rinse each of the pieces of chicken under cold running water and pat dry with a towel or paper towels.

• Tear off a piece of waxed paper about 14 by 12 inches and put it on the counter. Mix the flour, salt, and pepper together on the waxed paper.

• Roll each piece of chicken, one by one, in the flour mixture until it is completely coated with the flour. Shake each piece to get rid of excess flour. Set aside and continue to coat the remaining chicken. Don't do this ahead or the coating will get gummy; do it just before you fry the chicken.

Pan-Frying the Chicken

• Choose a skillet or frying pan large enough to hold all the chicken pieces in one layer. If you are cooking more than your skillet can hold, you will need to do the frying in 2 batches or in 2 skillets.

- Put the skillet on the burner and turn the heat to medium-high, heating it until it feels hot when you place your open hand—palm side down—an inch above the bottom of the skillet. Add 2 tablespoons of oil to the skillet, then tilt and turn the skillet so the bottom is completely covered with oil. Place the chicken pieces in a single layer in the skillet.

- Stand by the stove and let the pieces brown on one side; this takes about 4 or 5 minutes. Peek at the bottom of a piece to see how brown it is. It should be golden brown, not dark brown.

- When the pieces are brown on the bottom, turn each piece over with a fork and let brown on the other side.

- Turn the heat down to medium and if the skillet bottom seems dry add the remaining tablespoon of oil. Cook over medium heat for about 10 minutes, then turn the pieces over again and let cook for another 10 minutes.

- Test the doneness of the chicken by cutting into the thigh close to the bone. If the meat is not pink, it is done. If there's still some pink, cook for a few more minutes and test again.

- Serve hot.

◆

PEAS

Frozen peas are one of the good frozen vegetables. They are best boiled—not steamed or microwaved. Simply put them in a pot, cover them with boiling water, and simmer them for 3 minutes, breaking up the frozen block with a fork. Now taste a pea and see if it is tender; if not, cook a minute or two longer. When done, drain through a colander or strainer and toss the peas with a little butter and salt.

When fresh peas are in season they are a real treat. It may take some time to remove the peas from their pods, but get a friend or family member to sit with you on the porch or wherever and visit while you shell peas together. Cook them the same as you would frozen peas but be sure to taste because really young peas take only a minute or two. You will need at least ½ pound of unshelled peas per person.

◆

Chicken with Feather Dumplings

DUMPLINGS ARE SMALL BALLS of dough that are added to soups or stews. They take the place of potatoes and rice, and when they are prepared well, they are a treat. They used to be a staple in parts of America where Middle Europeans settled, but they have slowly fallen out of favor, probably because when poorly made they are apt to be heavy and coarse. But these dumplings are feather-light and flavorful, and you will have created something wonderful when you serve them.

THE CHICKEN

1 cut-up chicken (10–12 pieces) 4½ to 5 pounds	1 large yellow onion
	1½ teaspoons dried thyme
Water to cover chicken by 1½ inches	½ teaspoon dried rosemary
	2 teaspoons salt
2 carrots	½ teaspoon freshly ground
2 stalks celery with leaves	pepper

THE DUMPLINGS

1 cup flour	1 small onion
½ cup fresh bread crumbs (box, page 153)	A few sprigs parsley
	1 egg
2 teaspoons baking powder	⅓ cup milk
¾ teaspoon salt	Freshly ground pepper to taste
2 tablespoons butter	

Cooking the Chicken and Vegetables

• Rinse the chicken pieces under cold running water and put them in a large pot. Add enough water to cover the chicken by 1½ inches.

• Peel the carrots and cut them crosswise into ¼-inch-thick pieces; add to the pot.

• Trim off 1 inch of the stem end of the celery, cut the stalks crosswise into ¼-inch pieces, and add to the pot.

• Peel and coarsely chop the onion (for full details, see page 13). Add to the pot.

• Crumble the thyme and rosemary into the pot by rubbing the herbs in the palms of your hands. Add the salt and pepper.

• Turn the heat to high, bring the water to a boil, then reduce the heat to medium-low so it just simmers. Cover and simmer for 20 minutes.

■ BUYING CUT-UP CHICKEN

When buying a package of cut-up chicken, you can choose to buy 1 whole chicken cut-up with 2 legs, 2 thighs, 2 halves of chicken breast that you can cut in half after cooking. For this recipe, because you want 4½ to 5 pounds of chicken, you would probably have to augment 1 cut-up chicken with an extra package of whatever parts you prefer. Or if you like all dark meat, you can buy packages with only legs and thighs. Look and read the package carefully so you know what you are buying.

■

Preparing the Dumplings While the Chicken Cooks

- In a small bowl, mix together the flour, bread crumbs, baking powder, and salt with a fork.
- Melt the butter in a small pan and set aside.
- Peel and finely chop the onion (for full details, see page 13), and measure ¼ cup.
- Rinse the parsley, pat dry, and discard the stems. Finely chop the leaves (for full details, see box, page 12).
- Put the melted butter, onion, egg, and the milk in another bowl, and beat them with a fork to mix well.
- Stir the egg mixture into the dry flour ingredients to make a stiff batter. Stir until smooth, add most of the chopped parsley and the pepper, and mix well.

Cooking the Dumplings and Serving

- When the chicken has simmered for 20 minutes, scoop up rounded tablespoonfuls of batter and then with your finger push it off the spoon on top of the bubbling broth. Continue until you have used up all the batter and the entire surface of the liquid is covered with dumplings. Cover the pot and simmer over low heat for 20 minutes—without lifting the cover—so that the steam from the broth cooks the dumplings tenderly.
- When the chicken and dumplings are done, put a piece or two of chicken in each soup bowl, ladle in some broth, and top with a dumpling or two. Sprinkle the remaining chopped parsley on top and serve hot.

◆

**GETTING SHELL
OUT OF THE EGG**

It happens to everyone—sometimes a small chip of the shell will fall into the bowl with the eggs as you crack them. To extract, simply use a large piece of shell to fish the small chip out. Eggshell has this remarkable ability to cut through the whites, unlike anything else, and to make the fragment of shell adhere.

◆

Chicken Vinegar Sauté

Serves three or four

VINEGAR ADDS A tart accent here and it brings out the good flavor of chicken in the same way lemon juice does. The chicken cooks quickly, and so does the tiny pasta called orzo. You can put on the water for the orzo after you've started the chicken and both will be ready about the same time (see box, page 81, for cooking orzo). Putting some peas in with the orzo not only looks appetizing, it tastes good and supplies the vegetable accompaniment.

8 chicken legs or thighs, or a combination of both	¼ cup water
1 teaspoon salt	2 cloves garlic, about 1 teaspoon chopped
1 teaspoon pepper	2 sprigs parsley
4 tablespoons vegetable oil	½ teaspoon dried tarragon
½ cup red-wine vinegar	

Starting the Chicken

◆ Rinse the chicken pieces under cold running water and pat dry with paper towels.

◆ Sprinkle the chicken pieces all over with salt and pepper.

◆ Pour the vegetable oil into a heavy-bottomed skillet and put over medium-high heat. When you hold your hand about an inch above the oil in the skillet and it feels warm, add the chicken pieces, skin side down.

◆ After 2 or 3 minutes, using a fork or kitchen tongs, lift up a piece of chicken to see if the skin is nicely browned. Turn each piece over when the bottom has browned. Brown the other side—it should take about 8 to 10 minutes in all.

◆ Add half the vinegar and all the water to the pan, cover the pan, and turn the heat to low.

◆ While the chicken is cooking, peel and finely chop the garlic (for full details on garlic, see box, page 33). You'll need 1 teaspoon, a little more if you really like garlic.

◆ Remove the stems from the parsley, and finely chop the leaves (for full details on parsley, see box, page 12).

• Put the dried tarragon on top of the chopped parsley and chop the 2 herbs together. The moisture in the parsley will bring the tarragon flavor to life.

Finishing the Dish

• After the chicken has cooked 15 minutes more, test it for doneness by cutting into a piece to see that the meat is not red and the juice is clear. If the meat is still pink, cook another 5 minutes, and test again.

• When the chicken is done, remove the pieces to a serving dish and keep warm in the oven.

• Add the garlic to the skillet and cook for about 1 minute. Add the rest of the vinegar to the skillet, turn the heat to high, and boil for about 1 minute.

• Pour the pan sauce over the chicken and sprinkle the parsley and tarragon on top. Serve at once.

■

SAUTÉING

To *sauté* means to cook gently in a sauté pan, which is like a skillet but with straight 2½-to-3-inch sides, or you can use a frying pan. You brown the food first in less fat than is ordinarily used for frying, tossing the ingredients in the pan so they don't stick (the word "sauté" comes from the French verb for "to jump"—in other words, the ingredients are made to jump around). Then often a little liquid is added to the pan, and the meat or vegetables—in this case, chicken pieces—are cooked slowly on top of the stove, covered, until they are tender.

■

Ginger Chicken Breasts

THIS RECIPE ANSWERS THE NEED for a supper in a hurry. The skinless chicken breasts are rolled in ground ginger and quickly sautéed in a skillet, then the onions are placed on the chicken and they cook together for 5 minutes. Chicken, onions, and snappy ginger are wonderful together. Any leftover chicken can be used in salads or sandwiches. Serve with riso, a tiny pasta that looks like rice grains and cooks in 6 minutes (see page 159).

3 tablespoons ground ginger
1½ teaspoons salt
¾ teaspoon freshly ground
   black pepper
4 boneless, skinless half
   chicken breasts (for full
   details, see box, opposite)

4 medium-size yellow onions
⅓ bunch parsley
3 tablespoons vegetable oil
1 cup chicken broth, canned
   or homemade, or water

Special Equipment: 12-inch skillet or shallow, flat-bottomed frying pan with a lid (if you don't have a pan with a lid, use aluminum foil instead, covering the pan with it and crimping the edges)

Seasoning the Chicken

◆ Spread out a 12-inch-long piece of waxed paper on a work counter. Put the ginger, salt, and pepper in a heap on the center of the paper. Use your fingers to mix the seasonings together until blended.

◆ Rinse the chicken under cold running water and pat dry.

◆ Cut each half chicken breast in half crosswise. You will have 8 pieces of chicken.

◆ Roll each piece of chicken in the ginger mixture, which will stick because of the moistness of the chicken. Gently shake each piece to get rid of the excess seasoning.

Cutting the Onions and Parsley

◆ Remove the skin from the onions and cut each one in half from the stem down. Put the onions on a cutting board with the cut side facing down and slice across in ⅛-inch-thick slices.

◆ Remove and discard the stems from the parsley and finely chop the leaves.

Sautéing the Chicken

◆ Pour the oil into the skillet, set it over medium-high heat, and tilt the pan so the oil coats the bottom.

- Hold your hand about an inch above the bottom of the skillet. When it feels hot, put the chicken pieces in the pan, leaving a little space between them for even cooking.

- Stand right by the stove and use a fork to move the chicken pieces around from time to time (without turning them over) so they don't stick. After 2 to 3 minutes of sautéing, use the fork to lift up one of the pieces and look to see if it is nicely browned. If so, turn it over. Check on the other pieces in the pan and turn each one over as it is browned.

- Sauté the chicken on the second side another 2 to 3 minutes, until the pieces are browned.

Finishing Up the Dish

- Turn the heat down to low. Pour the broth or water over the chicken and lay the sliced onions on top of the chicken. Put the lid (or foil) on the skillet and set the timer for 5 minutes.

- After 5 minutes, check to see if the chicken is cooked by cutting into the center of one of the pieces with a small paring knife. If the meat is all white with no pink remaining, it is done. If it is still a bit pink, cook it another minute or two and check it again.

- Put the chicken pieces on a serving plate, spoon the onion slices over them, and sprinkle parsley over the top. Serve hot.

◆ ABOUT CHICKEN BREAST ◆

You can buy chicken breast labeled either "Half Chicken Breasts with Ribs," or "Half Chicken Breasts Skin and Bones Removed." The price of the skinned and boned chicken is 4 times that of the unboned, unskinned breast. Removing the ribs and skin is such a simple, quick task that you will wonder why anyone would ever spend so much to have so little done.

The easiest way to pry and peel the meat away from the rib bones is to use your hands. 1) After using a paring knife only to cut through a strand or two of cartilage, with your fingers between the rib bones and the meat, gently pry away the chicken. It will take only a minute or two to free the meat. 2) Last, pull the skin off the breast with your fingers.

1

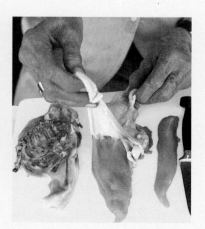

2

Chicken Pieces Roasted with Vegetables

SERVES FOUR

HERE'S A DISH that is one of the delights of home cooking. The juices from the chicken are absorbed by the potatoes and onions and richly flavor them. Plus, everything is done in one pan, minimizing cleanup. Serve this with Parsley Salad (page 44) or just a tossed green salad.

3 tablespoons olive oil

1 cut-up chicken (8 pieces), 2½ to 3 pounds

3 medium-size red onions

8 red potatoes

Salt and pepper to taste

2 teaspoons dried or several sprigs fresh rosemary

2 large garlic cloves

Preheat oven to 425°F.

Preparing the Baking Dish

• Spread 1 tablespoon of the olive oil over the bottom of a 9-by-13-by-2-inch baking dish with your fingers or a paper towel.

Preparing the Chicken and the Vegetables

• Rinse the chicken pieces under cold running water and pat dry with paper towels.

• Peel the red onions and cut into quarters. Wash the potatoes and cut them in half. There's no need to peel them. Salt and pepper the potatoes and onions.

• If you are using fresh rosemary, chop only the small, needlelike leaves, discarding the stems. You should have about 1 tablespoon.

• Peel and finely chop the garlic (see box, page 33, for full details).

• Put the potatoes in the middle of the baking dish and sprinkle the rosemary and garlic over them. Place the chicken pieces on top of the potatoes. Surround the chicken and potatoes with the onions.

• Drizzle the remaining 2 tablespoons of olive oil over the chicken; salt and pepper generously.

Cooking the Chicken and Vegetables

• Put the chicken in the oven and roast for 45 or 50 minutes, or until the skin is nicely browned.

• When the chicken is done, remove everything to a platter. Tilt the pan and carefully spoon off most of the fat, then pour the good pan juices over the chicken and vegetables. Decorate with fresh rosemary branches, if you have them. Serve hot.

◆

Meaty Main Meals

◆

INTRODUCTION

T HERE ARE RECIPES in this chapter that are so sat-isfying you'll be convinced that knowing how to cook is worth it.

Some of the dishes are quick to cook, some take longer. The longer-cooking ones can be pleasant to fix on a Sunday after-noon. Once the ingredients are in a pot simmering on the stove, or in the oven, they don't require your attention, except for an oc-casional peek to see how they're coming along, and the house will have those good aromas wafting around. Once the dish is cooked, you can have it that same day or put it in the refrigerator so that you have a good supper to look forward to.

Try the meatloaf recipe when you can. I have cut the baking time almost in half by making 2 smaller, flatter loaves. Depending on how many servings you need, leftover meatloaf sandwiches are a big favorite with most people. Remember, with any of these recipes, to prepare more than you need for just one meal so you can enjoy the ease of using your leftovers later.

RECIPES

POT ROAST WITH VEGETABLES AND GRAVY

ONE-HOUR BEEF ROAST

OLD-FASHIONED BEEF STEW

AMERICAN MEATLOAF

SUPPER STEAK SALAD SANDWICH

HAMBURGERS

ROAST BEEF HASH

PAN-FRIED PORK CHOPS

JAMES BEARD'S ROASTED SPARERIBS

PORK TENDERLOIN WITH JALAPEÑO SAUCE

PORK WITH SAGE AND BROWN RICE

BAKED HAM

WINTER WHITE BEANS AND HAM

HAM AND SOUR CREAM BAKED NOODLES

ROAST LEG OF LAMB

LAMB SHANKS

QUICK LAMB CURRY

POTATOES, CABBAGE, AND POLISH KIELBASA

Pot Roast with Vegetables and Gravy

SERVES SIX WITH LEFTOVERS

THIS IS A DISH that you can't buy anywhere—it has to be made at home. Once you prepare pot roast, it will become a frequent visitor at your table. Just follow these easy steps and you will love the result. First you brown the meat slowly, which creates a rich flavor and deep color. Then you add water to the pot, put on the lid, and let the meat cook slowly so it becomes tender and moist. This method of cooking with moist heat is called braising.

POT ROAST

4 teaspoons salt	1 cup water, or more
2 teaspoons pepper	3 bay leaves
4 to 5 pounds beef chuck roast, with or without bones	3 medium-size yellow onions
	6 carrots
3 tablespoons vegetable oil	5 medium-size russet potatoes

GRAVY

¼ cup all-purpose white flour	Cooking liquid from the pot roast
1 cup water	Salt and pepper to taste

Browning the Roast

◆ Sprinkle 2 teaspoons of the salt and 1 teaspoon of the pepper on all sides of the meat.

◆ Pour the vegetable oil into a large heavy-bottomed pot, one with a lid, and tilt it around so the oil coats the bottom. Set the pot over medium-high heat and let the oil get hot. To test, hold the palm of your hand about an inch above the oil, and if it feels very warm, the oil is hot enough. Set the meat gently in the pot and turn the heat down to medium.

◆ After about 5 minutes of browning the roast on one side, lift it with a fork and check to see if it has turned a rich brown color on the bottom. If not, let it cook another few minutes and check again. When it becomes a mahogany color, turn it over and let the bottom brown, then turn it again to brown the sides.

Braising the Meat

◆ When the meat has browned on all sides, insert a meat thermometer into the center of the roast not letting it touch the bone, add the water, and crumble the bay leaves into the pot. Put the lid on the pot and turn the heat to medium-low. The roast will take about 1½ to 2 hours to cook.

• Check the roast from time to time as it cooks to make sure the liquid in the pot is gently bubbling. If it is bubbling too rapidly, turn the heat down a bit; if it is not bubbling, turn it up a bit. Also, make sure that there is at least ½ inch of liquid in the bottom of the pot at all times. If not, add 1 cup of water.

Preparing the Vegetables

• While the meat is braising, peel and quarter the onions (for full details on cutting onions, see page 13).

• Peel and cut the carrots into 2-inch lengths (for full details on preparing carrots, see box, page 201).

• Peel and quarter the potatoes. Fill a bowl with cool water for the potatoes to sit in until it's time for them to go in the pot. Once peeled, they will discolor if exposed to air.

• Before adding the carrots and potatoes, season them with the remaining 2 teaspoons of salt and 1 teaspoon of pepper.

Adding the Vegetables and Finishing the Roast

• When the roast has cooked for 1 hour, add the onions, carrots, and potatoes to the pot, spreading them around so they sit alongside and on top of the roast. Cook, simmering, for 30 minutes.

• After 30 minutes, check to see if the roast is done. If the temperature is at least 180°F, it is done. If not, cook it another 20 minutes or so and check again.

Serving the Pot Roast

• Once the roast is done, use a large fork to lift it out of the pot and onto a cutting board. Transfer the vegetables to a warm serving platter and cover with foil. Set aside the pot with the cooking liquid, which you will use to make the gravy (recipe follows).

• Using a large sharp carving knife, cut the roast into ¼-inch-thick slices. Discard any bones. Arrange the meat on the center of the platter with the vegetables surrounding it. Cover the platter with foil and keep warm until you have made the gravy and are ready to serve the meal.

Making the Gravy

◆ Put the flour and water into a 2-cup jar, screw on the lid, and shake for about 5 seconds. If you don't have a jar, mix them in a small bowl with a fork or whisk.

◆ Set the pot with the cooking liquid over medium-high heat (don't worry if there are small bits of vegetables in the pot) and reheat until the liquid begins to bubble gently.

◆ Add the water-flour mixture and stir with a wire whisk for about 1½ to 2 minutes, until the mixture thickens to the consistency of a thick soup.

Seasoning and Serving the Gravy

◆ Taste, and add salt and pepper to the gravy, about ¼ teaspoon at a time, until it is well seasoned according to your personal taste.

◆ Pour into a small bowl or gravy boat and serve hot with the pot roast.

POT ROAST LEFTOVERS

Leftover pot roast makes a wonderful hot sandwich. Heat slices of cold pot roast with some of the gravy in a pan. Put slices of the beef on a slice of bread and spoon hot gravy on top. Serve with a green salad on the side. Or chop the leftover beef into small pieces and add it to cooked brown rice. The flavor of the beef is delicious with the rice.

One-Hour Beef Roast

SERVES FOUR TO SIX

THE TRI-TIP (or triangle, or triangle tip, or bottom sirloin) is a small cut of tender beef from the bottom sirloin. It is the perfect answer when you want the luxury of roast beef in a small version (the tri-tip weighs from 2 to 3 pounds). It serves 5 to 6 people nicely, but is far more affordable than the large cuts of prime beef and only takes an hour to roast. Surrounded with onions and potatoes that cook and brown, in the same amount of time, it makes a festive dinner and is simple to cook. The carrots are done in a foil packet to keep them moist. Serve this roast with a jar of Dijon mustard or horseradish.

3 medium-size yellow onions
6 medium-size carrots
2 tablespoons butter
Salt and pepper to taste

4 medium-size white potatoes
2½-pound tri-tip beef roast
(triangle or triangle tip,
or bottom sirloin)

Preheat oven to 350°F.

Special Equipment: A roasting pan large enough to hold the beef roast, onions, potatoes, and carrots

Preparing the Vegetables

• Slice the root and stem ends off the onions (for full details, see page 13) and discard. Peel the papery outer skin off and discard. Cut the onions in half from the stem end to the root end.

• Trim the stem tops off the carrots and discard. Peel the carrots, then cut them in half crosswise. Set aside.

• Melt the butter in a small saucepan.

• Tear off a large piece of aluminum foil. Pile the carrots on one half of the foil, lightly salt and pepper them, and drizzle or brush the butter over them. Fold the other half of the foil over so the carrots are snugly enclosed in the foil and roll up the edges to seal tight. Put the foil packet in the roasting pan.

• Place the onions cut side down next to the packet of carrots and lightly salt and pepper them.

• Wash and dry the potatoes and put them in the roasting pan.

The Last Little Step

• Salt and pepper the roast all over and put it in the center of the roasting pan, fat side up, if it has a layer of white fat on one side. Insert a roasting thermometer in the center.

Roasting the Beef and Vegetables

• Put the pan with the beef and vegetables in the oven.

• Roast for 50 minutes, then check for doneness. If the thermometer reads 140°F the beef will be rare; at 150°F it will be medium rare; and at 170°F it is well done. Remove the roast from the oven when it is done to your liking. Most tri-tip roasts don't yield much pan juices, but even if there are just a few drippings, spoon them over the potatoes, or slices of beef. If you want to remove the fat, tilt the roasting pan and pour the drippings into a little bowl. Spoon off the clear shiny fat that will float to the top of the drippings, leaving the good dark-brown meat juices.

Serving the Beef Roast and Vegetables

• Using a large fork, lift the roast onto a serving platter, and arrange the onions, carrots, and potatoes neatly around. Carve 2 or 3 horizontal slices for each serving.

◆

HORSERADISH

Horseradish is a slightly hot, peppery condiment that is pleasing with the roast beef and vegetables. Dijon mustard has the same effect, so serve either or both with the dinner.

◆

Old-Fashioned Beef Stew

THERE ARE TWO SECRETS to making a splendid beef stew. First, thoroughly brown the chunks of beef until they are a rich, dark brown, which will give them the deep flavor a good stew should have. Second, don't try to hurry the cooking time. It takes about 1½ hours for the beef to reach a tenderness that is just right. The stew will develop even more flavor a day or two after it's made, so be sure to cook enough for leftovers.

◆

BROWNING

Heat the shortening or oil in the pot and turn the heat on to medium-high. Give the fat (shortening or oil) a minute or two to get hot, and run some cold water over your fingertips. Shake the cold water into the fat, and if it sizzles and splatters it is time to add the flour-coated beef chunks to the fat. Don't crowd the chunks of beef; you want them to brown all over, and they need room to be moved and turned over. Be patient with the browning process, because it is the key to making a flavorful stew. If medium-high heat blackens or tends to burn the chunks, lower the heat to medium. Turn the meat so it gets a rich brown on all sides. Remove the pieces when they are browned and set aside, as you add more chunks and continue until they are all richly colored. You may have to add a little more shortening or oil, if your cooking pot gets dry.

◆

---

2 pounds stewing beef, cut into pieces	1 tablespoon Worcestershire sauce
⅓ cup flour	1 teaspoon sugar
2 teaspoons salt	2 bay leaves
½ teaspoon pepper	½ teaspoon ground allspice
1 large yellow onion	10 carrots
¼ cup vegetable shortening or vegetable oil	12 small red or white potatoes (about 1½ inches in diameter)
4 cups water	½ bunch parsley
2 teaspoons lemon juice	

Preparing the Beef and Onions

• Using a sharp knife, cut the beef into large chunks, about 1½ inches square.

• Mix the flour, salt, and pepper on a piece of waxed paper or aluminum foil about 16 inches long.

• Roll the beef cubes in the flour mixture to coat them lightly.

• Peel the onion and cut in half from the stem down. Put the halves on a cutting board, flat side down, and cut each crosswise into 5 slices.

Cooking the Meat

• Put the vegetable shortening or oil in a heavy-bottomed pot with a lid, and turn the heat to high. Wait a minute or two, until the oil gets very hot. To test if it's ready, flick a few drops of water into the fat, standing back so it doesn't spatter on you. If you hear a sizzling noise, the oil is hot enough. Turn the heat down to medium-high.

• Drop about a third of the beef chunks into the pot, leaving enough room between the pieces so that you can easily move them and turn them over. Resist the temptation to crowd them in.

• Turn the beef chunks when they take on a rich brown color and brown them on all sides.

• When the first batch of beef is browned all over, remove from the pot, set aside on a plate, and continue to brown more chunks of raw beef in same pot. Just cook as many in the pot at once as will fit easily with space between.

◆ While the last batch of beef is browning, pour the water into a separate, small saucepan and bring it to a boil over high heat.

Starting the Stew

◆ Once you have browned all of the meat, put the pieces and all the juices back in the browning pot and pour in the boiling water. It will bubble and sizzle at first and then simmer down.

◆ Stir the stew with a large spoon and add the lemon juice, Worcestershire sauce, sugar, bay leaves, allspice, and the onion slices. Stir again, cover the pot, and turn the heat to low. Simmer for 1½ hours.

◆ After about 5 minutes, check to make sure the stew is simmering. You don't want it boiling too hard but you want to be sure it is really simmering (for full details on simmering, see box). Adjust the heat if needed, cover, and continue simmering.

Preparing the Vegetables

◆ Meanwhile, peel the carrots and cut into 1½-inch-long pieces.

◆ Wash the potatoes, and if they are 1½ inches in diameter or smaller, leave them whole and unpeeled. If they are much larger than this, cut them in half or in quarters, depending on their size. Put the cut potatoes in a bowl of cold water so they won't discolor.

◆ Finely chop the parsley (for full details on chopping parsley, see box, page 12). You should have about ½ cup.

Finishing the Stew

◆ After 1½ hours, add the carrots and potatoes to the stew and continue to simmer the stew for another 20 to 25 minutes, or until the vegetables are just tender and can be easily pierced with a fork. Remove the pot from the burner.

◆ Taste the stew to see if it needs more salt. If so, add salt, ½ teaspoon at a time, stirring well after each addition, until it tastes well seasoned to you.

Removing the Fat and Serving the Stew

◆ It's important to remove as much fat from the stew as possible. Using a large spoon, skim off the fat, which looks clear and shiny and floats to the top of the stew, and discard it. Keep skimming until you see very little of the shiny fat remaining. Fish out the bay leaves and discard them.

◆ Ladle the stew into big bowls. Sprinkle a little chopped parsley on top and serve hot.

■

SIMMERING

Simmer means to boil so gently that the liquid barely bubbles. There should be just a few faint, lazy bubbles that rise to the surface and slowly pop.

American Meatloaf

SERVES SIX TO EIGHT

TRADITIONALLY MEATLOAF IS COOKED in one large loaf pan. I like to make mine in 2 free-form round loaves instead, cooking them side by side in a large rectangular baking dish. The 2 smaller loaves cook more quickly, and because the meat is not stuffed into a pan, a tasty crust forms on the entire outside of each loaf. Be sure to buy ground beef with 20 percent fat, which will give you a moist meatloaf with flavor. The spinach added to the meatloaf in this recipe gives it moistness, not to mention a little added nutrition. Leftover cold meatloaf mellows overnight in the refrigerator and makes wonderful sandwiches.

■

ALLSPICE

Allspice isn't a collection of spices; it is one spice that comes mainly from Jamaica. It is a berry that tastes of a mixture of spices—clove, nutmeg, cinnamon. You can buy it in whole tiny dried berries or ground. Buy the ground allspice; it is what most recipes call for.

■

½ bunch fresh spinach (about 2 cups of leaves pressed gently into a 2-cup measure), or ½ of a 9- or 10-ounce box of frozen chopped spinach, thawed

2 slices white bread with crusts

1 large yellow onion

2 pounds ground beef (about 20 percent fat)

¼ pound ground pork

2 large eggs

½ cup milk

1 teaspoon salt

1 teaspoon pepper

1½ teaspoons ground allspice

Preheat oven to 350°F.

Preparing the Spinach

• If using fresh spinach, remove and discard the coarse stems, and wash the leaves (for details on washing spinach, see box, page 47). Chop the spinach into pieces the size of small postage stamps.

• If you are using frozen chopped spinach, let it thaw and divide the contents of the box in half. Take one half of the spinach and squeeze out the liquid; no need to chop it. Refreeze the remaining half for another use.

Mixing the Meatloaf

• Pull the bread apart into large pieces and put them in the bowl of a food processor fitted with a metal blade. Process the bread for a few seconds, until it turns into bread crumbs. If you don't have a food processor, tear the bread into tiny pieces with your hands. A blender also does the job well.

• Peel and chop the onion (see page 13 for full details).

• Put the spinach, bread crumbs, onion, ground beef, ground pork, lightly beaten eggs, and milk in a large mixing bowl. Sprinkle the salt, pepper, and allspice over the meat.

• Use your hands to mix the meat lightly—just enough so that all the ingredients are evenly distributed throughout. Overhandling toughens the meat. Divide the mixture in half.

Cooking the Loaves

• Set the 2 portions of meatloaf side by side in a baking dish approximately 9 by 13 inches. Using your hands, form each into a round that measures 6 or 7 inches in diameter and 2 inches high. They will look like 2 meat cakes. Again, be sure not to pat them down—or you will have a tough, dry meatloaf.

• Put the baking dish on the middle rack of the oven and bake for 25 minutes. Use a little knife to cut into the center of one of the loaves. If it is not pink, it is done. If it is still pink, cook another 5 minutes and test again. The loaves may take as long as 40 minutes to cook.

• When the loaves are cooked, remove the pan from the oven. Let the loaves rest 10 minutes. Use 2 spatulas to lift the loaves out of the pan and onto a serving platter.

• Cut the meatloaves into 1-inch-thick slices and serve.

◆

GOOD WITH MEATLOAF

Frozen peas cook quickly and taste very good with meatloaf (see box, page 101). You might also scatter some small red potatoes, cut in quarters, all around the meatloaves when you put them in the oven. The potatoes will cook in about the same amount of time it takes to cook the meatloaves.

◆

Supper Steak Salad Sandwich

SERVES FOUR

THIS IS A SUPER MEAL, a whole supper on one slice of bread (see illustration, page 110). Everything comes together—onions, mushrooms, steak, and steak juices—to make the bread moist and flavorful. Just a glass of red wine and the meal is complete. It's an easy dish to make for yourself—simply use only one-quarter of the ingredients.

2 bunches watercress

2 large yellow onions

½ pound fresh mushrooms

5 tablespoons butter

4 6-ounce beef filet steaks
   (about 1 to 1¼ inches thick)

Salt and pepper

4 slices white bread (the
   thicker the better)

Preheat oven to 250°F and leave the oven door open a bit.

Preparing the Watercress, Onions, and Mushrooms

• Remove the coarse stems of the watercress and discard. Rinse the leaves and tender upper stems in cold running water; pat dry or dry in a salad spinner.

• Peel the onions and cut into thin rings (for full details, see page 13).

• Wipe the mushrooms clean of any clinging dirt with a damp paper towel. Remove and save the stems. Slice the mushrooms from the top of the cap down, in slices no more than ¼ inch thick. Cut the stems in half lengthwise, trimming off any tough ends.

• Put the butter in a 12-inch heavy-bottomed skillet over a burner turned to medium. Add the onions and mushrooms and cook for about 2 minutes, stirring constantly until they are just soft. Remove the vegetables to a plate and keep warm in a slow oven. Put the serving plates in the oven so the food will stay warm when served. Presetting the oven to 250°F and leaving the door ajar works well for warming plates and food without overheating.

Cooking the Steaks

◆ Set the pan over medium-high heat. It's hot enough when you hold your hand an inch above the surface of the skillet and it feels hot. Sprinkle the steaks with salt and pepper, put them in the pan in one layer, and fry for 2 minutes. Turn them over and cook for 2 minutes on the other side.

◆ After the second side has cooked for 2 minutes, cut into a steak with the tip of a knife. If it looks rosy and you like your steak rare, remove it from the pan. If you like it medium rare, cook for another minute or two and test again to see if it is cooked enough.

Assembling and Serving

◆ Remove the steaks from the skillet and put them alongside the vegetables in the oven. Now put the bread slices into the skillet and fry them, turning each one over once to sop up the pan juices.

◆ To serve, put a slice of bread on each of the 4 warm plates, and spoon a quarter of the onions and mushrooms over each piece. Pile on some watercress, then place the steak on top of all. Gently press down on the steaks with a spatula so some of the warm juices drip down into the bread. Serve at once.

■

WATERCRESS

Watercress is an often forgotten salad green with a peppery taste. It adds a liveliness to the rich flavors of the beef and mushrooms.

■

Hamburgers

GROUND BEEF IS one of the best allies a home cook can have. It can be stretched by working 1 cup of soft bread crumbs gently into each pound of ground meat and then making meatballs or patties. Even a little ground beef can be sautéed in a pan and added to a spaghetti sauce, or just tossed with pasta or cooked dried beans, or used as a topping for a baked potato.

An easy supper can be made of hamburger patties, as prepared in this recipe, served with corn on the cob and a salad. Or just put together that all-American favorite—hamburger on a bun. Be sure to have all the fixings ready and on the table before you start cooking the hamburgers—sliced tomatoes, chopped onions, lettuce, mustard, mayonnaise, ketchup, and other relishes that you like. It is nice to have the buns warm, too; either toast them or heat them in the oven.

You may be perplexed at the range of fat percentages on the packages of ground beef that your supermarket offers these days. Don't make the mistake of going for the one that has the lowest fat count. You need ground meat that has 20 percent fat in order to make a good hamburger; otherwise it will be dry and tasteless. If you're on a very restricted fat diet, it's better to forgo hamburgers than make ones that will disappoint you.

1 ½ pounds ground beef
(20 percent fat)
2 tablespoons vegetable oil

1 ½ teaspoons salt
½ teaspoon pepper

Preparing the Hamburger Patties

- Divide the ground beef into 4 equal parts. Handling the meat gently and lightly, form each portion into a patty ¾ to 1 inch thick. Don't slap the meat together and press down on the patty or you'll have tough hamburgers.

Cooking the Patties

• Pour the oil into a frying pan or a sauté pan that will hold the patties without crowding them. Tilt and turn the pan so that the oil covers the bottom, then set it over medium heat.

• In about 30 seconds, hold your hand, palm side down, about an inch over the pan, and if it feels hot, add the patties. Sprinkle about half the salt and pepper over them. Do not press down on them with a spatula while they are cooking or you will press out the juices and toughen the meat. Always handle hamburgers gently.

• After 4 minutes of cooking, lift one of the patties with a spatula, and if it has browned on the bottom, turn them all over. Sprinkle the remaining salt and pepper on top and cook another 4 minutes.

• Check for doneness by making a slit with a knife deep into the center of one of the patties and opening up the meat a little to judge the color. If the center is pink and you like your hamburgers rare, they are done. If you prefer them medium or well done, cook another minute or two. Remove from the pan and serve immediately.

◆

CORN ON THE COB

Fresh corn on the cob is so easy to prepare and tastes so delicious you'll want to enjoy it as often as possible when it is in season. Buy ears in their husks, and when you are ready to cook them, simply pull off the husks and the silk at the tip of the ear. Put a large pot filled with water on to boil—large enough so that all the ears of corn you plan to cook will be immersed. When the water comes to a boil, add the corn and cook at a brisk boil for just 5 minutes. Drain the pot into a colander or fish the ears out with tongs. If you want to keep some of the ears warm for a second helping, you can just leave them in the water with the heat turned off; they won't overcook. Be sure to have lots of room-temperature butter on the table as well as salt and pepper.

◆

Roast Beef Hash

SERVES TWO OR THREE

ROAST BEEF HASH IS a classic dish that has never lost its popularity. One of the best virtues it has for new cooks is that the amount of each ingredient is flexible, so a little more or a little less will still make good hash. The main ingredients are onions, potatoes, and your leftover roast beef (or any leftover meat, for that matter). Don't worry if you don't have quite enough of any of the ingredients, and if you don't have fennel, use celery instead, or just omit. The hash will taste good if you just follow the general directions of the recipe. A crisp green salad is good with this dish, or thick sliced tomatoes and buttered bread.

1 medium-size yellow onion	1 small green bell pepper
3 or 4 medium-size cooked potatoes	1 teaspoon salt
	½ teaspoon freshly ground pepper
½ pound cooked roast beef (about 1½ cups chopped)	2 tablespoons olive oil
1 small fennel bulb (optional)	¾ cup chicken broth or water

Preparing and Chopping the Vegetables and Meat

◆ Peel and chop the onion (for full details, see page 13) and put in a large bowl.

◆ Cut the cooked potatoes crosswise into ¼-inch slices, then stack the slices and cut into small squares or dice. Add to the bowl.

◆ Cut the roast beef into pieces about the same size as the onion and potato, and add to the bowl.

◆ Wash the fennel bulb, if you are using it, and remove any outer pieces if they are bruised or brown. Cut off the feathery leaves and the discolored root end (about ½ inch). Save the stems and the feathery leaves; put them in a plastic bag and refrigerate for later use. Cut the fennel bulb crosswise into ¼-inch slices, then chop the slices into small pieces. You want to have about ¾ cup chopped fennel; add any extra to the plastic bag for later use.

◆ Trim the pepper and discard the seeds and any white parts. Cut the pepper into strips, then bunch the strips together, and cut crosswise into small pieces (for full details, see box, page 31). Add to the bowl.

◆ Add the salt and pepper. Using your hands or a large spoon, toss and mix the vegetables and meat in the bowl. Taste and add more salt and pepper, if needed.

Cooking the Hash

◆ Put a large nonstick skillet on a burner turned to medium-high. Heat the skillet for a minute, and when it is hot add the 2 tablespoons of olive oil. Tip and tilt the skillet so the olive oil coats the bottom; if you need to add more oil to cover the bottom, add another tablespoon now.

◆ Put the vegetables and meat into the heated skillet, add the broth, and stir. Spread the hash evenly over the bottom of the skillet and press down on it with a metal spatula.

◆ Turn the heat to medium-low and cook for 15 minutes.

◆ Keep an eye on the hash, and press down on it from time to time with the spatula. After 15 minutes, using the spatula to lift the edge of the hash, peek at the underside to see if it is getting browned. When it is nicely browned, turn the hash over in the skillet.

◆ It's easiest to turn the hash if you cut it in quarters—or even smaller pieces, if you prefer—before turning with a good-size spatula.

◆ After you've turned over all the hash, cook the second side for 5 to 10 minutes, again peeking underneath after about 5 minutes to see that it isn't burning. When the second side is brown, serve the hash directly onto plates from the skillet.

■

DINNER FOR ONE

Many of us eat alone, and this is a dandy dish for one person. Also, the Supper Steak Salad Sandwich (page 122) is uplifting when eating alone.

■

Pan-Fried Pork Chops

SERVES FOUR

FRIED PORK CHOPS RETAIN their tenderness and moisture when they aren't cooked to death. Cook ½-inch-thick chops about 5 minutes on each side; ¾-inch-thick chops only 8 minutes; 1-inch chops 10 minutes a side. Anything thicker should be lightly browned and then braised in liquid. Pork chops are especially good served with Mashed Potatoes (page 184) and Applesauce (page 234), both of which can be prepared before you do the chops.

2 tablespoons flour	3 tablespoons vegetable oil
Salt and freshly ground pepper	½ cup apple juice or chicken
4 pork chops, ¾ inch thick	broth, canned or homemade

Cooking the Chops

♦ On a 12-inch piece of waxed paper, mix the flour, salt, and pepper together. Lay the chops in the flour mixture and coat them on both sides, then shake off any excess.

♦ Heat the oil over medium heat in a skillet large enough to accommodate all the chops in one layer.

♦ When the palm of your hand placed an inch above the pan feels hot, put the chops in. Cook for 5 or 10 minutes, depending on thickness, then turn them over and cook for another 5 or 10 minutes. To test for doneness, insert a paring knife into the center of the meat and see whether there are any pink juices. If there are, cook a little longer.

♦ Remove the chops to a warm platter. Pour off all but 2 tablespoons of the fat in the pan.

♦ Pour in the apple juice or broth and cook over medium-high heat for 1 minute, stirring as the juices bubble and thicken a little. Pour the pan sauce over the chops.

♦ Serve hot.

James Beard's Roasted Spareribs

YEARS AGO, in one of his famous cooking classes, James Beard showed us this simple, "can't fail" method for roasting spareribs. He predicted that this recipe would become an all-time favorite, and he was right. These ribs have the rich flavor of pork, which you can really taste, and they are also very tender and moist. Who needs all that BBQ sauce? The Red and Green Coleslaw (see page 54) is a good companion for ribs. If you can, get baby back ribs—they're best—but any pork spareribs will do.

4 pounds meaty pork spareribs   1 tablespoon freshly ground
2 tablespoons salt   black pepper

Preheat oven to 350°F.

Preparing and Roasting the Ribs

- Rub the ribs with salt and pepper on both sides.
- Set a roasting or broiler rack in a roasting pan. Arrange the ribs on the rack, meaty side facing up.
- Put the pan on the center rack of the oven and bake for 30 minutes. Using a pair of tongs, turn the ribs over, and cook for another 30 minutes.
- When the second 30 minutes are up, the ribs should be nicely browned and fairly crisp on the outside. If not, roast for another 10 minutes and check again.

Cutting and Serving the Ribs

- When you are serving the ribs, cut the rack into separate racks of 3 or 4 ribs per person and place on a platter or plates. Serve hot.

Pork Tenderloin with Jalapeño Sauce

SERVES FOUR

SLIM PORK TENDERLOINS ARE QUICK to roast and delicious. The simple sauce adds a peppy flavor and a moistness. Serve the pork with Yellow Cornbread (page 246) and black beans (box, page 135).

About 1½ pounds pork tenderloins	6 tablespoons jalapeño jelly, green or red
Salt and freshly ground black pepper	2 tablespoons water
	⅓ cup sour cream

Preheat oven to 425°F.

Preparing the Roasting Pan and the Pork

♦ Line a small roasting pan with heavy aluminum foil.

♦ Generously salt and pepper the tenderloins and place them in the roasting pan about 1½ inches apart with a meat thermometer in the center of one of them, if you wish.

♦ Melt 3 tablespoons of the jelly with the water in a small pan over low heat, whisking well until it's the consistency of a light syrup. Brush over the top of each tenderloin.

♦ Put the roasting pan in the oven and cook for 20 to 30 minutes, depending on the diameter of the tenderloins. (The tenderloin, a tender cylindrical muscle from inside the larger pork loin, usually measures about 2½ inches in diameter, but the size can vary.) Cook for 20 minutes, then check for doneness by cutting into the middle of a tenderloin with a paring knife. If it is still pink, cook for another 5 minutes and test again. The temperature when done should be 160°F. The tenderloins tend to dry out if overcooked, so keep an eye on them. When they are done, take them out of the oven, put on a carving board, and let them rest while you quickly make the sauce.

Making the Sauce

♦ Whisk sour cream and the remaining 3 tablespoons jelly in a small saucepan and heat over low heat until smooth and warm.

Serving the Pork

♦ Slice the tenderloins crosswise slightly on the diagonal making oval shapes about ½ inch thick. Put the slices on a warm platter and pour the warm sauce over.

♦

VARIATIONS ON THE TENDERLOIN

You could roast the tenderloin unadorned, sprinkling salt and pepper over it before roasting, and serve it with Applesauce (page 234) or Green Sauce (page 223).

♦

Pork with Sage and Brown Rice

SERVES FOUR

THIS RECIPE WILL INTRODUCE you to brown rice, which is often overlooked because it takes a little longer to cook than white rice. Try it, not only because the pork, sage, and brown rice are very good together, but also because the more you try new ingredients the more confident you will be as a cook.

½ cup all-purpose white flour	1 large onion
½ teaspoon salt	4 tablespoons vegetable oil
⅛ teaspoon pepper	1 cup brown rice
1 pound boneless pork (loin or	3 cups water
shoulder), cut into	2 teaspoons dried sage leaves,
bite-size cubes, about	or 1¼ teaspoons powdered
¾ inch (3 to 4 cups)	sage

Cooking the Pork

◆ Stir together the flour, salt, and pepper in a mixing bowl. Add the pork and toss lightly to coat the pieces. Shake off any excess flour.

◆ Peel and chop the onion (for details, see page 13).

◆ Heat 2 tablespoons of the vegetable oil in a large skillet over medium-high heat. The oil is hot enough when you place your hand an inch above the pan, palm side down, and you can feel the heat. Put the pork in the pan in one layer, and let cook for a minute or two, until the pieces start to turn brown. As they brown, turn them over and brown the other sides. The browning process should take about 5 to 7 minutes.

◆ When the pork is browned all over, remove to a plate.

◆ Add the remaining 2 tablespoons of oil and the chopped onion. Cook the onion for about 5 minutes, until it softens and turns translucent. Use a slotted spoon to remove the onion to the plate of pork.

Cooking the Brown Rice

◆ Put the brown rice in the skillet and cook, stirring constantly, for 2 or 3 minutes. The heat will lightly toast the rice and deepen the flavor.

◆ Put the onion and meat back in the skillet, add the water and the sage, and bring to a boil.

◆ When it boils, turn the heat to low, cover, and cook at a bare simmer for 45 minutes. It won't hurt to lift the lid from time to time and give the dish a stir. Brown rice can stick.

◆ After 45 minutes, the rice should be tender and the liquid nearly all absorbed by the rice. Taste the rice and a bit of pork, adding more salt and sage if the flavor seems too subdued. Serve hot.

Baked Ham

SERVES TEN OR MORE
(WITH LEFTOVERS)

T**HE WONDERFUL THING** about a baked ham is how many ways it can serve the family table. It's an ideal main dish for beginning cooks. Roast Beets (see box, opposite) make a particularly good accompaniment, and for a special dinner have as well a dish of Creamy Baked Potatoes and Turnips (page 188) (both can be cooked in the oven alongside the ham). Be sure to get the real thing, a half ham with the bone still in—not the jellied compressed ham in a can. And don't be afraid if all the hams are bigger than you think you need. Plenty of leftovers means more possibilities for meals during the weeks to come. Ham keeps well, can be frozen, and suffers no ill effects when reheated as a leftover. It is also good cold, of course.

½ fully cooked ham (about 8 to 10 pounds, often more)	3 tablespoons Dijon mustard
1 cup brown sugar	¼ teaspoon salt
2 tablespoons honey	2 tablespoons water

Preheat oven to 325°F.

Cooking the Ham

• Put the ham in a shallow roasting pan, fat side up, and insert a dial-type (not instant-read) meat thermometer into the fleshiest part of the ham, but not touching the bone. Bake the ham unglazed until the thermometer registers 140°F, approximately 2 hours.

HELPFUL HAM HINTS

■

I usually buy a 6- or 7-pound ham with the bone in, but the size depends on how many people you are feeding and how much you want left over. First, read the label carefully and completely. Hams are labeled "fully cooked" or "partially cooked." If the label reads "partially cooked" you must bake it until your thermometer reads 160°F. Even if the ham is fully cooked, baking not only heats it through but also enhances the flavor. Leftover ham will keep in the refrigerator several weeks. If you have more than you think you will eat up in that time, freeze the rest in carefully wrapped portions.

■

1   2

◆ Remove the ham from the oven. 1) Using a large sharp knife, cut off and discard the rough brown outer skin or rind of the ham.

◆ 2) Cut the fat in a diamond or crosshatch pattern about ¼ inch deep at 1 inch intervals.

◆ Mix together the brown sugar with the honey, mustard, salt, and water. Now brush this glaze on the ham, spreading it completely over the outside.

Making the Basting Sauce and Basting the Ham

◆ Return the ham to the oven, still at 325°F, and cook for 1 hour. Brush with the pan drippings 2 or 3 times. The ham is completely heated through when the thermometer reads 140°F.

◆ Remove the ham from the oven, let it rest briefly, and carve (see box).

◆ ROASTING BEETS ◆

Roasting beets slowly in the oven produces a delicious result. Begin by trimming with a sharp knife about an inch off the top (the stem end) and ½ inch off the bottom of each beet. Set the beets in a baking pan and cover with foil, crimping it around the edges of the pan to make a tight seal. Put the beets in a preheated 325°F oven and bake for 1½ hours. Test to see if they are done by piercing a beet with a paring knife. If it is tender and the knife goes in easily, the beets are done. Larger, older beets always take longer. If they are not done, bake another 5 or 10 minutes and check again. Let the cooked beets cool long enough so you can handle them without burning your fingers. Take each beet and firmly press against it all around until the skin is loosened and will slip off easily. Cut the beets into wedges or slice into rounds and serve with a little butter, salt, and pepper. Or dress with a good oil-and-vinegar salad dressing and serve on salad greens.

You will need about ½ pound of beets per person. But why not cook extras for that good salad?

CARVING THE HAM

Steady the ham with a large fork, and with a long sharp knife cut vertical slices.

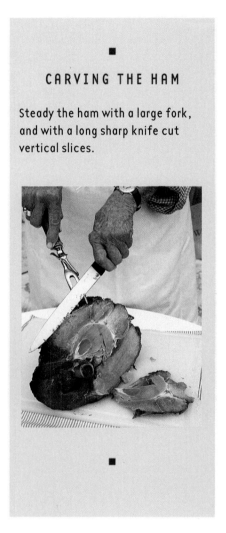

Winter White Beans and Ham

THIS DISH WILL WARM you from the inside out on a cold day. It is thick and filling, has a fine flavor, and is good served with rye bread. Remember to soak the beans overnight, or during the day for at least 6 to 8 hours—a step that will shorten the cooking time. Or you can use canned beans. Cooked beans are often more flavorful on the second day.

2½ cups dried, uncooked Great Northern beans (a 1-pound bag)	About ½ pound cooked ham (to make 2 cups cut up)
2 medium-size yellow onions	1 small bunch parsley (to make ½ cup chopped)
2 bay leaves	1 teaspoon freshly ground pepper
1½ teaspoons salt	

The Night Before

◆ Put the beans into a 4-quart pot (one with a lid), and add enough cold water to cover the beans by about 2 inches. Soak overnight, or for at least 6 to 8 hours. (See box, opposite, for full details on soaking and cooking beans.)

Chopping the Onions

◆ Peel and slice the onions. You should have about 1½ cups sliced onions. Add them to the beans.

Cooking the Beans

◆ Put the bean pot on the stove, add the bay leaves and salt, and turn the heat to high. As soon as the water boils, turn the heat down to low so the water is just simmering.

◆ A frothy scum will keep rising to the surface for about the first 30 minutes of cooking. Using a large spoon, skim this scum from the beans, and discard it. Do this several times, until the foaming stops. Now put the lid on the beans.

◆ Great Northern beans take about 1 hour to cook. If the water has reduced to the level of the beans, add enough water so that the level is where it was when you started. After the beans have simmered for 30 minutes, check again to see if they need more water.

Preparing the Ham and Parsley

◆ Cut the precooked or leftover ham into bite-size pieces, and add to the beans. Put the lid on and cook for another 15 minutes.

◆ Remove the stems from the bunch of parsley and discard. Finely chop the leaves; you should have about ½ cup.

Getting Ready to Serve

◆ When the beans are tender and soft, taste them, and add more salt if necessary. Add the pepper. Ladle helpings into bowls, making sure to put ample chunks of ham in each serving. Sprinkle the chopped parsley on top. Serve hot.

◆ The leftovers freeze well, or will keep refrigerated for three days.

◆

ABOUT DRIED BEANS

One cup of dried beans makes 3 cups when cooked (about 2 servings).

Each 15½-ounce can of cooked beans yields 1½ cups (about 1 serving).

There are two schools of dried-bean cooks, those who soak their beans before cooking and those who don't. Dried beans are like little sponges: they absorb water when soaked, they double in size, and they begin to soften. When cooked, they become soft and somewhat creamy. If beans are not soaked prior to cooking, they take at least another hour—and they remain firm, not creamy. The anti-soaking group insist their beans have better flavor and integrity.

I prefer soaking my beans. I cover each cupful with 4 cups of cold water. I don't pour the water off when it is time to cook the beans, just boil them in the water that they soaked in.

◆

Ham and Sour Cream Baked Noodles

SERVES FOUR

THIS IS A GOOD VERSION of the classic macaroni-and-cheese dish. Serve it with a fresh fruit salad and rye crackers. It's a good dish to take to a potluck dinner, or to a friend in bed with a cold.

3 quarts (12 cups) water	1 small onion
1 tablespoon plus ½ teaspoon salt	2 eggs
12 ounces wide egg noodles	1½ cups cottage cheese
6 tablespoons butter	1½ cups sour cream
1 green bell pepper	About ½ pound cooked ham (to make 2 cups chopped)
3 stalks celery	Pepper to taste

Special Equipment: 8-cup ovenproof casserole

Preheat oven to 350°F.

Cooking the Noodles

• Put the water in a large pot, add 1 tablespoon salt, and set over high heat. When the water boils, add the noodles, stir with a fork, and turn the heat down to medium-high. Cook the noodles for 7 to 9 minutes. Use a fork to fish a noodle out of the water, run it under cold water, and taste. If it is tender, the noodles are done; if a little firm, let cook 2 more minutes and taste again. When tender, dump the noodles into a colander set in the sink and let the water drain away. Put the hot noodles in the casserole. Add the butter in chunks to the casserole and stir to melt the butter in the hot noodles. Stir well, so the noodles are coated by butter; this will keep them from sticking together while you prepare the rest of the ingredients.

Preparing the Vegetables

◆ Finely chop enough of the pepper to make ½ cup (for full details, see box, page 31). Wrap any leftover pepper in plastic wrap and store in the refrigerator for later use.

◆ Trim the ends off the celery stalks, discard them, and finely chop the stalks.

◆ Peel and finely chop the onion (for full details, see page 13). Measure ¼ cup; wrap and store unused onion in the refrigerator.

Making and Cooking the Casserole

◆ Beat the eggs slightly with a fork or small whisk in a small bowl.

◆ Dump the cottage cheese, sour cream, chopped ham, the eggs, the ½ teaspoon salt, and the vegetables into the casserole. Mix well with a large spoon.

◆ Bake for 40 minutes, or until bubbling and set. The top should look crisp and browned in spots. Serve hot.

■

REHEATING THE NOODLES

Put leftovers in a skillet, add just enough milk to moisten—not so much that it's swimming in milk—and heat, stirring, for a few minutes. Taste to see if it is hot. Keep cooking and stirring until hot enough to serve.

■

Roast Leg of Lamb

SERVES SIX

A WHOLE ROASTED LEG of lamb is a good choice for a celebration. Serve with the Creamy Baked Potatoes and Turnips (see page 188) and Swiss Chard (see page 196). The chard takes only 5 minutes to cook, so you can do that while the roasted lamb is resting. You can prepare the potatoes the day before and then finish them in the same oven along with the roasting lamb. Put the gratin of potatoes into the oven the last 10 minutes that the lamb is roasting.

5-to-6-pound leg of lamb	Freshly ground pepper
3 cloves garlic	1 teaspoon dried rosemary
2 tablespoons olive oil	(or 2 teaspoons fresh, if you
1½ teaspoons salt	have it)

Preheat oven to 350°F.

Preparing the Lamb

• Have the lamb at room temperature. If it's been refrigerated, leaving it on the counter for 1 hour should be about right.

• Place the lamb, fat side up, in a shallow roasting pan. Cut the garlic cloves into slivers (for full details, see box, page 33). Make 10 or 12 slits in the meat—about an inch deep at the most—with the point of a paring knife. Tuck a sliver of garlic into each slit.

• Rub the lamb all over with the oil, and sprinkle on the salt and pepper. Crumble and rub the rosemary all over the lamb as well. Some of it will stick to the olive oil.

Roasting the Lamb

• Roast for about 1½ hours, with a dial-type (not instant-read) meat thermometer stuck into the fleshiest part of the meat. Don't let the thermometer rest on the bone or it won't read accurately. The lamb is done medium at 155°F, rare when the thermometer reads 140°F, well done at 170°F.

• Remove the lamb from the oven when it is done to your liking and let it rest for 15 minutes before carving.

■ CARVING THE LEG ■

There are two schools of thought about carving a leg of lamb. The British way is to cut across the grain downward but I prefer the French method, which is to cut horizontal slices. That way, those who like better-done meat can be served the first slices and those who like it rare can have the slices nearer the bone, which are always less well done. With your very sharp carving knife, remove a few thin slices lengthwise slicing from the underside of the roast, so you have a flat base on which to rest the lamb. Now turn it so that the meatier side faces up. Using a large fork to steady the roast, carve fairly thin horizontal slices from one end of the roast to the other. Keep slicing until you hit the bone. Dig out all the good meaty pieces, particularly around the knuckle bone— they are delicious.

◆

LEFTOVERS

You are bound to have lamb leftovers. And you will find them a treat. Turn them into the curry that follows (page 142). Or make a hash, using lamb instead of beef in the recipe on page 126. Cooked with small white beans instead of ham (page 134), lamb is almost as good as this first-day roast.

◆

Lamb Shanks

Serves four

LAMB SHANKS ARE TENDER, moist, and succulent. The carrots, onions, and potatoes cooked with the lamb make this a complete meal. Leftover lamb is wonderful cooked with lentils or with eggplant. See the Eggplant Filled with Roasted Vegetables (page 192); you can add chopped pieces of leftover lamb shanks to that dish.

2 lemons (⅓ cup lemon juice plus 1 tablespoon grated rind)

4 cloves garlic

4 lamb shanks

4 tablespoons flour

1½ teaspoons salt

1 teaspoon freshly ground pepper

3 tablespoons vegetable oil

1 bay leaf

2 cups water

6 carrots

3 medium-size yellow onions

4 small potatoes

Preparing the Lemon and Garlic

• Grate the zest of 1 or 2 lemons to make 1 tablespoon of grated rind. After you have removed the zest, cut the lemons in half and squeeze the juice from them. Strain and measure about ¼ cup.

• Peel the garlic cloves and slice each lengthwise into four slivers (for full details, see box, page 33).

Preparing the Lamb

• Using a sharp paring knife, cut 4 deep slits in the meaty part of each lamb shank, and insert a garlic sliver into each slit.

• Put the flour, salt, and pepper on a 12-inch piece of waxed paper and stir together. Spread the flour out a little and roll each shank in it so all sides are coated. Shake off the excess.

Starting the Cooking

• Put the oil in a large heavy-bottomed pot (one with a lid) and turn the heat to medium-high. After about 15 seconds, hold your hand about an inch above the bottom of the pot. If it feels hot, add the shanks and brown them on all sides, keeping the heat at medium-high. This will take about 5 to 10 minutes.

• When the shanks are all browned, turn the heat to low. Add the bay leaf, lemon rind, lemon juice, and 1 cup of the water to the pot. Put the lid on, and simmer the shanks over low heat for 1 hour.

Preparing the Vegetables While the Shanks Are Cooking

- Peel the carrots and cut crosswise into 1½-inch pieces.
- Remove the papery skin from the onions and cut them into quarters.
- Rinse the potatoes, leaving them unpeeled.
- After the shanks have been cooking for longer than 1 hour, add the carrots, onions, potatoes, and the other 1 cup of water to the pot and cook, covered, for another 30 minutes.

Finishing and Serving the Shanks

- Remove the lid and pierce the vegetables with a fork. If they are tender, they are done. The shanks should also be very tender by now. Put the shanks on a platter and surround with the vegetables. Serve hot.

■

ZEST

Zest is the outside, colored rind of citrus fruit. It is the most flavorful part of the fruit and it gives food a lovely fragrance and flavor of lemon, lime, or orange. When removing the zest, it is important to remove only the bright, shiny, thin outer part of the peel, leaving behind the white, bitter part of the skin (the pith). You can use a zester, a fine grater, a vegetable peeler, or a sharp paring knife to remove the zest. Or stack pieces of zest on top of one another and cut very thin slices lengthwise into strips, then chop the thin strips crosswise into very finely "minced" pieces.

■

Quick Lamb Curry

SERVES FOUR

THIS IS AN IDEAL WAY to use leftover leg of lamb. Serve the curry with long-grain white rice (see box, page 183—1 cup raw rice should be enough for 4). If you put the water on for the rice before you start the curry, everything should be ready at just about the same time. If the rice is ready a little earlier, put it in a warm oven, covered, until the curry is ready.

◆

USING OTHER MEATS FOR CURRY

You can use cooked leftover chicken, pork, or beef to make this curry. They are just as good as lamb—this is a flexible dish.

◆

---

2 medium-size yellow onions
2 tart green apples (Granny Smiths are the most available)
1¼ cups beef or chicken broth, canned or homemade, or 1¼ cups water
About ½ pound cooked lamb (2 cups ½-inch cubes)

2 tablespoons butter
2 tablespoons all-purpose white flour
1 tablespoon curry powder
1 tablespoon raisins
Salt
Freshly ground pepper

Preparing the Onions and Apples

- Peel and chop the onions (for full details, see page 13).
- Peel the apples, remove the cores, and cut into 8 wedges each.

Cooking the Curry

- In a small saucepan, heat the beef or chicken broth over medium heat. Keep the broth on the burner while you prepare the lamb.
- Cut the leftover lamb into medium-size cubes, about ½-inch pieces.
- In a large heavy-bottomed skillet, melt the butter over medium heat. Add the onions, and cook slowly until they are translucent, about 5 to 7 minutes.
- Add the pieces of cooked lamb and stir. When the lamb is just warmed, sprinkle on the flour, and stir it in with the lamb and onion until it is smooth and blended.
- Add the hot broth, and stir constantly for a couple of minutes, until the sauce thickens.
- Add the curry, apples, raisins, and salt and pepper to taste.
- Simmer, covered, for 5 to 10 minutes, then test for doneness. You'll know the curry is ready when the apples are easily pierced with a knife but still hold their shape. If they feel firm and crunchy, cook for another 5 minutes and test again.
- Serve with steamed white rice.

Potatoes, Cabbage, and Polish Kielbasa

SERVES FOUR OR FIVE

THEY OUGHT TO SEND St. Bernards into the Alps with this dish. It's warming, filling, and best of all it tastes very, very good. Smoked cooked sausages—available in the meat department of your supermarket—can be a great boon to the home cook. A few slices of sausage can be added to beans or lentils to make a main dish.

8 red potatoes (see page 67 for details on potatoes), about 1½ pounds

1 tablespoon salt

1 pound Polish kielbasa, completely precooked, cut into 1-inch lengths

1 head cabbage (round, firm, light-green head), about 1 pound

4 tablespoons olive oil

4 tablespoons white vinegar

Pepper

Cooking the Potatoes

- Wash the potatoes and cut them in half. Don't peel the potatoes.
- Fill a large pot (4 quarts or larger) about ⅔ full of water and put it on the stove. Turn the heat to high and add the salt. When the water boils, turn the heat down to medium so the water boils less furiously, add the potatoes, and cook for 15 minutes.

Preparing the Kielbasa and Cabbage

- Cut the kielbasa into 1-inch pieces.
- Cut the cabbage in half, slicing down through the stem, then cut out and discard the hard white core. Put each half flat side down on a cutting board, cut it in half one way, then cut it in half the other way, then slice it into 2-inch pieces. Pull the leaves apart. You should have about 6 loosely packed cups of cabbage—the amount does not have to be exact.

Finishing the Dish

- After 15 minutes, test the potatoes for doneness. Using a small sharp knife, pierce the potatoes in the water. If the knife slides in easily, they are done; if they feel hard to pierce, let them cook another 5 minutes. When the potatoes are just soft, add the sausage pieces to the pot and cook for 5 minutes.
- Set a colander in the sink.
- When the sausages have cooked for 5 minutes, dump the cabbage into the pot with the potatoes and sausage. Stand right there and count to 8, then take the pot to the sink and pour the contents of the pot—

water, potatoes, cabbage, and sausage—into the colander. The water will immediately drain away. Put the potatoes, cabbage, and sausage into a serving bowl.

♦ Add the olive oil, vinegar, and pepper, and toss and mix everything together, making sure that the olive oil and vinegar coat the pieces. Taste for salt and add some if needed.

♦ Serve hot with mustard and rye bread on the side.

■

ABOUT KIELBASA

Polish kielbasa is a flavorful sausage that can be kept frozen for weeks. Served with eggs, it is a filling meal; cut into slices and added to beans it is a first-rate supper. It is easily found in all supermarkets.

■

◆

Meals Without Meat

◆

INTRODUCTION

———

WE USED TO THINK that meat had to be the center-piece of our dinner but this attitude has changed. Many of us have vegetarian family members and friends we have to cook for. And more and more of us eat pastas, rice, polenta, and egg dishes combined with different vegetables and/or cheese and find they make wonderfully satisfying dinners.

Here are a dozen or so such dishes that you'll discover are easy to make and taste fresh and different from what you might get at your supermarket's "home replacement meal" section. The truth is that nothing can replace a home-cooked meal.

RECISES

———

SPAGHETTI WITH BUTTER AND PARMESAN CHEESE

MARIETTA'S SPAGHETTI

SPAGHETTI WITH PARSLEY, GARLIC, OLIVE OIL, AND BREAD CRUMBS

FUSILLI WITH TOMATO SAUCE AND BEANS

CAESAR PASTA

PASTA WITH GREEN CHILIES, TOMATOES, AND CILANTRO

RISO WITH MINT AND CURRANTS

ORIGINAL MACARONI AND CHEESE

CRUSHED MACARONI AND VEGETABLES

RISOTTO

POLENTA BAKED WITH VEGETABLES

BROWN RICE WITH MUSHROOMS AND ONIONS

GREEN CHILI PIE

Spaghetti with Butter and Parmesan Cheese

THE APPEAL OF THIS DISH is its simplicity and wholesomeness. The butter and Parmesan cheese are satisfying in a way that many fancier sauces simply never are. This is a lesson in how a simple dish can be far better than a complicated one. A cold lettuce salad and warm bread and butter complete the meal, with maybe some fruit for dessert.

4 quarts water

1 tablespoon salt (for cooking the pasta)

1 pound spaghetti

8 tablespoons (1 stick) butter

1½ cups grated Parmigiano Reggiano cheese (or other

cheese for grating, such as Romano; see box, page 49), plus more for the table

Salt and freshly ground pepper to taste

Preheat oven to 250°F.

Cooking the Spaghetti

• Put the water and salt in a large pot, and bring to a boil over high heat. When the water boils, add the spaghetti (for full details, see box, page 151).

• While the spaghetti is cooking, cut the butter into 4 to 6 pieces. Put them in a large heatproof bowl and put in the oven to warm, along with the serving plates or bowls. Leave the oven door ajar.

• After 10 minutes, test the pasta for doneness every minute or two.

• When the spaghetti is cooked, pour it and the cooking water through a colander set in the sink. Let the water drain away.

Serving the Pasta

• Remove the bowl from the oven and put the hot, drained spaghetti into it. Add the grated cheese and a sprinkling of salt and pepper. Toss the noodles with 2 large spoons, taking care to distribute the butter and cheese over all the spaghetti.

• Serve at the table, scooping up portions onto the heated individual plates or bowls. If you wish, put a dish of grated cheese on the table along with plenty of freshly ground pepper.

USING ONLY FRESHLY GRATED CHEESE

When you grate cheese, grate only what you think will be needed (you can always grate a little more if necessary). Grated cheese dries out and loses some of its flavor when sitting in the refrigerator. This is why buying already grated cheese is really not a saving; it begins to taste like sawdust after a while. Keep your cheese in a jar with a lid screwed on.

Marietta's Spaghetti

MARIETTA'S TOMATO SAUCE—made in this simple way— is the best I've ever tasted. Roasting the tomatoes has a magical effect and intensifies the flavors. Though especially delicious in summer, this recipe is also just the thing when you can't find perfect fresh tomatoes. The sauce brings out the best even in a winter tomato.

12 Roma or plum tomatoes (about 1¾ pounds)
Salt and pepper to taste
3 cloves garlic
½ bunch parsley
½ cup olive oil
4 quarts water

1 tablespoon salt (for cooking the pasta)
1 pound dried spaghetti
2 tablespoons butter
1 bunch fresh basil (½ cup chopped)

Preheat oven to 350°F.

Preparing the Tomatoes
- Cut the tomatoes in half lengthwise, and place them—cut side up—in a large shallow baking dish. Salt and pepper them lightly.

Preparing the Garlic, Parsley, and Olive Oil
- Peel and finely chop 3 cloves of garlic (for full details, see box, page 33).
- Wash the parsley and pat dry; remove and discard the stems. Finely chop the leaves (you want about ½ cup).
- Mix together the garlic, half of the parsley, and 2 tablespoons of the olive oil in a small bowl. Using a spoon or your fingers, pat the garlic mixture on the tomatoes, and drizzle on 2 more tablespoons of the olive oil.
- Bake for 45 minutes, uncovered. The tomatoes should be mushy; if not, bake for another 10 minutes and test again.

Cooking the Spaghetti
- After the tomatoes have baked for 30 minutes, fill a 6-quart pot about ⅔ full of water, stir in the 1 tablespoon salt, and set over high heat, covered. When the water reaches a full boil, add the spaghetti and stir. After about 10 minutes, start testing pieces of pasta every minute or so until the spaghetti feels tender but still firm.

◆ Pour the water and the spaghetti into a colander set in the sink. Let the pasta drain.

Finishing the Pasta

◆ Melt the butter in a small pot over medium heat.

◆ Chop the basil leaves into small pieces.

◆ In a large serving bowl, mix together the remaining parsley and olive oil, the melted butter, and the basil. Add the drained spaghetti and the baked tomatoes. Using two forks, lift small batches of spaghetti until it is all coated with the oil-butter mixture and the tomatoes are well distributed. Serve immediately.

■ COOKING PASTA ■

One pound of pasta will serve 4 people for a main course, depending on appetites and what else is served.

To cook 1 pound of pasta, use a large (at least 8-quart) pot and fill it with water 3 inches from the top. Add a tablespoon of salt and set over high heat. When the water comes to a rolling boil, add the pasta. Stir to make sure the pasta isn't sticking and all the pieces are immersed. If the water starts boiling over, turn the heat down a little, but you want to maintain a good rolling boil.

The cooking time will vary depending on the shape and size of the pasta. Most spaghetti types will take from 12 to 15 minutes, but fatter pieces like macaroni, fusilli, penne, and shells will take longer. Incidentally, you can use any shape of pasta you want in these spaghetti recipes. Look at the instructions on the pasta package for an estimated cooking time, although often American varieties recommend too-long cooking. So always taste your pasta a little before you think it may be done. Fish out a piece with tongs or a fork and bite into it. It should be just tender—not mushy—with no hard interior. Have a colander ready in your sink and then carefully take the pot to the sink and drain the pasta through the colander. (In spite of what you may have been told, do *not* rinse the pasta at this stage.) Put it in a warm bowl, add whatever sauce you are using, and toss to mix well.

Spaghetti with Parsley, Garlic, Olive Oil, and Bread Crumbs

SERVES FOUR

THIS IS A GOOD EXAMPLE of how a few humble ingredients can make a wonderful dish. It is important to serve this spaghetti hot, so have your bowl and plates warming in the oven. If you are worried about the raw garlic, don't. It gets tempered when it's tossed with the hot spaghetti.

4 quarts water

1 tablespoon salt (for cooking the pasta)

1 pound spaghetti

2 tablespoons plus ¼ cup olive oil

1 cup bread crumbs (see box, opposite)

A few sprigs parsley (to make ¼ cup chopped)

6 cloves garlic (to make 2 teaspoons finely chopped)

Salt and freshly ground pepper to taste

Preheat the oven to 250°F.

Cooking the Spaghetti

• Put the water and salt in a large pot, stir, and bring to a boil over high heat. When the water boils, add the spaghetti (for full details, see box, page 151).

While the Spaghetti Is Cooking

• Put the 2 tablespoons of olive oil in a small skillet and turn the heat to medium. Add the cup of bread crumbs and stir. It will only take a minute or two to toast the bread crumbs, so stir and watch carefully. Once the crumbs begin to turn a light golden brown, transfer them to a small dish and set aside. If you leave them in the skillet they will continue to brown from the heat in the skillet, and will turn too brown or taste burned.

• Wash the parsley and pat dry. Remove the stems, discard, and finely chop the leaves (for full details, see box, page 12).

• Peel and finely chop the garlic (for full details, see box, page 33).

◆ Put the serving bowl and the plates in a warm oven, leaving the oven door partially open.

Serving the Pasta

◆ After 10 minutes of cooking, taste the spaghetti for doneness. When ready, drain through a colander.

◆ Remove the bowl from the oven and put the hot, drained spaghetti into it. Add the olive oil, parsley, garlic, and a sprinkling of salt and pepper. Toss the noodles with 2 large spoons to distribute the ingredients evenly.

◆ Using your hands, sprinkle the bread crumbs over all.

◆ Put the pasta on the warmed serving plates and serve immediately. Or serve it at the table from the bowl.

◆

MAKING BREAD CRUMBS

Each slice of sandwich bread will yield about ⅓ cup of crumbs. Tear the slices of bread you will be using into bite-size pieces and put them, a handful at a time, into a blender. Blend very briefly, until they are irregular-size crumbs. Spread them out on a cookie sheet and bake in a 250°F oven for about 10 minutes. Check the crumbs to see if they are dry and golden. Remove. If you want to use them later, put them in a bag, snugly closed, and freeze until needed. This technique produces nice, irregular coarse crumbs instead of crumbs that are too fine.

◆

Fusilli with Tomato Sauce and Beans

THIS RECIPE MAY SEEM unusual but it tastes very good. The oven-roasted tomatoes add a fresh garden taste, the beans are all substance, and the tender pasta makes the dish complete. Serve with a small Parsley Salad (page 44) and perhaps Judith's Focaccia (page 248). A fine dessert would be the Lemon Pudding Cake (page 266). You could make the focaccia much earlier and freeze it.

1 ¾ pounds Roma or plum
   tomatoes (about 12)
2 teaspoons plus 1 tablespoon
   salt
1 teaspoon pepper
3 cloves garlic
½ small bunch parsley
½ cup olive oil

1 pound fusilli pasta (corkscrews)
2 cups cooked pinto beans (for
   details on cooking beans,
   see box, page 135), or
   2 15½-ounce canned pinto
   beans, drained and rinsed
¾ cup freshly grated Parmesan
   cheese

Preheat oven to 350°F.

Preparing the Tomatoes

♦ Cut the tip off each tomato to remove the stem, and cut each tomato in half lengthwise from the stem down.

♦ Arrange the tomatoes in a 9-by-12-inch baking dish with the cut side facing up. They should fit snugly side by side in the pan. Lightly sprinkle with 2 teaspoons salt and the pepper.

♦ Remove the papery skins from the garlic and finely chop (for full details, see box, page 33).

♦ Remove the stems from the parsley and finely chop the leaves (for full details, see box, page 12). You should have about ½ cup.

♦ In a small bowl, mix the garlic, parsley, and 2 tablespoons of the olive oil.

♦ Scoop up a small amount of the parsley and garlic with your fingers and pat it on top of a few of the tomatoes. Continue until all is evenly distributed over all the tomatoes.

♦ Drizzle the remaining olive oil over the tomatoes.

♦ Roast the tomatoes in the oven for 45 minutes.

Getting the Pasta and Beans Ready

◆ When the tomatoes have been cooking for about 15 minutes, fill a large pot with water and add 1 tablespoon of salt. Set the pot over high heat and bring to a full boil. Add the pasta and cook for 10 minutes. Test for doneness by removing a piece of pasta from the water and biting into it. When it's done, drain in a colander set in the sink.

◆ Heat the cooked pinto beans, over medium heat, in the same pot you used to cook the noodles. Add the cooked pasta, and turn the heat to low. Keep warm until the tomatoes are done.

Finishing the Dish

◆ When the tomatoes have cooked for 45 minutes, check to see if they are done. They should be soft, nearly mushy, and you should be able to pierce them easily with a fork. If they are done, remove from the oven. If not, cook another 10 minutes and check again.

◆ Mash the tomatoes with a fork right in the baking pan until the mixture looks like a sauce.

◆ Combine the tomato sauce, pasta, and beans in a large bowl and mix with a big spoon. Taste it to see if it needs more salt. If so, add salt, ¼ teaspoon at a time, until it tastes good to you.

◆ Bring the bowl to the table and serve along with good, freshly grated Parmesan cheese.

Caesar Pasta

HERE'S A DRAMATIC DISH that lets you have your Caesar salad and pasta all in one. The contrast of cold, crisp lettuce with hot pasta—mixed together at the last minute and all coated with lots of olive oil, garlic, and crisp croutons—is surprisingly good. Penne is a dried pasta shaped like little tubes with pointed ends, like quill pens.

2 cups toasted croutons
   (page 48)
4 quarts water
1 tablespoon salt
1 pound penne pasta

Caesar dressing (see below)
1 head romaine lettuce, about
   4 cups coarsely chopped
¼ pound Parmesan cheese

Caesar Dressing

2 large cloves garlic
1 cup extra-virgin olive oil
½ teaspoon Worcestershire
   sauce
1½ teaspoons lemon juice

1 tablespoon red-wine vinegar
⅓ cup heavy cream
¼ teaspoon salt
¼ teaspoon freshly ground
   pepper

Preparing the Croutons

◆ Toast the croutons according to the recipe on page 48. The croutons can be made well ahead of when you need them.

Cooking the Pasta

◆ Pour the water into a large pot, add the salt, and set over high heat. Bring to a boil, then add the pasta (for full details, see box, page 151).

While the Pasta Cooks: Making the Dressing and Preparing the Lettuce

◆ Peel the garlic cloves and chop them finely.

◆ The easiest way to make this dressing is to use a pint (2-cup) jar with a lid. Put the garlic, olive oil, Worcestershire sauce, lemon juice, red-wine vinegar, cream, salt, and pepper into the jar, put the lid on, and shake vigorously. You'll have about 1½ cups.

◆ Rinse the lettuce in cool running water, and dry using a salad spinner or paper towels. Cut the leaves crosswise into 1-inch pieces, and put back in the refrigerator so they are nice and cold when you add them to the pasta.

◆ Grate the Parmesan cheese, using the smallest holes on a metal grater. You'll want at least ½ cup of grated cheese.

Finishing the Dish and Serving

◆ After 10 minutes, test the pasta for doneness.

◆ When the penne is cooked, drain it into a colander set in the sink. Shake or gently stir the pasta in the colander to remove more water, which can get trapped inside this tubular pasta. Transfer the pasta to a large bowl.

◆ Pour about ⅔ of the dressing (about 1 cup) onto the hot pasta, and stir well with a large spoon to coat it. Taste a piece of pasta, and if the Caesar flavor isn't pronounced enough, add more of the dressing.

◆ Just before serving, add the chopped lettuce, the croutons, and the Parmesan cheese to the bowl and toss a few times. Grind some black pepper over the top.

◆ Serve on individual plates, with more Parmesan and freshly ground pepper on the table.

Pasta with Green Chilies, Tomatoes, and Cilantro

SERVES FOUR

THE ONLY INGREDIENT that might not be in your refrigerator is cilantro (for more information, see box, page 34). It is available in supermarkets, and combined with mild canned green chilies and vinegar, it adds a good Mexican dash to the spaghetti.

4 quarts water
1 tablespoon plus ¼ teaspoon salt
1 pound dry spaghetti or spaghettini
2 medium-size yellow onions
8 cloves garlic
4 tablespoons (¼ cup) olive oil

1 28-ounce can Italian crushed tomatoes
1 7-ounce can green chilies, chopped
Red-pepper flakes, to taste
½ cup red-wine vinegar
2 bunches cilantro (to make 1 cup chopped), plus some sprigs for garnish

Cooking the Pasta

◆ Put the water and 1 tablespoon of salt in a heavy-bottomed pot and place on a burner set to high. When the water boils, add the pasta (for full details, see box, page 151).

Preparing the Sauce While the Pasta Is Cooking

◆ Peel and chop the onions (for full details, see page 13).
◆ Peel and finely chop the garlic (for full details, see box, page 33).
◆ Put the olive oil in a skillet and set over medium heat. Add the chopped onion and cook—stirring occasionally—until the onions turn translucent, in about 5 to 7 minutes. Add the garlic, tomatoes (juice and all), the green chilies, red-pepper flakes (if you wish), vinegar, and ¼ teaspoon salt. Simmer for 5 minutes.
◆ Cut off the stems from the bunches of cilantro and discard. Chop the leaves coarsely to yield 1 cup, and stir into the sauce.

When the Pasta's Done

◆ After 10 minutes of cooking, taste the pasta for doneness. When the pasta is cooked, drain through a colander.
◆ Put the drained spaghetti into a large, warmed bowl. Pour on the hot sauce and mix well. Divide onto 4 warmed serving dishes and garnish with the cilantro sprigs.

Riso with Mint and Currants

RISO IS A TINY PASTA shaped just like rice. You'll find it in the pasta section of the supermarket. If you can't find riso, look for orzo, which is the same shape, only a bit larger. There is little difference between them, and one can be substituted for the other. You can serve riso and orzo unadorned, much as you would rice. Riso and orzo go especially well with chicken and pork dishes, and are good in soups. The currants and mint in this recipe give it a special appeal and a lively flavor. Currants are very small raisins and are available in the dried-fruit section of most markets.

6 CUPS

2 teaspoons salt (for cooking
    the pasta)
1½ cups riso
1 cup currants

Salt and pepper to taste
1 tablespoon finely chopped
    fresh mint
3 tablespoons butter

Cooking the Riso

◆ Fill a 4-quart pot about ¾ full of cold water and add the salt. Turn the heat to high and bring to a boil.

◆ Turn the heat down to medium-high and slowly add the riso. Use a large spoon to stir it for a few seconds to make sure the pasta doesn't stick to the pot.

◆ After 10 minutes, add the currants to the riso and stir again.

◆ With a small spoon, scoop up a few pieces of riso to test them for doneness. The ricelike pasta should be just tender, with no hard interior.

◆ When the riso is cooked, pour the contents of the pot into a colander with small holes or small mesh wire, that you have placed in the sink. Shake the colander to get rid of any excess water.

Flavoring the Riso

◆ Fill a large serving bowl with hot water and let it stand for a few minutes. Pour out the water, put the riso into the warm bowl, and taste the pasta again to see if it needs a bit more salt. If so, add salt, about ¼ teaspoon at a time, stirring to mix well, until it suits your personal taste. Add pepper to taste as well.

◆ Add the mint and butter, stir to blend, and serve hot.

Original Macaroni and Cheese

ABOUT 6 CUPS, SERVING 4

SOME CLASSIC RECIPES should be left alone, and this is one of them. Don't try to get tricky by using sour cream, chives, or any stylish new ingredients. This is a pure, wholesome, and delicious dish that cannot be bettered by gussying it up.

8 cups water (2 quarts)	¼ cup all-purpose white flour
1 tablespoon plus ½ teaspoon salt	2 cups milk
2 cups medium-size elbow macaroni	1½ cups grated sharp cheddar cheese
4 tablespoons butter (½ stick)	¼ teaspoon pepper

Cooking the Macaroni

♦ Pour the water and 1 tablespoon salt in a 4-to-5-quart pot and set over high heat. The water will come to a boil more quickly if you cover the pot.

♦ When the water boils, add the macaroni and stir so it doesn't stick to the bottom of the pot.

♦ After 10 minutes, scoop up a piece of macaroni and taste it. Be careful not to burn your tongue. If the noodle is tender, it is done. If it's still a bit firm, cook for 2 more minutes and check again.

♦ Dump the macaroni into a colander set in the sink, and let the water drain away.

♦ Put the macaroni in a heatproof bowl or casserole large enough to hold 6 cups.

Making the White Sauce

♦ While the macaroni is cooking, melt the butter in a small saucepan over medium heat, stirring regularly. Don't walk away from the stove; this whole process only takes about 6 minutes.

♦ Add the flour and stir continuously for about 2 minutes to blend the ingredients.

♦ Slowly pour in the milk and stir constantly, scraping the bottom and sides of the pot so nothing sticks. Continue stirring vigorously until the sauce thickens to the consistency of thick cream.

Adding the Cheese

◆ Add the cheese, ½ teaspoon salt, and the pepper to the white sauce, and stir until it is smooth and the cheese melts (2 or 3 minutes).

◆ Taste the sauce. If it is bland, add another ½ teaspoon of salt.

Finishing the Dish and Keeping It Warm

◆ Pour the cheese sauce over the macaroni and mix until the sauce evenly coats the pasta.

◆ If you are not quite ready to eat, put the dish in a 300°F oven to keep it warm. Leave it in the oven no longer than 20 minutes, though, or it will become dry.

◆ If you think the dish is a bit dry, you can moisten it by adding ½ cup hot milk and mixing it well.

Crushed Macaroni and Vegetables

SERVES FOUR

AS ODD AS CRUSHED MACARONI MAY SOUND, trust me, you will love this. It is very, very good. Crushing the dried elbow macaroni transforms the pasta into a wonderful new texture, and with the tomatoes and eggplant it becomes a complete meal in one dish. Serve a sourdough bread with this and one of the desserts of fresh fruit (page 291).

⅓ cup olive oil	⅓ cup water
1 cup small elbow macaroni	3 large cloves garlic
1 bunch fresh spinach (to make about 2 cups trimmed and chopped)	3 medium-size tomatoes
	¾ teaspoon salt
	¾ teaspoon pepper
½ bunch parsley	1¼ cups canned stewed tomatoes, with liquid
1 medium-size eggplant	

Preheat oven to 350°F.

Preparing the Baking Dish

• Pour 2 teaspoons of the olive oil in an 8-by-8-by-2-inch baking dish and smear it around the bottom and sides, using your fingers or a paper towel.

Crushing the Macaroni

• Put the macaroni in a plastic bag (the 1-gallon zip bags work well) and seal the end. Use a rolling pin to crush the macaroni, rolling it back and forth until each elbow is crushed into small pieces. Don't overcrush or you will end up with pasta powder.

Preparing the Spinach and Parsley

• Wash the spinach (for full details, see box, page 47), and chop into large pieces. Press the chopped spinach firmly into a measuring cup; you will need about 2 cups. Set aside in a bowl.

• Wash the parsley and pat dry. Remove the stems and discard; finely chop the leaves (for full details, see box, page 12). Put the parsley and spinach in the bowl and toss together.

Preparing the Eggplant

• Slice off about ¼ inch of the stem end of the eggplant and discard. Leaving the skin on the eggplant, cut the eggplant crosswise into ¼-inch rounds.

Preparing the Liquid

• Put the remaining scant ⅓ cup of the olive oil and the water in a small lidded jar.

• Peel and finely chop the garlic cloves (for full details, see box, page 33) and add to the jar. Screw the lid on tight and shake the mixture a few seconds, until it is well blended.

Putting the Dish Together

• Cut the tomatoes into slices ¼ inch thick and place them in a single layer—close but not overlapping—over the bottom of the baking dish. Add ½ teaspoon each salt and pepper.

• Spread ½ of the spinach-and-parsley mixture over the tomatoes.

• Sprinkle the crushed macaroni evenly over the tomatoes, add the remaining ¼ teaspoon salt and pepper, and put another layer of spinach and parsley over the macaroni.

• Spread the stewed tomatoes and all the liquid from the can over all.

• Place the eggplant slices on top of the stewed tomatoes.

• Shake the water-oil mixture again until well blended and drizzle it all over the top. Cover the dish snugly with foil.

• Bake for 1 hour. To test for doneness, *carefully and gently remove the foil—remember, there is hot steam trapped inside—*and, using a spoon, snag a piece of macaroni and bite into it. It should be tender. If not, cook for another 10 minutes and test again.

• Remove from the oven and allow to settle for a few minutes. Serve while still quite warm.

Risotto

RISOTTO IS A TRADITIONAL Italian comfort food made most often with a variety of short-grain rice called Arborio, which absorbs a lot of liquid and becomes quite plump and creamy. Here in this country, we usually prepare rice by adding the liquid to the rice all at once and leaving it to cook, covered and unattended (for full details on cooking rice, see box, page 83). With risotto, you add the hot liquid to the rice very gradually, stirring constantly. All this stirring may seem like a lot of work, but the warm, creamy risotto that results is well worth the effort. You can add an endless number of ingredients to this basic risotto to make a new and different meal each time.

1 medium-size yellow onion
4 tablespoons butter (½ stick)
5 cups or more chicken broth, canned or homemade
2 cups Arborio rice (available in many supermarkets or specialty food stores)
Salt and pepper to taste
¾ cup freshly grated Parmesan cheese

RISOTTO

Risotto is such a pleasing vehicle for flavors, and you can vary the basic recipe in many ways. Adding some leftover chicken, ham, or cooked shrimp makes a more filling dish; stir them in during the last ten minutes of cooking. To the right are two variations on the theme that are particularly delicious.

Preparing the Rice

- Peel and finely chop the onion (for full details, see page 13).
- Melt the butter in a 4-to-5-quart saucepan over medium heat, stirring regularly.
- Add the onion and cook, continuing to stir, until it turns soft and translucent. Turn the heat down if the onion starts to brown.
- Meanwhile, pour the chicken broth into a separate saucepan, set over medium heat, and bring to a gentle simmer. Adjust the heat as needed to maintain this simmer the whole time you are preparing the risotto.
- Once the onion is soft, add the rice and cook over medium heat, stirring constantly, for about 3 minutes. Adjust the heat as necessary—if the rice is cooked at too high a heat, it will turn brown and take on an undesirable flavor.

Adding the Liquid to the Rice

- Using a ladle, scoop up about ½ to ¾ cup of broth. Pour it in the pan with the rice, stirring constantly with a spoon. After the first addition of broth, the rice mixture will look a bit soupy.
- As the rice begins to cook, stir it constantly, making sure that you scrape along the bottom of the pan so that it does not stick. You should see little bubbles popping up in the liquid from time to time. If it bubbles more vigorously than this, turn the heat down to medium-low.

- When most of the liquid is absorbed into the rice and the rice begins to look a bit dry, add another ladle of broth to the pan and stir constantly, as before.

Determining When the Risotto Is Cooked

- Continue to add the broth in ½-to-¾-cup batches and stir the rice until you have used most of the broth (this will probably take about 20 minutes). It is now time to test whether the risotto is cooked. Spoon up a grain of rice and bite into it—it should be tender without being too mushy. If it is still crunchy and tastes a bit starchy, you will need to continue adding liquid and cooking further.
- If it looks as if you will run out of chicken broth and your rice is still not cooked, don't be alarmed. Because of variations in individual stoves and cooking temperatures, you may need more liquid than called for in the recipe. Simply heat up another cup or 2 of chicken broth. If you run out of broth, use hot water.
- When the rice is tender and the risotto has a creamy consistency, almost like thick oatmeal, it is done.

Serving the Risotto

- Add salt and pepper to the risotto, about ¼ teaspoon at a time, until it seems well seasoned to you. Stir.
- Add the grated Parmesan cheese and stir well.
- Serve the risotto immediately in warm bowls and have extra grated Parmesan on hand.

■

RISOTTO WITH TOMATOES AND BASIL

Take 4 Roma tomatoes, cut off and discard the stem tops, and cut the tomatoes into small pieces. Chop enough fresh basil leaves into small pieces to make about 1 cup. Put 2 tablespoons of olive oil in a skillet, and turn the heat to medium-high. When the bottom of the skillet feels hot when you put your open hand 1 inch from the bottom, add the tomatoes and sprinkle them with salt and pepper. Stir for 3 or 4 minutes, until they seem soft. Put the cooked tomatoes aside, and when the risotto is done, stir the tomatoes and basil into the hot risotto. Stir to mix well; taste for salt and add some if needed. Serve immediately and pass some grated Parmesan cheese.

■

◆

RISOTTO WITH SPINACH AND GARLIC

Peel and chop 3 large cloves of garlic (see box, page 33, for details) into small pieces, and put them on a piece of waxed paper. Rinse ½ bunch of spinach leaves, and shake off the excess water. Cut off the stems, bunch the leaves up, and cut them into thin strips, then cut crosswise into small pieces. Put 2 tablespoons of olive oil in a skillet and turn the heat to medium-high. When the bottom of the skillet feels hot when you put your open hand, palm side down, 1 inch from the bottom of the skillet, it is ready. Add the garlic to the oil and stir for a minute. Turn the heat to low, and add the spinach. Press the spinach down with a spatula, lightly salt and pepper it, and turn it over with a spatula. The spinach will wilt down almost immediately. Take the skillet off the stove, put a lid on the skillet, and when the risotto is done, stir the garlic and spinach into the risotto. Serve immediately, and pass some grated Parmesan cheese.

◆

Polenta Baked with Vegetables

SERVES FOUR AS A MAIN
COURSE OR SIX AS A SIDE DISH

POLENTA IS THE ITALIAN VERSION of our cornmeal mush. It has become very popular here recently, perhaps because the Italians have shown us different ways to liven it up with other ingredients. Polenta Baked with Vegetables is a very satisfying dish, and all it takes is stirring cornmeal, salt, olive oil, and water together in the baking dish, adding a few vegetables, and then, after about an hour of baking, sitting down to supper.

1 large red, ripe tomato
1 green bell pepper
1 bunch fresh or ½ box frozen chopped spinach (thawed)
1 medium-size yellow onion
1 cup polenta, not instant (use either an American yellow cornmeal or preferably an Italian brand of polenta or yellow cornmeal)
3¼ cups lukewarm water
1¼ teaspoons salt
¼ cup olive oil
⅓ cup grated Parmesan cheese

Preheat oven to 350°F.

Preparing the Vegetables

◆ Cut the stem off the tomato and chop the tomato into bite-size pieces (for full details on cutting tomatoes, see page 27).

◆ Cut the stem off the bell pepper and cut the pepper in half lengthwise (store one half for future use). Remove the veins and seeds and chop the pepper (for full details on cutting peppers, see box, page 31).

◆ If using fresh spinach, remove any large, tough stems and wash the leaves (for full details on washing spinach, see box, page 47). Take about half the spinach, pile it on a cutting board, and, using a large knife, chop into pieces the size of large postage stamps. Press the leaves firmly into a measuring cup and measure out 1½ cups of chopped spinach. Wrap and store any extra spinach for future use.

◆ If using frozen spinach, be sure it is defrosted, and squeeze out any excess water with your hands.

◆ Peel and cut the onion in half lengthwise, from the stem down. Store one half for another use. Chop the remaining half of the onion (for full details, see page 13).

Mixing the Polenta

◆ Put the polenta, water, salt, and olive oil into an 8-inch square baking dish and stir with a fork until blended. There's no need to grease the pan.

◆ Add the tomato, pepper, spinach, and onion to the polenta and stir to distribute the vegetables evenly.

Baking the Polenta

◆ Put the baking pan on the center rack of the oven and bake for 30 minutes, then check to see if the liquid is boiling around the edges of the baking pan. If so, leave the temperature as is. If not, turn the oven up to 400°F. Bake for another 15 minutes, or until the water has all been absorbed—that's your signal that the polenta is done.

◆ Remove the pan from the oven and put it on a heatproof counter. Sprinkle Parmesan cheese evenly over the top and let sit for 5 minutes.

◆ Cut the polenta into squares, then lift portions from the pan with a spatula. Serve warm.

◆

LEFTOVER POLENTA

If you have any leftover polenta, you can enjoy it by frying squares of it in olive oil until they are golden on each side. Serve for supper, and sprinkle with Parmesan cheese. In fact, you'll find it so delicious, you might want to bake an extra dish of polenta so you can enjoy it again this way.

◆

Brown Rice with Mushrooms and Onions

7 CUPS, SERVING FOUR TO FIVE

THIS DISH MAKES a first-rate supper. All you need to round out the meal is a tossed Green Salad (page 42), and fruit with cheese or cookies for dessert. Brown rice, which has a good chewy texture and a delicious, nutty flavor, takes considerably longer to cook than ordinary white rice. So make this on an evening when you have an hour to relax before supper, or on a weekend.

3½ cups water	3 tablespoons butter
2 teaspoons salt (for cooking the rice)	Salt to taste, about 1 teaspoon
1½ cups brown rice	1 teaspoon freshly ground black pepper
½ pound button mushrooms*	
1 large yellow onion (to make about 1½ cups chopped)	

Cooking the Rice

- Put the water in a pot (I use a 3-quart pot) with a lid. Stir in 2 teaspoons salt and turn the heat to high. When the water begins to boil, pour the rice into the boiling water, and stir a second with a large spoon. Turn the heat down to low, put the lid on, and cook for 50 minutes.

While the Rice Is Cooking:
Preparing the Mushrooms and Onions

- Clean the mushrooms by wiping them with a damp paper towel (see box, opposite). Cut or break the short stems off the mushrooms and keep them—you'll be cooking the stems, too. Cut the mushroom caps in quarters. Set aside.
- Peel and chop the onion (for full details, see page 13).

Sautéing the Vegetables

- Set a large skillet over high heat and add the butter. Turn the heat down to medium when the butter melts, and tilt the skillet so the butter coats the entire bottom of the pan.
- Add the mushrooms and the chopped onion.
- Using a large spoon, stir the onions and mushrooms. Be sure to keep them moving around the pan so they cook uniformly. When the mushrooms soften, and the onions turn translucent—in about 4 or 5

* Standard white mushrooms found in the supermarket produce section.

minutes—they are done. It is a good idea to taste a piece of mushroom and a piece of onion to make sure they are tender.

Finishing the Dish

- After 45 minutes, taste a little bit of the rice; if it's tender it is done.
- Put the cooked brown rice in a serving bowl. Add the sautéed mushrooms and onions and stir to mix them in thoroughly. Salt and pepper to taste. Serve hot.

■ CLEANING THE MUSHROOMS ■

It is better to clean mushrooms by wiping them with a damp paper towel. If you soak them, they absorb water and lose some of their flavor. The stems are very good, so don't discard; just cut off a thin slice of the dark root end, then slice or quarter the stems and add them to the caps.

Green Chili Pie

THIS GOOD DISH IS a pantry friend, because you can keep canned, roasted green chilies (which are very mild) on your shelf indefinitely, and the eggs, cheese, and milk should also be regulars in your refrigerator. You may not always have fresh cilantro, but a sprinkle of parsley on top will do instead. Serve with corn tortillas warmed in the oven. The "pie" doesn't actually have a crust—only green chilies lining the pan —so it's quick to make.

1 tablespoon butter	1½ cups whole milk
2 7-ounce cans roasted whole green chilies	½ teaspoon salt
	Freshly ground pepper to taste
½ pound Jack or Fontina cheese	A few sprigs cilantro
4 eggs	

Preheat oven to 425°F.

Preparing the Pan

- Smear the bottom and sides of a 9-inch pie pan with the butter.
- Drain the liquid from the canned chilies, and pat the chilies dry with paper towels. Using your fingers, open up the chilies and spread them out so they are in one layer; remove and discard the seeds. Line the pan with the chilies, placing the pointed tips toward the center of the dish, and the tops up the sides of the dish to the rim. The chilies will hold the filling much as a pie crust would.
- Grate enough cheese on the large holes of the grater to yield 1¼ cups, then sprinkle it evenly over the chilies. You will have cheese left over; just wrap it well and refrigerate.
- In a mixing bowl, beat the eggs until well blended. Add the milk, salt, and pepper, mix well, and pour over the chilies.
- Put the pan on a baking sheet and set on the middle shelf of the oven. Bake for 15 minutes, reduce the heat to 325°F, then bake the pie for another 20 minutes.

Preparing the Cilantro

- While the pie is baking, wash and pat dry a few sprigs of cilantro. Pull off the whole leaves and discard the stems.
- Test for doneness by sticking a knife into the center of the custard. If the knife comes out clean, the pie is done. If not, cook for another 5 minutes and test again.
- Garnish with cilantro leaves and serve hot—or cold.

◆

Good Vegetables

◆

INTRODUCTION

───

IN THE PAST, on the American table, vegetables were always considered side dishes. But that has changed today, and more and more vegetables are treated as the main part of the meal.

Certainly some of the vegetable recipes in this chapter should be promoted to center stage. I love a baked potato for supper, either just with sour cream or with one of the stuffings you'll find here. Eggplant Stuffed with Roasted Vegetables; Carolina Green Beans, Potatoes, and Bacon; or the Vegetable Cobbler will make a whole meal.

There are also some recipes here for vegetables that serve more as accompaniments. And throughout the book you will find some formulas for simple vegetables that go well with a particular main dish. So check the index under vegetables for further simple recipes.

RECIPES

———

VEGETABLE CHART

BAKED POTATOES

BAKED POTATOES STUFFED WITH HAM AND CHEESE

MASHED POTATOES

PARSLIED SMALL RED POTATOES

OVEN-ROASTED POTATOES

CREAMY BAKED POTATOES AND TURNIPS

BAKED SWEET POTATOES/YAMS

ROAST ZUCCHINI

EGGPLANT FILLED WITH ROASTED VEGETABLES

CAROLINA GREEN BEANS, POTATOES, AND BACON

SWISS CHARD

BAKED BUTTERNUT SQUASH

CABBAGE WITH BACON AND SUNFLOWER SEEDS

SAUTÉED SWEET PEPPERS

CARROTS WITH FRESH MINT

VEGETABLE COBBLER

STEAMING VEGETABLES

Vegetable Chart

Limited to Vegetables Called For in This Book

Vegetable	Look For	Storage	Will Keep
Asparagus	Firm straight stalks, green about ⅔ of their length with firm tips. Size can vary from pencil-size stalks to thick as your thumb. Choose uniformly sized stalks so that they will cook evenly—avoid shriveled or discolored stalks and wilted tips.	Leave them in a loosely closed plastic bag and refrigerate. Or loosen the bunch and set the stalks upright in a jar, add 1 inch of water, cover the jar loosely with a plastic bag, and refrigerate.	2–3 days in plastic bag, longer with jar/water method.
Avocado	Either Hass (black, pebbly-textured skin) or Fuerte (green, smooth skin) avocado (technically a fruit). Usually sold hard and unripe. Hold in the palm of your hand and squeeze gently: if hard to very firm, it needs to ripen. If softer but not mushy (mushy indicates spoilage), it's ready to eat.	If avocado is hard, ripen it at room temperature 2–5 days. Check it daily until it yields slightly when squeezed in the palm of your hand. Once ripe, refrigerate in a loosely closed plastic bag.	4–7 days.
Beets	Hard, medium-size to large, fairly smooth-skinned, garnet-red beets—may be sold in a bunch with "greens" (stems and leaves); if so, choose those with fresh-looking greens. May also be sold individually without greens.	If purchased with greens and you want to store beets for longer than a few days, cut greens off, leaving an inch or so of the stem attached to beet, and refrigerate beets in a loosely closed plastic bag, separate from greens. (Greens may be cooked and eaten like spinach or discarded.)	Beets—a month or more. Greens—1–2 days.
Broccoli	Tender but firm stalks that are not "woody" (resembling the cut end of a stick of wood) at the bottom of the broccoli stem, a strong green color with tight "buds" (the top of the stems), and crisp leaves.	Refrigerate in a loosely closed plastic bag.	3–4 days or more.

VEGETABLE	LOOK FOR	STORAGE	WILL KEEP
Butter-head lettuce	Smallish, round, loosely formed heads with soft pale-green outer leaves and crisper pale-yellow inner leaves—avoid those with wilted, brown, or bruised leaves and discolored stem ends. Similar varieties: "Boston," "Bibb," and "limestone" lettuce.	Refrigerate unwashed in a loosely closed plastic bag. Or separate leaves, discarding tough, wilted, or damaged ones, gently rinse, and dry using a salad spinner or pat dry with paper towels or clean dish towels, and store refrigerated in a tightly closed plastic bag.	2–3 days in plastic bag, up to a week if washed, dried, and stored.
Cabbage	Compact heads, heavy for their size, may be waxy greenish-white or bright reddish-purple	Refrigerate in a loosely closed plastic bag.	Up to a month.
Carrots	Freshest carrots have lacy greens attached to firm, longish orange roots (the carrots). Carrots may be bagged or sold individually without greens. Avoid limp, rubbery, or cracked ones and black or discolored stem ends (the big end).	If purchased with greens, cut greens off (without cutting carrot) before storing. Dispose of greens and store carrots unwashed in a loosely closed plastic bag.	Up to a month.
Celery	Firm, greenish-white, tightly formed bunches with crisp green leaves.	Refrigerate in a loosely closed plastic bag.	A week or more.
Celery root (celeriac)	Very firm, medium-size (about the size of a baseball or softball), with pebbly, tough, brown skin. Sometimes will have fresh green tops like little celery stalks. Hold in your hand and feel around for soft spots and heft—should feel heavy for its size.	Refrigerate in a loosely closed plastic bag.	2–3 weeks.

VEGETABLE	LOOK FOR	STORAGE	WILL KEEP
Corn	Refrigerate corn with husks (leaves that cover corn) left on. Pull husk down 2 inches or so and look for worms or worm damage. Rows should be filled with plump kernels. Look for tip: some stores remove ends and part of husk, which may be OK or may be a way to disguise old corn. To tell, prick a corn kernel; if fresh, it will almost squirt a sweet milky liquid.	Refrigerate in a loosely closed plastic bag.	Use immediately! (The sugar in corn quickly turns to starch, and you lose that great taste.)
Crisp head lettuce or "iceberg" lettuce	Firm, large, round, tight heads of pale-green leaves, heavy for their size with no signs of browning. Butt end or where head was cut from root should be creamy color and smell sweet, not bitter.	Refrigerate in a loosely closed plastic bag. Sometimes sold wrapped in plastic mesh—leave mesh on until you use it, but put it, mesh and all, in the loosely closed plastic bag.	Up to a week.
Cucumbers	Firm, dark-green cucumbers 6–9 inches long. Avoid yellowing, shriveled, or soft specimens. Small are good, too.	Refrigerate in a loosely closed plastic bag.	Up to 10 days.
Eggplant	Firm shiny purple-black with a fresh-looking green cap. Avoid brown or soft spots and shriveled skin.	Refrigerate in a loosely closed plastic bag. Eggplants are quite fragile and bruise easily, so don't stack or crowd them against harder produce.	2–3 days.
Fennel	Clean, crisp yellowish-white bulbs with bright-green lacy leaves. Avoid signs of browning.	Refrigerate in a loosely closed plastic bag.	Up to a week.
Garlic	Good-size, very firm bulbs that feel heavy for their size, with dry paperlike covering through which you can feel large "cloves" (the sections that make up the bulb). Can be white or purplish. Avoid soft, sprouting cloves or those with cloves that have begun to separate from the bulb.	At room temperature, in a dark place, away from other food.	Up to a month. Discard when it becomes spongy or moldy and/or begins to sprout.

Vegetable	Look For	Storage	Will Keep
Green beans	Slender beans, firm, crisp, and free of blemishes.	Refrigerate in a loosely closed plastic bag.	Up to 5 days.
Green onions or scallions	Crisp bright-green tops with a firm white base that is straight and not bulblike—should have firm roots	Refrigerate in a loosely closed plastic bag.	Up to a week.
Leaf lettuce	Crisp, evenly colored leaves that show no sign of damage, wilting, or yellowing. Varieties include redleaf, greenleaf, oakleaf, and salad-bowl.	Refrigerate in a loosely closed plastic bag. Or separate leaves, discarding tough, wilted, or damaged ones; gently wash, dry (use salad spinner), layer with paper towels or clean dish towels, and store refrigerated in a tightly closed plastic bag.	2–3 days in a plastic bag. Up to a week washed, dried, and stored.
Leeks	Bright-green tops with a firm white base that extends several inches up from the root. Often white part is all that is needed in recipes, so choose those with the most white.	Refrigerate in a loosely closed plastic bag.	A week or more.
Mushrooms	Common or cultivated mushrooms ½–3 inches in diameter, firm, unblemished, with tightly closed caps (look on the flat underside; the cap will be closed around the stem and you will not see the "gills" or dark variegations on the underside of the mushroom).	Air should circulate around mushrooms—place in a paper-towel-lined basket, plate, or baking sheet; arrange in one layer with space between them; cover with a damp paper towel; and wrap loosely with plastic wrap or plastic bag. Refrigerate.	Up to a week.
Onions	Firm, dry onions with dry paperlike skin. Check stem end (opposite of root end) for wetness or softness. May be yellow, white, or red. The "sweetness" of onions depends more on their age than their variety, with younger onions being better for raw use.	In a cool dark place away from potatoes.	Up to 3 months. Discard when they become spongy or moldy and/or begin to sprout.

Vegetable	Look For	Storage	Will Keep
Peas	Fairly small, shiny, green, unblemished pods. Avoid pods that appear "stuffed" with peas. Peas inside pods should be "pea-green" and on the small side. Avoid large, tough, and starchy whitish-green peas.	Refrigerate in a loosely closed plastic bag	3–4 days.
Peppers, bell or "sweet" peppers	Firm, thick-fleshed, shiny, brightly colored peppers. Avoid soft or brown spots. Stem end should be firm and dry. May be green, red, orange, or yellow. Green peppers have the most pronounced flavor; red, orange, and yellow peppers are milder, sweeter.	Refrigerate uncovered in a paper-towel-lined basket or plate.	Up to a week.
Potatoes	Firm, well-formed potatoes. Avoid greenish, sprouting, soft, shriveled, cut, or cracked potatoes. (Generally, any variety—brown, white, or red—will be suitable. For specific recommendations, see box, page 67, About Potatoes.)	In a cool, dry, well-ventilated and dark place (away from onions: the moisture from potatoes causes onions to rot).	2–3 weeks.
Romaine lettuce	An elongated head with dark-green leaves on the outside having a fairly wide white rib down their center; inner leaves are a much lighter green and curl inward like a scoop. Avoid wilted or damaged heads. Stem end should be creamy-colored, not brown.	Refrigerate in a loosely closed plastic bag. Or separate leaves, discarding tough, wilted, or damaged ones; gently rinse and dry, using a salad spinner or patting dry with paper towels or clean dish towels. Store refrigerated in a tightly closed plastic bag.	A week or more.
Shallots	Firm shallots with bulbs from ¼–¾ inch in diameter with a smooth and dry outer skin. Avoid those that are soft, shriveling, and/or sprouting.	In a cool, dry, well-ventilated and dark place.	A month or more. Discard when soft and sprouted.

VEGETABLE	LOOK FOR	STORAGE	WILL KEEP
Spinach	There are two common varieties: one with dark-green crumpled leaves and quite thick stems (which have to be removed); the other with smoother, smaller leaves and tender stems. Avoid wilted, bruised, or yellowish leaves.	Refrigerate in a loosely closed plastic bag.	3–5 days.
Squash—"summer"	All are soft-shelled. Varieties include: zucchini or Italian, crookneck, and patty pan or scallop. Buy firm, small-to-medium-size. Avoid those that are overly large, soft, or light in weight for their size.	Refrigerate in a loosely closed plastic bag.	3–5 days.
Squash—"winter"	Winter squash are all hard-shelled. Small varieties include acorn or Danish and butternut. Large varieties include banana and Hubbard and are sometimes sold cut into pieces. Look for hard, smooth-skinned winter squash. Avoid any with signs of softening.	In a cool, dry, well-ventilated place, or refrigerate, uncovered, if whole; in a sealed plastic bag or tightly wrapped in plastic wrap if cut.	Uncut—several months. Cut—a week or more.
Sweet potatoes and yams	Sweet potatoes have light yellowish-tan skin, yams coppery-brown skin; they are interchangeable in cooking. Buy firm, small-to-medium-size squash that taper at both ends and are smooth-skinned. Avoid those with cracks, soft spots, discoloration, or shriveled skin.	In a dark, fairly humid place—near your potatoes would be fine.	About 2 weeks.
Swiss chard	Bunches with wrinkled but firm green leaves with silvery-white or red stalks. Avoid wilted, bruised, or yellowing leaves.	Refrigerate in a loosely closed plastic bag.	3–5 days.

VEGETABLE	LOOK FOR	STORAGE	WILL KEEP
Tomatillos	Tomatillos have a papery brown covering called a "husk." Inside the husk is a smooth green fruit about the size of a golf ball. Look for snug husks and firm unblemished fruit.	Refrigerated in a loosely closed plastic bag.	3–4 weeks.
Tomatoes	Look for smooth, firm, unblemished tomatoes. They can be a light orange-red to red. Tomatoes (technically a fruit) may need ripening after purchase. If they are very hard and more light orange than red, they are not ripe.	If necessary, ripen 2–3 days or more at room temperature. Check them daily, like fruit. When they turn red and yield slightly when gently squeezed, they are ripe. Refrigerate when ripe.	When ripe and refrigerated, 3–5 days.
Turnips	Very firm, small-to-medium-size turnips, heavy for their size. Avoid large ones that can be hollow and bitter and those with cuts or punctures. May be sold with "greens" (stems and leaves) or individually without greens.	If purchased with greens, cut them off if you want to store turnips for longer than a few days. Refrigerate turnips in a loosely closed plastic bag. (Greens may be eaten like spinach or discarded.)	A month or more.
Watercress	Bunches with small stems and bright-green, unwilted leaves.	Untie the bunch and sort out any bad sprigs. Rinse remainder in cool water, drain on paper towels or dry in salad spinner, and refrigerate in a loosely closed plastic bag.	Up to a week.

Baked Potatoes

SERVES TWO

A BAKED POTATO, just out of the oven, split down the center, and the center mashed with butter, salt, and pepper, is a perfect food. Quite honestly, I don't think anything can improve it. But for the sake of variety, stuffing a baked potato with leftovers such as ham and cheese can be mighty good too. There is no end to stuffing possibilities. The best varieties of baking potatoes are russet and Idaho. A good side dish to a baked potato is a plate of sliced tomatoes with a little pile of chilled sugar snap peas that have been salted. (Sugar snap peas are wonderful for their crunchy, slightly sweet taste. Most supermarkets have them in cellophane packages.)

2 large baking potatoes
2 tablespoons butter

Salt and pepper to taste

Preheat the oven to 425°F.

Preparing the Potatoes

• Rinse the potatoes under cold running water and pat dry. Pierce the skin of the potato in 2 or 3 places with the tip of a paring knife, so that, as the potatoes bake and get steamy inside, they won't explode.

Baking the Potatoes

• Put the potatoes a couple of inches apart on the middle rack in the oven. Set a timer for 45 minutes to check for doneness. It sometimes takes 50 to 60 minutes to bake large potatoes. Test by piercing a potato with the tip of a paring knife, then pushing the knife into the center of the potato. If it feels tender, it is done; if not, bake another 10 to 15 minutes.

Finishing the Potatoes

• Remove the potatoes from the oven. Using a paring knife, cut each potato lengthwise down the center. Put a tablespoon of butter in each potato and lightly salt and pepper. Using a fork, mash the potato a few times to move the butter, salt, and pepper around. Serve hot.

Baked Potatoes Stuffed with Ham and Cheese

SERVES TWO

HERE IS A SIMPLE AND satisying meal all in one. You will want the stuffing warm too, so don't turn off the oven when you first take the potato out.

1 green onion or scallion
½ cup chopped cooked ham
   (about 2 ounces)
½ cup grated sharp cheddar
   cheese
⅓ cup sour cream
2 large freshly baked potatoes
   (preceding recipe)
Salt and pepper

Preparing the Stuffing

• Finely slice the white and some green of the onion (for full details see page 51).

• Chop the ham into small pieces; you should have about ½ cup.

• Put the grated cheese in a bowl. Add the onion, ham, and sour cream, and mix well.

• Hold each potato with a towel or pot holder—remember, it's hot—and split it lengthwise with a paring knife. Scoop out all of the potato, leaving the skin with just a thin layer.

• Put the scooped-out part of the potato in the sour-cream mixture and mash with a fork. Don't worry about making it smooth—it isn't suppose to be.

• Lightly salt and pepper the mixture and taste it. If it needs more salt or pepper, add some.

• Divide the filling and fill each potato shell. Don't pack down the filling.

• Put the stuffed potatoes in a baking dish, and bake for 15 minutes. Serve hot.

■

BAKED POTATO STUFFED WITH VEGETABLES

The possibilities for stuffing potatoes are endless. Small amounts of vegetables are called for in this recipe—it is a good example of using up tidbits of food left in the refrigerator. Think of it as conceptual—as a guide—and use whatever small bits of vegetable you have.

½ small carrot
½ cup frozen peas
Leftover bell pepper (to yield
   about 2 tablespoons grated)
⅓ cup milk
2 tablespoons butter
2–3 sprigs parsley, chopped
2 large freshly baked potatoes
   (see opposite)

Using the medium-size holes of the grater, grate the carrot into a small mixing bowl. Put the peas in the bowl. Grate the bell pepper—red or green—and add it to the bowl. Heat the milk slowly in a small (1-quart) saucepan to lukewarm, then add the butter to the milk and stir until it melts. Add this to the bowl, along with the parsley. Stuff this mixture into the potatoes, following recipe directions.

■

Mashed Potatoes

4 CUPS

THERE IS A WORLD of difference between instant mashed potatoes and your own homemade. The trick to making creamy mashed potatoes is to heat the milk and butter together before you start the mashing. Mashed potatoes taste good with so many things, particularly with Trout with Celery Root (page 82), Smothered Chicken with Mushrooms (page 98), or Pot Roast with Vegetables and Gravy (page 113)—invite friends to share the pot-roast dinner. Note that you can keep the potatoes warm for up to an hour if you want to do them ahead.

6 medium all-purpose potatoes	4 tablespoons butter
	Salt
1 cup milk	Freshly ground pepper

Cooking the Potatoes and Heating the Milk

◆ Peel the potatoes and cut them into quarters. Put them in a pot and add just enough cold water to cover them. Turn the heat to high, bring to a boil, and boil gently for 15 to 20 minutes. Turn the heat down to medium-high if the water bubbles too violently. The potatoes are done when a fork pierces them easily.

◆ Near the end of the potato-cooking time, put the milk and butter in a small pot and heat on a burner set to medium. Don't let the milk boil; you just want it hot.

Mashing

- When the potatoes are done, drain them in a colander set in the sink. Shake to remove all the excess water.

- Put the potatoes in a bowl and mash them with a potato masher or a fork. Briskly mash until the big lumps disappear, slowly adding half the hot milk-and-butter. Move the potatoes around in the bowl to mash every bit of them well. Add more milk—a little at a time—until the lumps disappear and the potatoes smooth out. The moisture content of potatoes varies so greatly that it is hard to say exactly how much milk and butter you will need.

- When the lumps are gone, whip the potatoes with a whisk or a fork until they are as smooth as you like. Add salt and pepper to taste.

- Serve immediately in the same bowl. Or, if you want to keep them warm for up to an hour before serving, cover the bowl with foil and put the bowl in a 200°F oven.

BEATING THE POTATOES

You can mash and beat the potatoes with an electric mixer, or a hand-held electric mixer. Don't use a food processor, because it will turn the potatoes into a gummy gray mess.

Parslied Small Red Potatoes

Serves six

Small red potatoes are in a category all their own, and are delicious either hot or cold. Any leftovers can be reheated, or used in a salad. Serve these with Trout with Celery Root (page 82), or with the Smothered Chicken with Mushrooms (page 98), or any simple roast or steak.

2 pounds small red potatoes	4 tablespoons butter
3 teaspoons salt	¼ teaspoon freshly ground
A few sprigs parsley (to make	black pepper
about ⅓ cup chopped)	

Preparing and Cooking the Potatoes

◆ Wash the potatoes in cold water. There's no need to peel them—the skins look good and taste good.

◆ Put the potatoes into a 3- or 4-quart pot. Fill the pot with water so the water is about 2 inches above the level of the potatoes. Add 2 teaspoons of the salt, turn the heat to medium-high, and let the water come to a boil. When the water boils, turn the heat down to medium and cook the potatoes for about 15 to 20 minutes.

◆ After 15 minutes, test the potatoes for doneness. Pierce the center of a potato with a small paring knife. If the knife slides in easily, the potatoes are done. If not, cook for another 5 minutes, then test again.

Preparing the Parsley

◆ While the potatoes are cooking, remove the stems from the parsley and finely chop the leaves (for full details, see box, page 12).

Serving the Potatoes

◆ When the potatoes are done, dump them into a colander in the sink, and let the water drain away. Put the potatoes back into the pan, add the butter, parsley, 1 teaspoon salt, and the pepper. Using a fork, stir the potatoes until they are well coated with the mixture. Serve hot.

Oven-Roasted Potatoes

THESE POTATOES HAVE the flavor and look that most of us love in fried potatoes—without being fried. They are welcome at breakfast and/or supper. They reheat well, and you can do this quickly by adding a couple of tablespoons of oil to a skillet and quickly heating them. Stand right by the stove and stir them with a fork as they get hot.

SERVES TWO OR THREE AS A SIDE DISH

2 medium russet potatoes
3–4 tablespoons olive oil

1 teaspoon salt, plus more to taste

Preheat oven to 425°F.

Preparing the Potatoes
• Peel potatoes and cut into bite-size cubes. The cubes should all be about the same size, no bigger than ½ inch.
• Put the potatoes in a small pot and add water until it reaches about 2 inches above the top of the potatoes. Add 1 teaspoon salt.
• Put the pot on high heat and bring the water to a boil. Cook the potatoes until they are just tender and can be fairly easily pierced with a knife—but not so soft that they crumble when handled. This takes about 5 minutes after the water starts to boil.

Roasting the Potatoes
• Drain the potatoes in a colander set in the sink. Shake the colander well to eliminate any excess water.
• When the potatoes are well drained, dump them onto the baking sheet and drizzle with most of the olive oil. Using your hand, toss the potatoes around in the oil until it coats all the potato cubes, using the rest of the oil if necessary, and the entire surface of the baking sheet.
• Using a salt shaker, sprinkle the potatoes liberally with salt.
• Set the baking sheet on the center rack of the oven and cook for 30 minutes, turning the potatoes over with a spatula about every 10 minutes for even browning.
• After 15 minutes, check to see if the potatoes are golden brown all over and are soft when pierced with a fork. If so, remove from the oven. If not, cook another 5 or 10 minutes and check again.
• Once the potatoes are cooked, taste a piece. Sprinkle on more salt if needed. Serve hot.

Creamy Baked Potatoes and Turnips

SERVES FOUR TO SIX

WHEN I TAUGHT this dish to beginners in my classes, everyone loved it—even those who had always said, "I don't like turnips!" Turnips are mildly sweet and delicate, and they are natural partners with potatoes in this creamy, rich dish. This is a recipe that will make your reputation as a first-rate cook. Make it for a special dinner, or give yourself a special dinner. Serve with the Roast Leg of Lamb (page 138), or the Lamb Shanks (page 140), or with the Roast Chicken with Vegetables (page 96). You can prepare the dish ahead and put it in the same oven with your meat for the last 20 minutes of cooking.

2 garlic cloves
1 medium-size yellow onion
3 russet potatoes (see box, page 67)
2 white turnips, medium-size
3 tablespoons butter
1 cup heavy cream

1¾ cups or more milk
1 teaspoon salt
Pepper to taste
½ teaspoon freshly grated nutmeg (or ¼ teaspoon ground nutmeg)

Preheat oven to 325°F.

Preparing the Vegetables
• Peel the papery outside skin off the garlic cloves. Slice each clove into thin slices lengthwise, then chop them into tiny pieces crosswise. Set aside on a plate.
• Peel the papery skin off the onion, then trim off the root end and the top stem. Cut the onion in half, lay the flat sides down, then cut the halves into thin slices. Pile the onion slices on the plate with the garlic bits and set by the stove.
• Wash and peel the potatoes and turnips, then cut them crosswise into ¼-inch-thick slices. Set them near the stove.

Cooking the Garlic, Onions, Potatoes, and Turnips
• Put the butter in a large pot with a 4½-quart capacity and place on a burner set to medium. (I use a sauté pan 11 inches in diameter and 4 inches deep—a very useful piece of equipment.)
• Melt the butter, then add the garlic and onion. Stir for about 3 minutes, until the onion is limp but not brown. Add the potatoes and turnips to the pan, and stir to mix with the garlic and onion. Add ¾ cup

of the cream, the milk, salt, pepper, and nutmeg. Taste the sauce. If you think it needs more nutmeg, add a little more. Taste again. Stir so the vegetables all get coated with the liquids and the seasonings. Cook for about 15 minutes, stirring often, and if the vegetables seem to be sticking on the bottom of the pan, add another ½ cup milk. You want to cook the potatoes and turnips until they are tender but not soft or mushy when pierced with a fork or a paring knife.

    ◆ Transfer the potato-turnip mixture to a shallow baking dish large enough to hold it. I like to use a round Pyrex or ovenproof earthenware dish, one that looks good when you just want to set the completed dish right on the table.

    ◆ Bake in the oven for 15 to 20 minutes, or until the top begins to brown a little. Remove from the oven.

Finishing the Dish

    ◆ Place an oven rack 5 or 6 inches beneath the broiler and set the oven to broil. Drizzle the remaining ¼ cup cream all over the top of the potatoes and turnips, put the dish on the rack closest to the broiler, and stand right there watching until the top gets nicely browned. This only takes 2 or 3 minutes. Serve hot.

Baked Sweet Potatoes/Yams

YAMS AND SWEET POTATOES look inviting served together, side by side on a plate. They go particularly well with Pan-Fried Pork Chops (page 128).

2 sweet potatoes	4 tablespoons butter
2 yams	Salt and pepper to taste

Preheat oven to 375°F.

Cooking the Potatoes

- Rinse the potatoes and scrub them with a kitchen brush.
- Cut a small piece off the end of each potato so it won't explode during cooking.
- Place the potatoes a few inches apart on a baking sheet, and put the sheet in the oven. Bake for 1 hour.
- To test for doneness, stick a fork in the potatoes. It should go in easily once you've pierced the rather tough skin.

Serving the Sweet Potatoes and Yams

- The traditional way to serve these is to cut them open lengthwise with a fork, drop in a pat of butter—or two—and season with salt and pepper.
- I like to slice the potatoes crosswise with a sharp knife, into disks about ¾ inch thick, then peel off and discard the tough skin, and top with a good bit of butter. The slices add color to a plate and are rich, smooth, and flavorful.

■

ABOUT SWEET POTATOES AND YAMS

Sweet potatoes and yams are both round and long, and we often confuse them. Sweet potatoes are tan and are mildly sweet, rather dry, but very, very good with butter mashed in. The reddish-purple yams are more popular because they are more moist and sweet. Try baking one of each and see which you prefer.

Roast Zucchini

ROASTING ZUCCHINI in the oven develops that delicious flavor you get only from oven-browning. Roast some extra and enjoy the leftovers the next day.

SERVES FOUR

2 pounds zucchini (about
    6 medium-size)
Olive oil

1 teaspoon salt
Pepper to taste

Preheat oven to 400°F.

Preparing the Zucchini and Baking Sheet

◆ Rinse the zucchini and pat dry with paper towels. Cut off and discard about ¼ inch from either end of the squash, and slice them in half lengthwise.

◆ Using a pastry brush or your fingers, spread olive oil on the zucchini, both the cut sides and the dark-green rounded outer parts. Sprinkle with salt and pepper, and place them—cut side down—on a baking sheet. Since the zucchini are well oiled, there's no need to oil the baking sheet.

Cooking the Zucchini

◆ Roast the zucchini for 12 minutes, then check for doneness. Using a metal spatula, lift up a piece of the squash to look at the flat, cut side. The zucchini should be turning a light brown and softening slightly, but they should not be limp and mushy. If they have not started to change color, cook for another 3 or 4 minutes, then check again.

◆ When the zucchini are cooked, use the spatula to lift them onto a platter. Avoid overcooking, since the squash will turn to mush if left in the oven too long. Serve immediately as a vegetable, or chill and serve with a vinaigrette.

Eggplant Filled with Roasted Vegetables

SERVES FOUR TO SIX

THIS IS ANOTHER REMINDER for beginning cooks—the oven really is your good friend. Here is a simple combination of eggplant, onion, and summer squash that all roast together in your oven for about 40 minutes. Your reward is a delicious vegetable supper that can be particularly pleasing with warm wheat bread, and strawberries and cream for dessert.

5 tablespoons olive oil	2 medium-size yellow onions
1 long eggplant (6 or 7 inches long, about 1 pound)	1 teaspoon dried thyme
	1 teaspoon salt
1 pound yellow crookneck squash (or zucchini)	½ teaspoon black pepper

Preheat oven to 350°F. Spread about 1 tablespoon of the olive oil over the bottom of a baking sheet. (My baking sheet is 13 by 17 inches, which easily holds these vegetables.)

Preparing and Roasting the Vegetables

◆ Cut the root and stem ends off the eggplant and discard. Cut the eggplant in half lengthwise from top to bottom and place the halves cut side down on the baking sheet.

◆ Cut the crookneck squash (or zucchini) crosswise into ½-inch pieces.

◆ Peel and chop the onions (for full details, see page 13).

◆ Put the squash and onions in a mixing bowl. Rub the dried thyme between the palms of your hands for a few seconds, then sprinkle it over the vegetables in the bowl. Sprinkle the remaining olive oil over the vegetables, and add the salt and pepper. Reaching to the bottom of the bowl, toss and turn all the vegetables so they are coated with the thyme, olive oil, salt, and pepper.

◆ Spread the vegetables in a layer on the baking sheet. Put the baking sheet in the oven and cook for 20 or 30 minutes. It usually takes about 30 minutes to bake the vegetables, but test doneness after 20 minutes. Pierce the middle of one of the eggplant halves with a sharp knife. If it feels tender, not resistant, it is done. If it still feels firm, test again in 10 minutes. Bake until it feels tender.

- Remove the eggplant from the baking sheet and continue to cook the remaining vegetables for about 10 or more minutes, or until they are slightly brown on top. When done, remove the baking sheet from the oven.

Finishing and Serving the Vegetables

- Prepare the baked eggplant for serving by using a large spoon to scoop out the center, leaving the shell with just a thin layer of flesh. The eggplant shell will be soft, but it will hold the vegetable filling. Combine the scooped-out eggplant with the other roasted vegetables. Cut each half eggplant in half to make 4 pieces, or, if serving 6, cut each half into thirds. Put the eggplant shells on a serving platter or on individual serving plates and pile some of the squash mixture into the shells. Taste for salt and add if necessary. Serve.

◆

A SALAD MADE WITH LEFTOVERS

For a lunch on the weekend, chop up the leftover cooked vegetables, and mix them with a little salad dressing. Let the vegetables sit for about an hour and then add some chopped lettuce.

◆

Carolina Green Beans, Potatoes, and Bacon

SERVES FOUR

FOR THE LAST FEW YEARS, most of us have been following the recommended way of cooking green beans until they are just tender, because we think long cooking destroys flavor and vitamins. But this Southern dish has a fullness of flavor and a depth of character that crunchy green beans don't have. Serve with warm Yellow Cornbread (page 246) for a complete supper.

4 slices hickory-smoked bacon	1 cup water
1 pound green beans	½ teaspoon salt
3 green onions or scallions	¼ teaspoon freshly ground
2 medium-size russet or Idaho potatoes	pepper

Preparing the Bacon and Vegetables

◆ Stack the slices of bacon on top of each other, and cut the slices in half lengthwise. Chop the bacon into small pieces crosswise. Separate the bacon into small pieces (don't worry about separating all of them—when they are cooking, you can easily separate them with a fork).

◆ Put the green beans in a colander and rinse them under cold water, shaking the colander so they are well washed.

◆ Trim the ends off the beans and discard, then cut the beans into 1-inch pieces.

◆ Trim the root end off the scallions, and trim off some of the coarser, green top, usually about 2 or 3 inches. Chop the remaining white and green part into tiny slices.

◆ Peel the potatoes and cut them down the center lengthwise. Place the halves flat side down on a cutting board, and slice the halves in half again lengthwise. Cut the 4 pieces crosswise into 1-inch squares.

Cooking the Bacon, Green Beans, Potatoes, and Scallions

◆ Set a heavy-bottomed pot or pan with a lid over medium-high heat. When you place your hand about 1 inch from the bottom of the pan and it feels hot, add the bacon.

- Using a fork, push and move the bacon around the pot, then separate the little chunks of bacon that are stuck together. Stand right by the stove, stirring and moving the pieces until they are lightly browned, about 5 minutes.

- Add the green beans and the water, and stir to mix everything together. Put the lid on the pot and turn the heat to low.

- After 10 minutes, add the scallions and the potatoes. Sprinkle the salt and pepper all over. Leave the heat on low and put the lid on again. Cook for 30 more minutes. Check once after cooking for 15 minutes to make sure that water hasn't all evaporated. If so, add another ½ cup of water, cover, and cook the remaining 15 minutes. Serve hot.

ABOUT BACON

Bacon is a good staple to have around. If there are only one or two of you in your household, don't be afraid to buy a whole pound. You can break the slices up and make packages of ¼ pound or less; wrap them tightly in plastic and freeze them. It's handy to have some bacon when you want a good Sunday breakfast, bacon and eggs for supper, or a BLT for lunch, and it makes a fine flavoring for dried bean and cabbage dishes, as well as for soups and pastas.

Swiss Chard

THERE ARE TWO KINDS of chard: Swiss chard, with white stems and green leaves; and red chard, with red stems and green leaves. They are interchangeable. Chard is very good with lamb shanks or firm-fleshed fish like halibut or shark. It is good in soups, and the tart leaves add a piquant taste served with pastas. It is quick to cook, and if you have any left over, add a little vinegar and olive oil to it and eat it cold with a toasted cheese sandwich.

1 bunch Swiss chard or red chard (usually about 16 to 18 ounces)	3 cloves garlic (to make about 2 teaspoons chopped)
2 teaspoons salt (for boiling)	3 tablespoons olive oil
	Salt to taste after cooking

Preparing and Cooking the Chard

◆ Rinse the chard leaves and stems under cold water, then shake off excess water. Trim off the tough ends of the stalks and discard.

◆ Cut the stalks off at the base of the leaves and cut them into ½-inch pieces. If the stalks continue up through the leaves and are wide, fold the leaves in half and cut the thick white or red rib out.

◆ Cut or tear the leaves into big bite-size pieces.

◆ Bring a large pot of water with 2 teaspoons salt to a boil. Put only the pieces of stem into the boiling water. Set a timer for 4 minutes.

Preparing and Cooking the Garlic

◆ Meanwhile, peel the papery skin off the garlic cloves and discard.

◆ Chop the garlic into tiny pieces (see box, page 33).

◆ Put the olive oil in a small skillet and set over medium-high heat. When the skillet is quite hot, add the garlic and stir it around in the oil with a fork. The garlic will turn slightly golden around the edges; when it does it is done. Don't let it turn brown.

◆ Remove the skillet from the heat, and shove the garlic to the side of the skillet so the pieces stop cooking in the hot oil.

Finishing Cooking the Chard

◆ After 4 minutes of cooking the stems, add the chard leaves to the pot. Cook for 2 more minutes after the water comes to a boil again.

◆ Put a colander in the sink and drain the chard leaves and stems. Transfer the chard to a bowl, and stir in the garlic and oil. Taste for salt, and add more, a little at a time, if needed. Serve hot.

Baked Butternut Squash

B UTTERNUT SQUASH IS a good stand-in for potatoes, and can be done in no time when peeled, sliced into rings, and baked in a hot oven. It has an earthy, rich taste and a creamy texture. Serve it with honey brown butter (see box, page 79).

SERVES FOUR TO SIX

1 butternut squash, 2½ to 3 pounds	About 4 tablespoons butter Salt and pepper to taste

Preheat oven to 400°F.

Preparing the Squash

• Peel the squash with a vegetable peeler or a sharp paring knife. Cut off and discard about 1 inch from each end.

• Using a large sharp knife, cut the peeled squash crosswise into rings about ½ inch thick, starting at the neck. When you get to the more rounded base of the squash, remove the seeds and stringy material with a spoon and discard. Continue cutting the base into rings.

Cooking the Squash

• Melt the butter in a small saucepan over medium heat. Brush some of the butter onto a baking sheet to grease it all over. Lay the rings on the sheet, and brush them generously with melted butter. Sprinkle with salt and pepper.

• Bake for 20 minutes. The slices should be soft when pierced with a fork.

• Put the squash slices on a platter and serve hot.

Cabbage with Bacon and Sunflower Seeds

WHENEVER I SEE SOMEONE turn up his nose at the mention of cabbage, I know it's because he's never had this version. It will make cabbage seem like a brand-new vegetable to you. Barely cooked, it maintains its crunchiness, its fresh flavor, and its light-green color. And it's quick—once the water boils, the cabbage cooks in just seconds. This makes a fine lunch with some hearty, sliced dark rye bread, but if hearty appetites are eating, you might include big cups of Quick Tomato Stew (page 26). For a country supper, serve with the Ham and Farm Cheese Butter-Fried Sandwiches (page 218), or Potato, Pepper, and Onion Frittata (page 212).

2 teaspoons salt, plus more to taste	5 slices bacon
1 head green cabbage, about 2 pounds (light green, no curly leaves)	¾ cup salted shelled sunflower seeds
	1 teaspoon sugar

Preparing the Cabbage

◆ Fill a 4-to-5-quart pot with water, and 2 teaspoons salt, and set over high heat.

◆ Cut the cabbage in half from the top down to the core end, then split each half down the center again, so you have 4 quarters. Cut the solid white core out of each piece of cabbage and discard. Put the quarters down flat on a cutting board and cut each crosswise at 2-inch intervals.

◆ Use your hands to separate the cabbage leaves. You don't need to separate each and every leaf.

Cooking the Bacon and Rendering the Fat

◆ Separate the bacon slices and lay them flat, and side by side, in a skillet. Turn the heat to medium.

◆ When the white part of the bacon (the fat) begins to turn brown, use a fork to turn the slices over. When the white fat becomes completely brown on the second side, the bacon is cooked. Remove the bacon and put it on a paper towel to drain and cool.

◆ Turn off the heat, pour the bacon fat into a small bowl, and set aside. You should have about 4 tablespoons. If you have a little more or a little less, don't worry—just use what you have.

◆ When the bacon cools, chop it into bits with a large knife or break it up with your fingers. Set aside on a paper towel.

Finishing the Dish

◆ Once the water in the large pot reaches a boil, add the cabbage and use a large spoon to push it down into the water. When it is fully immersed, count to 8 slowly.

◆ After 8 long seconds, dump the contents of the pot into a colander in the sink, and let the water drain away. Shake the colander to get rid of excess water.

◆ Put the warm cabbage in a large serving bowl and add the bacon fat, bacon, sunflower seeds, and sugar. Toss everything together, using 2 large forks.

◆ Taste the cabbage to see if it needs salt. If so, add salt, about ¼ teaspoon at a time, and taste again. Do so until it tastes good to you. Serve hot.

Sautéed Sweet Peppers

THIS COLORFUL DISH is unusual, quick to prepare, and—like a good condiment—will enhance the flavor of other foods. It tastes as good as it looks, and it makes spaghetti, noodles, steak, or fish seem a little more exciting. If you chop the strips of peppers into pieces like confetti, they'll do wonders for rice, barley, or lentils.

1 red bell pepper

1 green bell pepper

1 yellow bell pepper

2 tablespoons vegetable oil

1 teaspoon salt

½ teaspoon freshly ground
    black pepper

Preparing the Peppers

◆ See box, page 31, for details on preparing peppers. When you have opened up each of the 3 peppers and scraped off the seeds and ribs, stack the pepper rectangles on top of each other, and slice them into ¼ inch strips.

Cooking the Peppers

◆ Pour the vegetable oil into a skillet (about 10 inches in diameter) set over medium-high heat. After a minute, put your hand—open palm down—about an inch above the bottom of the skillet; if it feels hot, the skillet is ready. Tilt the skillet so the oil covers the bottom.

◆ Put the peppers in the skillet and, using a fork, spread them so they are in one layer and can cook evenly. Stir slowly and constantly to move them about, to cook all over. Salt and pepper them.

◆ After cooking for 2 or 3 minutes, turn the heat to medium-low and put a lid on the skillet. Let them steam for about 2 minutes. Take the lid off, stir the peppers around, and spear a strip with a fork and taste it. It should be soft, but not floppy and limp. Remove from the stove, and serve hot.

◆ If you are not using the peppers right away, let them cool and then transfer them to a plastic container with a lid. They will keep about 10 days in the refrigerator.

Carrots with Fresh Mint

CARROTS WITH FRESH MINT always taste like supper in the garden. There is a real difference between eating a whole mint leaf and little snippets. So use tiny whole leaves if you can.

SERVES FOUR

1 pound carrots (about
    5 medium)
2 cups water
Salt to taste

3 tablespoons butter
2 teaspoons brown sugar
⅓ cup whole fresh mint leaves,
    small if possible

Cooking and Serving the Carrots

♦ Peel the carrots and slice them into pieces ¼ inch thick (see box). Put the carrots in a small pot with the water and salt and bring to a boil. Turn the heat to low and simmer for 5 minutes, or until the carrots are just tender. Remove from the heat and pour the water and carrots into a colander or strainer. Drain well.

♦ Using the same pot you cooked the carrots in, melt the butter and sugar together over low heat. Add the cooked carrots, stirring well for about 1 minute to coat. Put the carrots in a serving dish and toss with the fresh mint leaves. Serve warm.

♦ ABOUT CARROTS ♦

Carrots have been used throughout this book in soups and stews and surrounding chicken and meats as they roast. There they are simply peeled and cut into 1- or 2-inch chunks, and they always add flavor to whatever they touch. Here they come into their own as a star dish. After trimming off the ends and peeling them, slice them thin so that they will cook quickly. Holding the carrot in one hand with your fingers tucked under, cut even ⅛-to-¼-inch slices firmly with a large sharp knife, moving your fingers back after each slice. The more you chop and slice, the more expert you will become. Carrots keep well in the vegetable bin of the refrigerator and are handy to have around. Make sure, particularly for this dish, that your carrots are still firm, not limp.

Vegetable Cobbler

ROOT VEGETABLES GO very well together in this dish. It is a full meal all by itself, not just a side dish. Serve with cornbread and cheese. Making the dough for the crust is a good lesson that can be applied to making pie dough. Beginners often fear blending flour and fat and rolling out the dough. But the worst thing that can happen is that your crust might be a little dry. The good thing is that we home cooks can eat our mistakes and feel philosophical, knowing next time it will be better.

THE COBBLER FILLING

1 turnip	½ cup chicken broth, canned or
1 russet (the brown) potato	homemade, or ½ cup water
1 celery root	1 tablespoon cornstarch
1 yellow onion	1 teaspoon salt
3 carrots	Freshly ground pepper to taste
½ bunch parsley	4 tablespoons (½ stick) butter

THE COBBLER DOUGH

1¾ cups flour	6 tablespoons (¾ stick) butter
1 tablespoon baking powder	(should be very cold)
½ teaspoon salt	¾ cup heavy cream

Preheat oven to 325°F. I like to use 13-by-9-by-2-inch Pyrex baking pan (3-quart capacity).

Preparing the Vegetables and Seasoning Them

• Peel the turnip and cut into ½-inch slices. Stack the slices and cut into ½-inch strips, then cut the strips crosswise into ½-inch cubes or "dice." Since all these vegetables have rounded edges, there will be lots of pieces that aren't cubes, but just include them.

• Peel the potato and cut lengthwise into ½-inch slices. Stack the slices and cut lengthwise into ½-inch strips. Cut the strips crosswise to make ½-inch cubes.

• Cut off and discard the stem and root ends of the celery root. Using a sharp knife, slice away the gnarled, rough brown outer surface. It yields easily to the knife to reveal the fragrant white interior. Slice the root into ½-inch slices. Stack the slices, and cut into ½-inch strips. Cut the strips crosswise to make ½-inch dice.

• Peel and coarsely chop the onion (for full details, see page 13).

- Peel the carrots, cut off and discard a bit of the rounded stem end, and cut them in half lengthwise. Cut crosswise into ½-inch pieces.
- Wash and pat dry the parsley, discard the stems, and finely chop the leaves (you want about ½ cup).
- Put the vegetables in the baking dish and, using your hands, stir them around so they are well mixed.

Preparing the Cornstarch Mixture
- Put the chicken broth in a small bowl and stir in the cornstarch. Pour this over the vegetables and stir so it coats all of them. Sprinkle the salt and pepper over all.
- Cut the 4 tablespoons butter into bits and scatter them over the top of the vegetables. Set the dish aside.

Mixing the Dough
- Put the flour, baking powder, and salt in a mixing bowl. Using your hand, or a fork, stir to mix the dry ingredients together.
- Cut the chilled butter into small bits and scatter over the flour mixture. Rub the butter and flour together, scooping the flour from the bottom of the bowl and rubbing the butter and flour together with your thumbs and fingers. Continue doing this until the mixture looks like a bowlful of loose flour with lots of little lumps of flour and butter, then stir in the heavy cream.
- Using a fork, stir and mix the dough. Now, with your hands, reach down and scoop up the dough from the bottom and all around the sides of the bowl to incorporate any dry flour into a rough mass. Press the dough firmly between your hands so it holds together.
- Flour your cutting board and dust your rolling pin with flour. Plop the dough onto the floured board. You want to roll the dough out into a piece the shape and size of the baking dish; the dough should be about ¼ inch thick.
- Starting at the center, roll toward the edge with the rolling pin, and pat and stretch the dough a little with your hands. It isn't fragile. Continue to roll until it's the size of the dish. When it is the right size, gently run a metal spatula under the dough to loosen it, fold it in half, lay the folded dough over half the vegetables in the baking dish, then unfold it so the dough covers all the vegetables. Press it against the sides of the dish. Now make a few vents on top by piercing the dough all the way through with the tines of a fork. The vents allow the steam to escape.
- Put the dish in the oven, and bake 55 to 65 minutes. The crust should be browned and the vegetables tender. Serve hot.

■ STEAMING VEGETABLES ■

Steaming is one of the best and quickest methods for cooking vegetables and preserves all the good nutrients in them. Artichokes, asparagus, broccoli, cauliflower, green beans, new potatoes—all can be steamed in a collapsible steaming basket set over boiling water or, if you have one, in a metal insert with holes made to fit into a particular pot. Simply fill a large pot with 1½ to 2 inches of boiling water—enough to come to the bottom of your steamer—and set the steaming basket inside, filled with your prepared vegetables, cover, and let steam over medium heat until the vegetables are just tender.

Here are some approximate guidelines for timing the cooking, but be sure to taste and use your own judgment as to when they are done to your liking. If you have several layers of vegetable in your steamer, stir them around once or twice while steaming so they are cooked evenly. Check to make sure the water hasn't boiled away before the vegetable is steamed, and add more if necessary. When done, remove your vegetable from the heat immediately and toss with some butter or olive oil, salt, and perhaps a little lemon juice.

VEGETABLE	PREPARATION	STEAMING TIME
Artichokes	Leave whole, any tired leaves removed	50 minutes
Asparagus	Leave whole, tough stems trimmed	5 minutes
Broccoli	Cut into flowerets, stems quartered	8 minutes
Cauliflower	Cut it into flowerets, hard core removed	8 minutes
Green beans	If young, leave whole, stems removed If large, stem and cut in half or quarters	10 minutes
New potatoes	Leave whole and unpeeled, any blemishes scraped off	15–25 minutes (depending on size)

◆

Breakfast Can Be Supper, Too

◆

INTRODUCTION

———

TOO MANY WONDERFUL DISHES—traditionally considered only for breakfast—are getting lost by the wayside in our busy lives. No one has the time to make waffles and pancakes or scrambled eggs before rushing off to work. So why not enjoy them for supper?

Egg dishes particularly can be enriched with fillings made from good leftovers. And we've forgotten how delicious a Welsh Rarebit or a ham-and-cheese sandwich fried in butter can be.

These things take but a few minutes to prepare at the end of a day—probably less time than you'd spend standing in line at the "Home Food Replacement" or deli counter (and they're cheaper than anything you'd buy, too).

RECIPES

———

SCRAMBLED EGGS

OMELETS

SOME OMELET FILLINGS

POTATO, PEPPER, AND ONION FRITTATA

WELSH RAREBIT

RAISED WAFFLES

THIN YELLOW CORNMEAL PANCAKES

J.B.'S FRENCH TOAST

HAM AND FARM CHEESE BUTTER-FRIED SANDWICHES

Scrambled Eggs

THE SECRET OF GOOD SCRAMBLED EGGS is to cook them over low heat, stirring gently, until they thicken but are still moist. Just remember: the more you cook them, the drier and tougher they will become. Remove them promptly from the skillet and turn them out onto a warm plate when they reach the stage you want, since they will continue to cook from the heat of the pan even after you turn off the heat or remove the pan from the burner.

2 eggs
¼ teaspoon salt
Pepper to taste

2 tablespoons water
2 tablespoons butter

1

Scrambling the Eggs

- Crack the eggs into a small bowl. Sprinkle in the salt and pepper, and add the water. Stir with a fork until the yolks and whites are well blended and a uniform yellow.
- Put the butter in an 8-inch nonstick skillet and set it over medium heat. Tilt and turn the skillet so that the fat coats the bottom of the pan completely. When the butter just starts to foam, pour in the eggs. 1) Let them set for about 5 seconds, then stir them gently with a fork and 2) tilt the skillet to let the runny part in the center spread to the edge. The goal is to have the mass of egg cook gently until it is tender and moist with large, lumpy curds. Remove quickly from the heat while some of the egg is still shiny—it will continue to cook for a few seconds. The entire cooking process should take less than a minute. Serve immediately.

2

◆ ABOUT EGGS ◆

When I was a child, eggs were considered the perfect food—inexpensive, nutritious, and very quick to cook. I still think they make the most satisfying breakfast, lunch, or supper. The most important lesson in cooking eggs (except for hard-boiled eggs) is that they don't like high heat. They'll get tough and rubbery with high heat, but a gentle, low heat will preserve the tender, pleasing texture and good flavor. Nonstick skillets are a great help when cooking eggs. And remember that eggs must be kept in the refrigerator so they don't spoil.

Omelets

A N OMELET IS a tender, fluffy blanket of egg that can be served plain or wrapped around any filling you want—as long as the filling is not too wet. Vegetables or a little ham or cheese tucked into an omelet makes a delicious meal. There are so many possibilities for fillings, many of which are sitting right in your refrigerator disguised as leftovers. So make good use of them and have yourself a fine omelet lunch or supper.

1

2

2 eggs	⅛ teaspoon pepper
1 tablespoon water	1 tablespoon butter
¼ teaspoon salt	

Starting the omelet

• Break the eggs into a small bowl, add water and the salt and pepper, and beat thoroughly with a fork for about 10 seconds, just enough to blend the yolks and whites.

• Set an 8-inch nonstick skillet over medium-high heat until hot. To test whether it is hot enough, sprinkle a few drops of water in the pan; if they sizzle and disappear, the pan is ready.

• Add the butter and tilt the pan, swirling the butter in all directions to coat the bottom and sides. The butter should not turn brown. If it does, throw it out and start over.

• When the butter has foamed in the pan for about 10 seconds, pour in the beaten eggs. Leave them alone for about 5 seconds to set.

• 1) Using a fork, lift the cooked part of the egg away from the rim of the pan toward the center, allowing the liquid egg to run under and toward the edge of the pan.

Filling and Finishing the Omelet

• After about 30 seconds, while the eggs are still very moist and creamy, but not liquid, 2) spread the filling in a line just to one side of the center of the omelet, then slip the spatula under the egg mass on the other side of the pan and 3) flip that half of the omelet over onto the other half to enclose the filling. If you are not using any filling, simply flip one half of the omelet over onto the other. 4) Now quickly tilt the pan over a plate so the omelet falls out bottom side up. Serve immediately.

FOR A 2-EGG OMELET, 4 tablespoons or ¼ cup filling is just about right. Don't use a wet or saucy filling, because the liquid dilutes the egg. Here are a few suggestions for both savory and sweet omelets.

Ham Omelet

Add ¼ cup finely chopped cooked ham to the beaten eggs before cooking.

Cheese Omelet

Spread ¼ cup grated cheese such as cheddar or Jack over the eggs just before folding.

Bacon Omelet

Add ¼ cup crisp, crumbled cooked bacon to the beaten eggs. To cook bacon, see pages 194–5.

Herb Omelet

Mix 2 tablespoons finely chopped parsley with 1 teaspoon chopped fresh sage, tarragon, or thyme and add to the beaten eggs.

Mushroom Omelet

Sauté ½ cup raw sliced or chopped mushrooms in 2 tablespoons butter and add to the eggs just before folding.

Apple Omelet

Put ¼ cup applesauce or cooked diced apples over the eggs just before folding.

Jelly Omelet

Put about ¼ cup of your favorite jelly onto the eggs just before folding over.

3

4

Potato, Pepper, and Onion Frittata

SERVES FOUR

A FRITTATA IS EASY to make. Italian by birth, it has been adopted by Americans with enthusiasm. It is firmer than an omelet but tender and takes well to all kinds of fillings.

1 green bell pepper	2 cloves garlic
1 medium-size yellow onion	6 eggs
1 medium potato	Salt and pepper to taste
3 tablespoons olive oil	

Preparing the Vegetables

- Wash the pepper and chop it into ¼-inch pieces (for full details, see box, page 31).
- Peel and chop the onion (for full details, see page 13).
- Peel the potato, cut lengthwise, then crosswise, into quarters. Slice the quarters lengthwise into pieces ¼ inch thick.
- Peel and chop the garlic (for full details, see box, page 33).

Cooking the Potato

- Pour the oil into a 12-inch skillet and set over medium heat. Add the potato slices, lightly salt and pepper, and cook, still over medium heat, about 5 minutes, turning the potatoes over several times so they cook on both sides.
- Add the pepper, onion, and garlic to the skillet and continue to cook, stirring every couple of minutes, for another 8 to 10 minutes.
- While the potatoes, peppers, onions, and garlic are cooking, prepare the eggs.

Beating the Eggs

- Crack the eggs into a bowl and beat lightly, just until the yolks and whites are blended into one color. Don't overbeat them.
- Sprinkle salt and pepper over the eggs and stir them again, then pour them over the vegetables in the skillet. Reduce the heat to low, cover the skillet, and cook for 8 to 10 minutes, or until the top of the frittata looks set, with no puddles of uncooked egg across the top.

Serving

- When the frittata is done, remove the skillet from the heat. Cut the frittata into wedges, and serve while still hot, turning the wedges over as you put them on the plates so that the golden-brown bottom side is now facing up.

■ FRITTATA VARIATIONS

Here are a couple of variations on the frittata theme. Once you get the hang of this versatile dish, try your own variations.

1. Instead of sautéing the chopped onion, potato, and garlic filling in the main recipe, use 1 large potato, peeled and chopped, and 1 leek, rinsed, trimmed, and chopped (for full details on preparing leeks, see page 24). After the leeks and potatoes have cooked in 4 tablespoons butter for 8 to 10 minutes, add the 6 eggs and cook the frittata just as described in the recipe for Potato, Pepper, and Onion Frittata.

2. Instead of the chopped onion, potato, and garlic filling for the main recipe, make one of ½ cup chopped zucchini, ½ cup chopped tomatoes, and 2 garlic cloves chopped, all sautéed in 4 tablespoons butter for 8 to 10 minutes. After you have added the eggs, sprinkle ½ cup grated Parmesan cheese on top (for full details on cheese grating, see box, page 149) and cook the frittata as described in the recipe for Potato, Pepper, and Onion Frittata.

■

Welsh Rarebit

SERVES FOUR

WELSH RAREBIT OR RABBIT CAN be a delicious, simple dish. It is made with a melted sharp cheddar cheese, dry English mustard, and a little dark beer, which is poured over a slice of toast. This dish hits the spot on a cold, rainy day.

5 ounces sharp cheddar cheese	1 teaspoon dry mustard
4 tablespoons butter	¼ teaspoon salt
2 tablespoons flour	6 slices whole-wheat or rye
1 cup beer	bread
1 teaspoon Worcestershire sauce	

Making the Sauce

- Grate the cheese. You should have about 2 cups grated.
- Melt 2 tablespoons of the butter in a medium-size skillet set over medium-low heat. Add the flour and stir constantly with a spoon or whisk until the flour blends smoothly into the butter (about 2 minutes).
- Slowly pour the beer into the skillet, stirring constantly, until the sauce thickens and becomes smooth.
- Add the Worcestershire sauce, mustard, and salt, and stir until blended.
- Add the grated cheese and cook, stirring, until smooth and thick.

Finishing the Dish

- Toast and butter the bread with the remaining 2 tablespoons of butter.
- Put 1½ slices of buttered toast on each plate. Spoon the Welsh Rabbit sauce over the toast and serve right away.

Raised Waffles

EVERYONE WHO HAS EATEN these waffles says they are simply the best. If you are serving them for breakfast, the batter, which is made with yeast, should be mixed the night before you want to bake them. If you want to have them for supper, make the batter in the morning. They are crisp on the outside and tender on the inside—you really have to make them to know how good they are. Incidentally, do not buy a Belgian waffle iron. The crevices are too deep and the waffles won't have the same delicacy.

½ cup warm water
1 package dry yeast
½ cup (1 stick) butter,
    cut in 8 pieces
2 cups milk
1 teaspoon salt

1 teaspoon sugar
2 cups all-purpose white flour
2 eggs
¼ teaspoon baking soda
Warm maple syrup

Special equipment: a waffle iron.

Making the Batter Ahead of Time

• Put the warm water in a large mixing bowl. Sprinkle the yeast over the water. Leave it alone for 5 minutes to allow the yeast to dissolve.

• Melt the butter slowly in a small saucepan. Add the milk and stir until just warm, but not hot.

• Add the warm butter and milk, along with the salt, sugar, and flour, to the yeast mixture, and beat with a wire whisk or hand rotary beater until smooth.

• Cover the bowl with plastic wrap and let the batter stand overnight (or from breakfast until supper time) at room temperature. It will bubble up and then subside.

Finishing the Waffles

• Just before cooking the waffles, crack the eggs into the bowl of batter, then add baking soda and beat until smooth. The batter will be very thin.

• Turn the waffle iron on and, when warm, grease both sides with nonstick cooking spray, butter, or oil. Close the lid and wait until the waffle iron is very hot. Pour about ½ to ¾ cup of batter into it. Close the lid.

- After a few minutes, check to see if the waffle is done. Lift the top of the waffle iron up carefully—you don't want to tear the waffle—and open it just enough so you can peek at the edge of the waffle. It should appear golden brown. If it is still pale, close the top and bake another minute or two.

Serving the Waffles

- When the first waffle is done, lift the top of the waffle iron and gently pry out the waffle with a fork. Serve hot with a pitcher of warm maple syrup.
- While the first round of waffles are being eaten, make a second batch.
- If you don't use up all the batter, it will keep well for several days in the refrigerator.

◆

LEFTOVER WAFFLE BATTER

Even if you have only a little waffle batter left over, don't throw it away. Put it in the refrigerator in a covered jar and one morning when you feel like a few pancakes for breakfast, you'll find you have a treasure ready and waiting. Just give the jar a shake, ladle spoonfuls of batter into a hot, greased skillet and cook them just as you would the cornmeal pancakes in the recipe on the next page. Eat them with butter and warm maple syrup—I can assure you they'll be wonderful.

◆

Thin Yellow Cornmeal Pancakes

2 DOZEN 3-INCH PANCAKES

NOTHING I CAN TELL YOU will really describe how good these small yellow pancakes are. If you double the recipe, try serving them with Salsa Verde (page 229), and then make more yellow pancakes for dessert and serve them with butter and maple syrup.

½ cup water
½ cup yellow cornmeal
4 tablespoons (½ stick) butter
1 large egg
½ cup all-purpose white flour

½ teaspoon salt
1 tablespoon sugar
1 tablespoon baking powder
½ cup milk

Getting the Ingredients Ready to Mix

• Pour the water into a small saucepan and bring to a boil over high heat.

• Put the cornmeal in a mixing bowl and pour the boiling water over, stirring briskly until well blended.

• Melt the butter in that same small saucepan over medium-low heat.

• Crack the egg into a small bowl and beat until it is one uniform color.

• Add the butter, egg, flour, salt, sugar, baking powder, and milk to the cornmeal mixture. Beat until the batter is thoroughly mixed.

Cooking the Pancakes

• Set a large frying pan over medium-high heat. When the pan is hot, brush the bottom with butter, oil, or nonstick cooking spray.

• Pour or spoon about 2 tablespoons of batter into one corner of the hot pan and let it spread, then spoon in equal amounts of batter nearby until you have as many pancakes as will fit easily into the pan without touching. Cook until you see little bubbles breaking on the topside of the batter, then turn the pancakes over with a spatula. Cook on the second side for about 10 or 12 seconds, or until the bottoms of the pancakes are lightly browned. Remove to plates, serving 3 or 4 pancakes per person. Serve hot.

• While the first round of pancakes is being eaten, cook the rest. Or keep the first batch warm in the oven while you prepare the rest.

J.B.'s French Toast

FRENCH TOAST UNDOUBTEDLY originated as a way for the frugal housewife to use the last slices of stale bread from a loaf. It is an ingenious creation, and here it has been enhanced by James Beard's addition of crumbled cornflakes. They give a pleasing crunch to the pan-fried bread.

3 large eggs

½ cup milk

½ teaspoon nutmeg

¼ teaspoon salt

2 cups cornflakes

6 slices white bread

4 tablespoons (½ stick) butter

6 tablespoons sugar

Warm maple syrup

Preheat oven to 250°F.

Mixing the Batter

• Put the eggs, milk, nutmeg, and salt in a bowl and beat with a wire whisk until well blended.

• Spread the cornflakes on a piece of waxed paper or aluminum foil. Press the palm of your hand down on the cornflakes to break them up a bit (to reduce each flake to about half its original size).

Dipping and Pan-Frying the Bread

• Dip (don't soak) both sides of each slice of bread into the egg-milk batter. Press each slice into the cornflakes to coat one side of the bread well, then turn and coat the other side.

• Melt 2 tablespoons of butter in a 12-inch skillet over medium heat. Set 3 slices of bread in the skillet and fry until golden brown on one side. Flip the bread over with a spatula and fry on the second side until equally brown.

• When done, sprinkle about 1 tablespoon of sugar on top of each slice and keep warm in the oven while you fry the other 3 slices of bread in the remaining 2 tablespoons of butter. Sprinkle these with the remaining sugar. Serve hot with a pitcher of warm maple syrup.

Ham and Farm Cheese Butter-Fried Sandwiches

2 SANDWICHES

NOWHERE IN THE WORLD do people eat as many and as varied sandwiches as we Americans do. And sandwiches fried in butter are particularly irresistible. Try this combination, and add a Green Salad (page 42) to the plate.

4 slices whole-wheat or white
   bread

4 tablespoons (about 3 ounces)
   cream cheese, softened to
   room temperature

4 thin slices cooked ham

4 tablespoons (½ stick)
   butter

Making the Sandwiches

• Spread each slice of bread on one side with 1 tablespoon cream cheese.

• Place a ham slice on top of the cream cheese on each slice of bread, then put another slice of bread on top to make a sandwich.

Frying Them in Butter

• Melt the butter over medium-low heat in a skillet large enough to fit both sandwiches.

• Place the sandwiches in the pan and fry gently until the bottom is golden, pressing down on each sandwich occasionally with a spatula to help melt the cheese.

• When golden brown, turn the sandwiches over and fry on the other side until equally brown. Serve warm.

Extras That Make a Meal

INTRODUCTION

———

THESE EXTRAS DO just what jewelry does to a plain dress. They can pick up the simplest of meals. Try a spoonful of Green Sauce with a slice of cold meat, a little salsa with yesterday's chicken, a basketful of biscuits with a bowl of soup, a dish of Country Spoonbread with a mixed salad, a dollop of Fresh Pineapple Chutney on Baked Butternut Squash, and you'll have a very special meal.

Make one or two of the sauces ahead on a leisurely Sunday afternoon so that you can use them creatively during the week on a pasta or a baked potato—any dish that needs a little sparkle. They all keep well, and you'll be surprised at how often you want to dip into them so they can perform their magic.

RECESPES

GREEN SAUCE

WHITE SAUCE

MUSTARD SAUCE

SOUR CREAM CAPER SAUCE

CRANBERRY SAUCE

SALSA VERDE

FIRE AND ICE RELISH

GUACAMOLE

FRESH PINEAPPLE CHUTNEY

APPLESAUCE

FRESH CITRUS SALAD DRESSING

A CAESAR DRESSING

CREAMY GARLIC DRESSING

BAKING POWDER BISCUITS

GARLIC ROLLS

POPOVERS

LIGHT CORNMEAL MUFFINS

COUNTRY SPOONBREAD

YELLOW CORNBREAD

JUDITH'S FOCACCIA

Green Sauce

THIS IS A SAUCE, a salad dressing, a good "fix-it" potion. You can use it on the Parslied Small Red Potatoes (page 186), the Roast Zucchini (page 191), or as a dressing for Beef Salad (page 70). And if your fish seems dry, spread some Green Sauce on top.

ABOUT 2 CUPS

4 large cloves garlic
1 bunch parsley
3 green onions or scallions
1 cup olive oil
⅓ cup water

3 tablespoons cider vinegar
1 teaspoon kosher or coarse salt
Freshly ground pepper
2 tablespoons Dijon mustard

Preparing the Garlic, Parsley, and Green Onions

♦ Remove the papery outer layer from the garlic cloves and finely chop (for full details, see box, page 33).

♦ Rinse the parsley and pat dry with paper towels, or dry in a salad spinner. Remove the stems from the parsley and discard. Finely chop the leaves. You should have about ¾ cup.

♦ Finely chop the scallions or green onions (for full details on scallions, see page box, page 60).

Making the Sauce

♦ Put the olive oil, water, vinegar, salt, and pepper to taste in a bowl, and stir with a large spoon or a whisk until well blended. Add the mustard, garlic, parsley, and scallions. Blend well, taste, and add more salt if needed.

♦ Use the sauce immediately, or store in an airtight jar in the refrigerator until needed. It will keep for a week, but it's always best to taste before using to make sure the sauce still tastes fresh and lively.

White Sauce

THIS IS AN ALL-PURPOSE SAUCE that can lift a dull dish out of the doldrums. Try it with cooked chicken, seafood, or ham or over hard-boiled eggs. Use it to thicken a soup. Add ¼ cup of grated sharp cheddar cheese to the sauce just before taking it off the heat, and serve it over cauliflower, or broccoli. Or stir in 2 teaspoons of curry powder just before taking it off the heat, and serve it over sliced leftover turkey, chicken, or lamb.

2 tablespoons all-purpose white flour	1 cup milk
¼ cup water	¼ teaspoon salt
2 tablespoons butter	Pepper, if desired

Mixing the Flour and Water

◆ Put the flour and water in a small jar with a lid and shake vigorously until well blended. This little step helps to really blend the flour and water—so you're already on your way to making a smooth sauce.

Cooking the Sauce

◆ Put the butter into a small pan and set over low heat. Stand by the stove and stir the butter as it melts. When it has melted, stir in the flour and water from the jar. It is important to stir constantly during the short time it takes to make this sauce.

◆ In a matter of seconds, the butter, flour, and water will thicken. The goal is to keep it smooth, so don't stop stirring while you slowly add the milk. Using a whisk can help smooth out lumps as you cook the mixture.

◆ Add the salt and continue to stir.

◆ If you are adding any flavorings, take the pan off the heat and add them now. Return the pan to the stove and continue to cook about 5 minutes, stirring.

◆ Taste the sauce. If the flavors or salt seem too faint, add a little more.

◆ This sauce can be made early and reheated. To cool sauce for later use, lay a piece of waxed paper or plastic wrap right on top of the sauce, so that a "skin" doesn't form.

◆ You can also make a thicker sauce by adding 3 tablespoons of flour instead of 2 tablespoons.

Different Flavors You Can Add to Your White Sauce

Curry Cream Sauce

- Add 1 teaspoon curry powder and ¼ teaspoon ground ginger to the sauce during the last couple minutes of cooking.

Lemon Sauce

- Add 1 tablespoon of lemon zest and 1 tablespoon of lemon juice to the finished sauce. Stir well to blend.

Cheese Sauce

- Add 4 tablespoons of grated Parmesan cheese, or cheddar or Swiss cheese, to the sauce during the last minute of cooking. When you add it, stir, of course, and keep stirring until the cheese has melted and the sauce is smooth.

Mustard-Flavored Sauce

- Add either 1 tablespoon of plain ballpark mustard, or 1 tablespoon of Dijon mustard to the finished sauce. Stir to blend well, taste, and add more if you want a peppier sauce.

Mustard Sauce

2 CUPS

THIS SIMPLE, EASY-TO-MAKE SAUCE gives an added sparkle to a variety of meats. It's also delicious spooned over cooked cabbage, bok choy, carrots, or celery. It keeps for several weeks.

3 tablespoons flour
2 cups water
2 tablespoons butter

¼ teaspoon salt
5 tablespoons Dijonnaise
    mustard blend

Mixing the Flour and Water

◆ Put the flour and 1 cup of the water into a pint (2-cup) jar, screw on the lid, and shake vigorously until well blended.

Cooking the Sauce

◆ Put the butter in a small saucepan and set it over medium heat to melt, giving it a stir or two as it melts. This will only take a minute or two. When the butter has melted, tilt the pan around so the melted butter coats the bottom of the pan. Leave over medium heat.

◆ Give the jar containing the flour and water a few good shakes, and pour the contents into the pan with the butter. Stir constantly; the mixture will thicken quickly. While stirring, add the remaining cup of water. Continue to stir so the sauce remains smooth.

◆ When the sauce has thickened a little, add the salt and mustard. Stir steadily, and cook for 2 or 3 minutes, until the sauce is smooth and creamy.

◆ Remove from the heat. Taste the sauce, and add a little more salt if needed. Serve warm over meat or vegetables.

◆

DIJONNAISE BLEND

Dijonnaise mustard is a blend of mustard and mayonnaise, which is a nice combination. But you may buy just Dijon mustard and use it, if you like a sharper taste to your mustard. Or mix your own blend of mustard and mayonnaise in the proportions you like.

◆

Sour Cream Caper Sauce

THIS IS A SMOOTH, SNAPPY DRESSING—and a good change from the usual olive-oil-and-garlic mixture that we often have on steamed broccoli, zucchini, or cauliflower. It is also very good with cold leftover fish.

1 CUP

1 tablespoon grated yellow
    onion (see procedure)
½ cup sour cream

2 teaspoons capers
⅛ teaspoon salt

Grating the Onion

◆ Before peeling a whole onion, check in your refrigerator to see if you have some leftover onion in there just waiting to be used up. If not, then peel an onion, cut in half, and grate some of it. You need about 1 tablespoon. Wrap the remaining onion in plastic and refrigerate for later use.

Making the Sauce

◆ Put all the ingredients in a small bowl and stir until the sauce is mixed up. Let it sit a few minutes for the flavors to blend. Cover any leftover sauce with plastic wrap and put in the refrigerator; it will keep 10 days to 2 weeks.

Cranberry Sauce

WE THINK ABOUT cranberry sauce during the holidays, but it is very good through the year as a relish with pork, ham, or chicken, or on sandwiches. It keeps months covered in the refrigerator.

4 cups fresh cranberries (usually found in 12-ounce packages in the produce section of the supermarket; buy 2 packages and freeze the remaining 2 cups)

¼ cup water
1 cup or more sugar

Cooking the Cranberries

* Put the cranberries in a large heavy-bottomed skillet. Add the water, sprinkle 1 cup of sugar over the berries, and set over medium-high heat.

* Using a large spoon, stir the cranberries constantly. As soon as the water boils, the sugar will melt. When the sugar has dissolved, set the spoon aside and use a large fork to mash the cranberries as they cook. They will make popping noises. Mash for 2 or 3 minutes. Remove the pan from the heat when all the rounded berries have been roughly mashed.

* Taste. If the cranberries don't taste quite sweet enough, add another ¼ cup sugar and stir a few times. The heat will melt the additional sugar.

* When the cranberries have cooled, put into a pint jar with a lid and refrigerate until needed. The sauce should keep indefinitely in the refrigerator.

Salsa Verde

ABOUT 1 CUP

THIS IS ONE of those sauces that can travel around and improve potatoes, rice, pork, and chicken, or serve with some beans (see box, page 135), topping each serving with sour cream and this Salsa Verde. If you want it to be fiery, add a few drops of Tabasco sauce, stir, and taste.

This sauce was originally made with Mexican green tomatillos, which is why it is called a Salsa Verde. But tomatillos are seasonal and hard to find in many parts of the United States, so I have substituted firm red tomatoes. If you can find tomatillos, by all means use them.

3 large cloves garlic
1 bunch cilantro
1 medium-size yellow onion
2 medium firm tomatoes
   (or 6 tomatillos, peeled)
2 teaspoons fresh lemon
   juice
½ teaspoon salt

Chopping the Ingredients

◆ Finely chop the garlic (for details, see box, page 33).

◆ Take about a third of the bunch of cilantro, remove the stems, and finely chop the leaves (for details, see box, page 34). Measure out 2 tablespoons of the cilantro. Wrap and refrigerate any extra for later use.

◆ Cut the onion in half and finely chop one half (for details, see page 13). Wrap and refrigerate the other half for another use.

◆ Finely chop the tomatoes (for details, see page 27).

Mixing It All Together

◆ Put the garlic, cilantro, onion, tomatoes, lemon juice, and salt in a small bowl and mix well. This sauce will keep refrigerated for 3 or 4 days.

Fire and Ice Relish

TRY A SPOONFUL OF Fire and Ice Relish on corn, chicken, salmon, or on a baked potato with olive oil. The fire is in the cayenne pepper and the cool element is in the tomatoes, bell pepper, and onion.

3 cups cherry tomatoes	1½ teaspoons mustard seed
1 large green bell pepper	4 teaspoons sugar
1 large red onion	⅛ teaspoon cayenne pepper
¼ cup cider vinegar	½ teaspoon black pepper
½ teaspoon salt	¼ cup water
1½ teaspoons celery seed	

Preparing the Vegetables

♦ Finely chop the cherry tomatoes and put them in a bowl, with their juices.

♦ Remove the seeds from the pepper, finely chop (for full details, see box, page 31), and add to the tomatoes. Finely chop the onion and add it.

Mixing the Relish

♦ Mix together the cider vinegar, salt, celery seed, mustard seed, sugar, cayenne pepper, black pepper, and water in a small pot and bring to a boil over high heat. Boil for 1 minute. Remove from the heat and immediately pour over the prepared vegetables. Cool, then cover and refrigerate for at least 3 hours before serving.

♦ This fresh relish will keep for about 10 days in the refrigerator.

■

WORD OF CAUTION ABOUT HOT SEASONINGS

Be cautious using cayenne pepper—it is very fiery. Add a tiny bit at a time and taste as you blend it with the other ingredients. The same holds true if you are using fresh hot peppers and don't know how potent they are.

■

Guacamole

GUACAMOLE CAN BE many things: a sauce, a dip, or a topping for dishes. It is a sauce when used in a taco or a tortilla, a dip for chips, and a topping for dishes such as beans and tamales. It is a favorite addition for almost everyone. Because avocados turn brown quickly, guacamole doesn't keep long, so try to use up what you make in a day, or make half the recipe.

2 large ripe avocados
4 canned, peeled mild green
   chili peppers
1 clove garlic

3 tablespoons fresh lemon juice
   (about 2 lemons)
½ teaspoon salt
¼ teaspoon black pepper

Preparing the Avocados

- See box, page 61, for details on preparing avocados.
- Put the avocado flesh into a small bowl and mash it with a fork. It doesn't need to be perfectly smooth.

Adding the Other Ingredients

- Finely chop the chili peppers and add to the avocados.
- Mince the garlic (for details, see box, page 33) and add to the avocados.
- Add the lemon juice to the avocados.
- Add the salt and pepper and stir all ingredients well. Taste and add more salt if the guacamole seems dull. Cover and refrigerate for several hours before serving.

Fresh Pineapple Chutney

4 CUPS

ONDIMENTS SUCH AS this Fresh Pineapple Chutney can lift and improve the flavor and taste of dishes that are good but need a little enhancement. This is easy to make and can be served with chicken, ham, pork, or fish. The salsa keeps, refrigerated, for a month.

1 medium-size fresh, ripe pineapple	3-inch piece of fresh gingerroot (to make
1 lemon	3 tablespoons
2 or 3 limes	chopped)
½ cup sugar	1 medium-size yellow onion
½ teaspoon salt	1 small bunch cilantro

Preparing and Mixing the Ingredients

• Peel and chop the pineapple according to the directions in the box.

• Cut the lemon and 2 limes in half crosswise and, using a citrus squeezer or juicer, squeeze the juice from the lemon and 2 of the limes through a strainer onto the pineapple. Add the sugar and salt and taste. If the lime flavor is undetectable or too subtle, add the juice of the third lime.

• Peel the piece of ginger, slice it crosswise into thin "coins," and cut the coins into thin slivers. Cut the slivers crosswise to make about 3 tablespoons of finely diced ginger, and add to the pineapple.

• Peel and finely chop the onion (for full details, see page 13). Add to the bowl.

• Wash the cilantro and pat dry with a paper towel; remove the stems and discard them; chop the leaves coarsely (you should have about ¼ cup), and add to the bowl.

• Stir the ingredients together and taste. There should be a nice balance between sweet, salty, citrus, and pineapple flavors. Add sugar and salt to taste, if needed, and refrigerate the salsa.

Serving and Storage

• It will keep in a jar with a lid for a week in the refrigerator, and you can put it in plastic bags with baggie ties and freeze it indefinitely.

◆

GINGER

Choose a piece of gingerroot that looks smooth and is firm. When very fresh, the beige outer skin of ginger will have a sheen. Gingerroot will last about 1 month in the refrigerator crisper.

◆

ABOUT PINEAPPLE, CHOOSING, PEELING, CUTTING UP

To pick a ripe pineapple, look at the color and smell it. If the color is yellow and it has a fragrant pineapple smell it is probably ripe. If it feels heavy, that, too, is a good signal that it is ripe. If the fruit isn't very sweet, after you have prepared it, add sugar and let it sit in the refrigerator a few hours before using. The pineapple will absorb the sugar and it will be fine to eat.

2

off the "eyes," the tiny brown spots that dot the surface.

3) With the fruit still standing on end, cut it in half from top to bottom, then cut each half in half again lengthwise. Running along

the inside of each quarter is part of the harder, fibrous core of the pineapple.

4) Cut off and discard the core. Cut the quarters lengthwise into ¼-inch slices, and cut those crosswise into ¼-inch pieces. Put the chopped pineapple in a large glass bowl.

4

1

To peel: with a large sharp knife, 1) cut off the leafy green top and ½ inch of the root end of the pineapple. 2) Stand the fruit on its bottom, and slice away the bumpy outer part of the fruit. Make sure you hold the pineapple firmly as you slice down in steady strokes.

When the "peel" is all trimmed away—revealing the juicy yellow fruit—use the knife to trim or slice

3

Applesauce

ABOUT 3 CUPS

APPLESAUCE IS DELICIOUS by itself, or with a little cream poured over the top it can be a dessert. It also makes a good side dish with pork, ham, or chicken. You can make applesauce from any kind of apple.

6 firm apples	¼ cup water
2 tablespoons sugar	

Making the Applesauce

◆ Peel the apples with a paring knife, then cut them into quarters off the core. Cut each of the quarters into about 4 pieces.

◆ Put the apple pieces in a skillet with a lid, sprinkle the sugar over them, and add the water.

◆ Set the skillet on the stove, cover it, and turn the heat to medium-low. Cook the apples for about 12 minutes. After about 7 minutes, check to make sure the water hasn't evaporated. If it has, add 4 tablespoons of water and continue to cook with the lid on.

◆ After 12 minutes, test the apples for doneness. They should be very soft and easy to mash with a fork when they are done. When they are soft, take the skillet off the fire and taste for sweetness. If they need a little more sugar, add it now—a teaspoon at a time—and stir into the apples. The sugar will melt quickly in the hot apples.

◆ Mash the apples with a fork. They should have some texture, so don't try to make the applesauce smooth.

◆ Serve warm if using the applesauce as a side dish with the main course, or chilled as a dessert with a little cream poured over the top.

◆ Store the sauce in the refrigerator in a covered container.

Fresh Citrus Salad Dressing

FRESH, TART, AND MILDLY SWEET, this dressing lends itself to balancing and enhancing cold cooked shrimp, fish, and fruit salads. If you don't have a blender or food processor, don't pass up this snappy good dressing. Just chop the grapefruit and onion as finely as you can.

1 grapefruit	½ cup salad oil
1 lemon	3 tablespoons tarragon vinegar
1 medium-size yellow or red onion (about 5 tablespoons chopped onion)	1½ tablespoons sugar
	1 teaspoon prepared mustard
	½ teaspoon salt

Peeling Grapefruit or Orange

• Remove the peel from the grapefruit by holding the grapefruit firmly in one hand on a cutting board and, with a large sharp knife, cutting down from the top of the fruit to the board, following the curve of the fruit. Turning the grapefruit after each cut makes this an easy process. See illustrations for peeling oranges, page 59.

• When you've peeled the grapefruit, cut it into pieces and remove and discard the seeds.

Making the Dressing

• Peel the lemon, remove the seeds, and quarter the peeled fruit.

• Peel and chop the onion (for full details, see page 13) and measure out 5 tablespoons.

• Put grapefruit, lemon, and onion along with the oil, vinegar, sugar, mustard, and salt into the bowl of a food processor or blender and process until thoroughly mixed. Or put all of the ingredients into a jar with a lid, put the lid on, and shake the dressing vigorously until it's mixed up.

• Look at the dressing to see if there are any seeds that slipped by. Remove them with a spoon, or strain the dressing through a wire-mesh strainer.

• Refrigerate in a covered container until needed. It should keep quite well for up to a week, but taste before using. It should still have its tangy citrus flavor.

A Caesar Dressing

1 ⅓ cups

DON'T LIMIT THIS creamy version of A Caesar Dressing to lettuce only. It can improve the flavor of many dishes. Try a spoonful on a baked potato, a little on pasta, or pour some over broccoli to give it a good flavor boost.

4 large cloves garlic
1 cup olive oil
1 teaspoon Worcestershire
   sauce
1½ teaspoons lemon juice
1½ teaspoons red-wine
   vinegar

⅓ cup mayonnaise (Best Foods
   or Hellmann's)
½ teaspoon salt
¼ teaspoon freshly ground
   pepper

Preparing the Garlic

• Peel and finely chop the garlic cloves (for full details, see box, page 33). Put the garlic into a pint (2-cup) jar with a lid.

Measuring and Mixing the Dressing

• Add the olive oil, Worcestershire sauce, lemon juice, red-wine vinegar, mayonnaise, salt, and pepper to the jar.

• Screw on the lid and shake the jar vigorously until all the ingredients are well blended.

• Keep the dressing refrigerated right in the mixing jar, and shake again just before use.

Creamy Garlic Dressing

SAUCES AND DRESSINGS ARE a rich bank of helpers that can wake up dull and flat foods with just a spoonful. This creamy dressing has many such uses: it is a fine salad dressing, and it is good spooned over a baked potato, over hot or cold green beans or broccoli, or added to a mild broth or soup. That one spoonful can do wonders.

1½ CUPS

1 cup olive oil

4 cloves garlic

1 teaspoon Worcestershire
    sauce

3 tablespoons red-wine
    vinegar

⅓ cup mayonnaise

¼ teaspoon salt

Mixing All the Ingredients Together in a Pint Jar

- Put the olive oil in a pint jar.
- Peel and finely chop the garlic cloves (for full details, see box, page 33) and add to the jar.
- Measure all the remaining ingredients and add to the jar, put the lid on tightly, and shake the jar vigorously.
- Taste the dressing and add a little more salt if needed. The flavor of the dressing will become stronger and smoother after a few hours. Refrigerate until needed.

Baking Powder Biscuits

ABOUT 16 2-INCH BISCUITS

IF THERE IS ONE FOOD that symbolizes how good home cooking can be, it is Baking Powder Biscuits. Measuring and mixing them is a snap, they don't take more than 10 minutes to make and 12 minutes to bake, and you can easily make double the amount and freeze any that you aren't going to use right away. You will have learned a good basic lesson in baking when you get the hang of rubbing flour and shortening together with your fingertips, until they are blended into small bits the size of grains of rice. The same technique is used to make pie crust. You can transform the plainest supper with the addition of these light, golden biscuits. Plus they can do double duty. Use them as a main-dish accompaniment, or spread them with strawberries and whipped cream for that American dessert—Strawberry Shortcake (see box, page 241).

1

2

⅓ cup vegetable shortening (such as Crisco), plus a little extra for greasing the pan

2 cups all-purpose white flour, plus extra for dusting your hands and the board

2½ teaspoons baking powder

1 teaspoon salt

1 cup milk

Preheat oven to 450°F.

Preparing the Pan

• With your fingers or a paper towel, scoop up a little vegetable shortening and smear it all over the sides and the bottom of an 8- or 9-inch baking pan—just enough to cover it.

Putting the Ingredients Together

• Put the flour, baking powder, and salt in a large mixing bowl and stir with a fork.

• 1) Add ⅓ cup shortening in one piece, then roll it around in the flour to make it less sticky. Break up the lump of shortening into 4 or 5 smaller pieces and coat them with the flour mixture.

Mixing the Biscuits

• 2) Now you need to turn the few big clumps of shortening into many tiny lumps distributed throughout the flour. Plunge your fingers

3

4

5

into the bowl and pick up a lump of shortening and some of the flour. 3) Lightly rub the shortening and flour between your thumbs and fingers and, lifting your hands, let the blended flour and shortening fall back into the bowl. Repeat this step over and over, reaching to the bottom of the bowl and scooping up some of the loose flour, then rubbing it and the shortening into irregular bits. Work lightly—don't squeeze the dough too hard. After a few minutes, when the dough has the look and feel of coarse sand, you will know that you have worked it enough.

◆ 4) Add the milk to the flour and shortening and stir with a fork just enough so that the milk is mixed in with the other ingredients and there are no dry streaks of flour left. Don't mix too much. The dough will be moist and sticky, qualities that make these biscuits rise high and taste tender.

Kneading the Dough

◆ Sprinkle about ¼ cup of flour on a large cutting board or smooth countertop and spread it out in a circle. Coat your hands with flour, then scoop the dough from the bowl and place it on the floured surface.

◆ Knead the dough as follows: 5) Press down on the dough with the palm of one hand and push it away from you (if it is more comfortable, use both hands to push the dough). The dough will stretch into an oval shape. 6) Lift the far end of the oval and fold it in half back toward you. Give the dough a quarter turn and press and push it away again. Repeat these steps about 10 times, using a light hand. If the

6

dough sticks to your hands or to the board, sprinkle on a little more flour.

• When you have finished kneading, pat the dough into a rough circle, about 8 inches in diameter and ½ inch thick.

Cutting Out the Biscuits

• You can cut the biscuits into any size or shape you like. I use a 2-inch round cookie cutter. If you don't have one, use the rim of a small drinking glass to cut the dough. You can also pat the dough into a square and use a knife to cut square biscuits.

• 7) Press the cookie cutter firmly into the dough at the edge of the circle, and then lift it off. Repeat this step, cutting the next circle close to the first.

• Place the rounds in the greased baking pan, leaving a little room between the biscuits. Once you have cut as many circles as you can from the dough, you will have some scraps left. Gather them up and pat the dough into a small circle, the same thickness as before, then cut out as many biscuits as you can.

7

◆ TIPS FOR SUCCESSFUL BISCUITS ◆

MEASURING THE SHORTENING: To measure shortening, use a spoon to scoop up the shortening from the can and press it into a measuring cup. Pack it down firmly as you fill the measuring cup, and level it off with a knife. Use your fingers to remove the shortening from the measuring cup, scraping around the sides and the bottom to get it all out.

BAKING POWDER: Check the expiration date on your can of baking powder. Be sure to replace it; otherwise your biscuits—or cakes or cookies—won't rise properly.

Baking the Biscuits

- Put the pan on the center rack of the oven.
- After 12 minutes, check to see whether the biscuits are done. They should be golden brown on top. Break one open to see if it is cooked through in the center and not sticky. If the dough feels sticky and damp, continue to bake another 3 to 5 minutes.
- Take the biscuits out of the oven and let them sit for about 3 minutes to cool just slightly. Remove them from the pan with a spatula and either serve immediately or store, tightly wrapped, for later use. Biscuits should always be served warm, so if they have cooled reheat in a preheated 350°F oven for 5 to 6 minutes.

■

FROM BISCUITS TO SHORTCAKE

It is a breeze to make Strawberry Shortcake with Baking Powder Biscuits. To serve 4 people, buy 1 quart of strawberries (4 cups). Rinse them, remove the green hulls, and slice them. Put the slices in a bowl and sprinkle ½ cup of sugar over them. Use a fork to toss and turn the slices, so they are coated with sugar. Whip ¾ cup whipping cream (this will give you 1½ cups whipped cream); add 1 tablespoon of sugar to the cream before you begin beating it. The last step in this easy dessert is to split each baking powder biscuit in half and place each half, cut side up, on a dessert plate (it is a nice touch to warm the biscuits, if they have gotten cold, before assembling them with the strawberries and whipped cream). Now pile a quarter of the berries over the biscuit. Spoon a quarter of the whipped cream on top. There will be a little of the strawberry juices in the bottom of the bowl. Drizzle a bit of the juices over each serving.

■

Garlic Rolls

8 ROLLS

THESE DRESSED-UP STORE-BOUGHT ROLLS are so sensational they will upstage the most delicious dish. When you read the recipe, you imagine they will just taste like garlic bread. But these rolls are in a category all their own. You can even justify having several, since you won't be using butter. Find good dinner rolls made in your supermarket or bakery and buy them there.

½ teaspoon kosher salt
1 tablespoon water
2 cloves garlic (to make
    1 teaspoon chopped)

A few sprigs parsley (to make
    2 teaspoons chopped)
¼ cup vegetable oil
8 soft dinner rolls, heated

Preheat oven to 350°F.

Preparing the Dressing

• Stir the salt into the water in a small bowl and let stand for 5 minutes, then stir again.

• While the salt is dissolving, peel the papery skin from the garlic and finely chop the cloves (for full details, see box, page 33).

• Remove the stems from the parsley sprigs and finely chop the leaves—you'll need about 2 teaspoons (see box, page 12 for chopping details).

• Put the garlic, parsley, and vegetable oil into the bowl with the water, and mix well. Set aside while the rolls heat.

Preparing the Rolls

• Place the rolls close together in a shallow baking dish, and heat them in the oven for 6 minutes. If the rolls are coming straight from the freezer, heat for 8 to 10 minutes.

• Remove the rolls from the oven. Stir the oil-and-parsley mixture and drizzle it evenly over the rolls. Serve immediately.

THE GLORY OF POPOVERS IS their incredible size, crusty outsides, and creamy, tender, and almost hollow insides, just waiting for butter and strawberry jam. The key to making good popovers is to have a forceful amount of heat surrounding each baking cup holding popover batter. Muffin pans don't work as well as separate Pyrex cups, unless you just fill the outside muffin cups and leave the center cups empty. Popovers must be eaten hot from the oven so have the rest of your meal ready and serve them before they deflate.

ABOUT 7 POPOVERS

1 ½ cups all-purpose white flour	1 teaspoon salt
1 ½ cups milk	3 eggs
	3 tablespoons melted butter

Preheat oven to 425°F.

Mixing the Popover Batter

♦ If you're using a hand-held mixer, put the flour, milk, salt, eggs, and butter in a mixing bowl and beat until the batter is smooth. (See box for other ways of mixing.)

Filling the Baking Cups

♦ Pour the batter into a pitcher or a quart-size glass measuring cup with a spout. This makes it easy to fill each baking cup with batter.

♦ Grease with butter or nonstick cooking spray 7 ¾-cup Pyrex glass cups. Fill each cup about ⅔ full of batter.

Baking the Popovers

♦ Arrange the cups on a baking sheet so they are not touching, and place the sheet in the bottom third of the oven. Set the timer for 25 minutes. When it rings, peek into the oven. If the popovers are high, mighty, and nicely browned, they are done. Remove them from the oven quickly, and with a sharp paring knife make 3 or 4 little slits on the top and sides of each popover. This will let the steam escape and keep them from collapsing. Eat them hot.

◆

MIXING UP THE BATTER

The easiest way to mix up the batter is with a hand-held mixer, or for popovers you can blend all the batter in a food processor or a blender. But if you don't have these pieces of equipment, you can mix it by hand, beating vigorously with a wooden spoon or a wire whip until the batter is completely smooth.

◆

Light Cornmeal Muffins

ABOUT 12 MUFFINS

LIGHT CORNMEAL MUFFINS—more delicate than the typical rustic version because of the refined cake flour—are very good with fish, seafood, fruit salads, and eggs.

½ cup butter (1 stick)
1 egg at room temperature (see box, opposite)
¼ cup vegetable oil
1 cup milk

1 cup cake flour*
⅔ cup yellow cornmeal
1 tablespoon baking powder
½ teaspoon salt
1 tablespoon sugar

Preheat oven to 400°F.

STORING LEFTOVER MUFFINS

■

If you have a one- or two-person household, don't hesitate to make muffins. You can always put the extras away in plastic baggies. First let them cool completely and seal the bags securely, then freeze them. Reheat as you need for Sunday breakfast—or any day for that matter. You'll be glad you put those muffins away. In fact, it's worth making a double batch to have them on hand.

■

Mixing the Batter

• Put the butter in a small pan, turn the heat to medium-high, and melt the butter. Don't walk away—it will melt quickly.

• Crack the egg into a mixing bowl, add the melted butter and oil, and beat with a spoon or wire whisk until well blended.

• Pour the milk into the same little pan used to melt the butter, and turn the heat to medium.

• When the milk is warm, not boiling, stir it into the egg and butter.

• In another bowl, mix together with a fork the cake flour, cornmeal, baking powder, salt, and sugar. Add these dry ingredients to the egg-and-milk mixture and stir until well blended. As soon as the batter is smooth and you don't see any lumps, stop mixing. The batter should be light yellow in color and medium thick.

• Grease or spray with nonstick cooking spray a 12-cup muffin pan.

• Pour the batter into a pitcher or a large measuring cup with a spout, then pour the batter into each muffin cup until it is ¾ full.

Baking the Muffins

• Set the timer for 15 minutes. When it rings, check to see if the edges of the muffins are slightly golden. Insert a toothpick into the center of a muffin. If it comes out clean, they are done. If the toothpick comes out sticky with batter, cook the muffins for another 5 minutes.

• When the muffins are done, place the muffin tin on the stovetop or a counter. Run a knife blade around the edge of each muffin and lift the muffins out carefully to avoid breaking them. Put them in a basket and serve warm from the oven, with plenty of butter, and honey or jam.

* You will find cake flour in boxes in the baking section of the supermarket. Do *not* buy self-rising flour.

Country Spoonbread

SPOONBREAD IS a wonderful old Southern cornmeal recipe. It isn't really a bread that is sliced, buttered, and eaten out of hand. Spoonbread is soft and creamy and is eaten with a spoon or fork. It takes the place of potatoes or rice when served with meat or chicken. It can be the main dish for supper with some melted butter and cheese, or sour cream dribbled on top. Serve it with Swiss Chard (page 196). Spoonbread is also good with bacon and applesauce on the side, and a little maple syrup poured over the top. Leftover spoonbread can be wrapped and frozen and reheated when needed. Thaw the leftover spoonbread, fry it in butter, and serve it with a good sausage like Polish kielbasa.

4 eggs	2 tablespoons butter, plus
2½ cups water	1 tablespoon for casserole
1 cup yellow cornmeal	1 cup buttermilk
1 teaspoon salt	

Preheat oven to 400°F.

Cooking the Cornmeal
- Beat the eggs well in a small bowl and set aside.
- Put the cornmeal in a small bowl and pour in ½ cup cold water. Stir to dampen all the bits of cornmeal. (This keeps the cornmeal from lumping when you add it to boiling water.)
- Bring 2 cups water to a boil in a 3-quart pot. Add the salt to the boiling water, then slowly add the cornmeal. Turn the heat down to medium, and keep stirring constantly, cooking for 1 minute. It will look thick and yellow.
- Add the 2 tablespoons butter, beaten eggs, and buttermilk to the cornmeal mixture and beat until smooth.

Cooking the Spoonbread
- Smear the bottom and sides of a 1½-quart casserole with the 1 tablespoon butter, then pour the cornmeal batter into it. Bake for 35 minutes; insert a toothpick into the center of the spoonbread to check for doneness. If the toothpick comes out clean, the spoonbread is done. If not, cook for another 5 minutes, then check again. Remove from the oven.
- Cut the spoonbread into squares and lift them out with a spatula. They are best when served hot from the oven.

ROOM TEMPERATURE EGGS

You will notice that in some recipes that call for eggs you are cautioned to have the eggs at room temperature. This is because there is quite a bit of butter or shortening used in the recipe. If the eggs are chilled from the refrigerator and the butter or shortening has been melted, the chilled eggs will firm up the butter, which spoils the mixing process.

Bring a cold egg to room temperature by putting it in a bowl of hot water and letting it stand for 10 minutes.

Yellow Cornbread

ONE 8-INCH SQUARE OR
ROUND CAKE

YOU'LL BE SURPRISED how easy and quick it is to make cornbread. If you think about home cooking during the days of the pioneers, you know baking had to be as simple as eating, and cornbread, then called corn pone, was made with the most primitive kitchen tools. So don't be intimidated about trying baking.

1 cup all-purpose white flour
¾ cup yellow cornmeal
1½ teaspoons baking powder
1 teaspoon salt
4 tablespoons butter (½ stick)
1 cup milk

2 large eggs
⅓ cup honey
1 tablespoon soft butter or nonstick cooking spray for greasing pan

Preheat oven to 425°F.

Mixing the Batter

• Measure the flour, cornmeal, baking powder, and salt right into a large bowl. Stir with a fork 5 or 6 times, until the ingredients are well mixed.

• Put the butter in a small saucepan and melt over medium-low heat, stirring occasionally.

• Put the milk, eggs, honey (scraping with your finger is the best way to get the honey out of the measuring cup), and melted butter in a separate, medium-size bowl. Beat these liquid ingredients with a large spoon until they are smooth and all one color.

• Add the liquid ingredients to the flour mixture. Using a large spoon, stir until the ingredients are thoroughly blended and all one color.

Baking and Serving the Cornbread

• Smear an 8-by-8-by-2-inch square baking pan with butter, or spray with nonstick cooking spray.

• Pour the batter into the greased baking pan, using your spoon or a rubber spatula to scrape up any batter remaining on the sides and bottom of the bowl. Smooth over the top of the batter so it is evenly distributed in the pan.

- Put the cornbread on the center rack of the oven and set the timer for 20 minutes.

- When the timer rings, check to see if the cornbread is done by inserting a toothpick or small paring knife in the center of the bread. If it comes out clean and doesn't have any wet batter adhering to it, remove the pan from the oven. If you see wet batter on the toothpick, bake the cornbread for another 10 minutes and check it again.

- When the cornbread's done, put it on a heatproof counter and let it sit for 5 minutes.

- Run a small sharp knife along the outside edge of the cornbread to loosen it from the pan. If you've baked the bread in a square pan, cut it into squares. Use a small spatula to remove the bread gently from the pan.

- Serve piping hot with butter and jam or honey.

■

SERVING SUGGESTIONS

This moist, tender cornbread is good for supper with a simple homemade soup, and with almost any vegetable dish. Leftover cornbread makes a good Sunday breakfast, fried in a skillet on both sides in butter until lightly browned. Serve with maple syrup poured over it and sausages on the side.

■

Judith's Focaccia

12 PIECES ABOUT 1½ INCHES WIDE BY 4 INCHES LONG

THIS IS THE EASIEST of breads to make, and when you make this recipe you will be ready to make all kinds of yeast breads. Baking has a magic about it, and the foods you can bake give such a lot of pleasure both to you and others. Focaccia is in the pizza family and is eaten as a snack in Italy. It rounds out any meal, particularly one of a simple pasta and salad. The dough is baked in a rectangle about 8 by 10 inches, and the finished bread is about 1 inch thick.

2 tablespoons olive oil, plus more for greasing baking sheet and mixing bowl
1½ cups warm water
1 package active dry yeast
2¼ cups all-purpose white flour
½ teaspoon salt

3 big cloves garlic
3 sprigs fresh rosemary, about 1 tablespoon of the needlelike leaves; or 1 tablespoon dried rosemary
1½ teaspoons coarse kosher salt, or 1 teaspoon table salt

Mixing the Yeast and the Dough

- Grease a baking sheet with olive oil.
- Fill a ½-cup measure with warm—not hot—water. Pour the water into a large mixing bowl, add the yeast, and give it a stir. Let stand for 5 minutes so the yeast has time to dissolve.
- Add the remaining 1 cup warm water to the large mixing bowl and stir. Add 2 cups of the flour and the ½ teaspoon salt. Using a large spoon or your hands, blend the wet and dry ingredients together. They have to be well mixed, not just briefly blended. Mix vigorously at least 1 minute.
- Scrape the bottom and sides of the bowl to incorporate all the loose flour into the dough.
- Sprinkle some flour on a board or countertop. Scoop the dough out of the bowl, using a scraper if it is too sticky to handle, and dump it onto the floured board.
- Flour your hands and start kneading gently, pushing the dough away from you and scooping it up again with the help of a dough scraper or a spatula. Keep flouring your hands, and lightly pushing and bringing or folding the dough back toward you. This step will exercise the yeast dough so it develops some stretching strength. Continue to knead lightly for just a couple of minutes, sprinkling a little more flour on the board and your hands to keep the dough from sticking to them.

- When the dough is well kneaded, put it in a clean mixing bowl that has had some olive oil smeared around the inside.
- Cover the bowl with a towel or plastic wrap and let the dough rise until it is approximately double in size. The measurement doesn't have to be exact, and the process will probably take about an hour, depending on the warmth of your kitchen.

Preparing the Garlic and Rosemary

- Remove the papery outer skin from the garlic cloves. Cut each clove into 6 lengthwise slices, then cut the cloves crosswise into tiny pieces.
- If using fresh rosemary, pick the small needlelike leaves from the woody stem of the rosemary. You'll need about 1 tablespoon of the leaves, whether you are using fresh or dried.
- Preheat oven to 400°F.

Finishing the Dough

- Plop the dough onto a lightly floured board. Using your fingers, pat and press the dough into a rough rectangle the size of an 8-by-10-inch baking sheet or a bit smaller. Sprinkle the slivers of garlic over one half of the length of the dough, and fold the other half over it.
- Grease the baking sheet or sprinkle it with cornmeal.
- Lift the dough into the baking sheet, and pat and press it into a rectangle about 8 by 10 inches. Let the dough settle and rise for about 10 minutes, then smear 2 tablespoons olive oil all over the top. At intervals of about an inch all over the top of the dough, poke 2 of the little rosemary leaves into the focaccia. Don't bury them; you should see the little leaves sticking up. Sprinkle the kosher salt evenly over the top.

Baking the Focaccia

- Put the focaccia in the bottom third of the oven to bake. Cook for 25 minutes, then check to see if it is golden brown all over the top. If it is very light-colored, let it bake another 5 minutes. Remove from the oven. Let cool about 10 minutes and cut into 1½-inch-wide strips, each about 4 inches long. Serve warm.

◆

ABOUT YEAST

Yeast is different from any other ingredient that you use in cooking because it is alive. The live yeast cells are too small to see, but when you make bread you will see and feel how the yeast changes the bread dough. The dough grows bigger and becomes soft and puffy from the little air pockets the yeast creates. When you punch the air out of the dough, you get rid of all the air pockets, but the yeast will get busy and put them all back again. This is just what we want them to do, because that action is what makes our bread strong enough to hold together instead of crumbling apart. And light enough so that we can eat it without breaking our teeth. When you put your bread in the hot oven, the bread will rise and slowly set.

When yeast is called for in a recipe it usually means dried yeast, which needs to be brought back to life with some warm water. Once it is activated, the yeast loves to live in bread dough, feeding on the starch and sugar in the flour, and it thrives in warm temperatures. To dissolve dried yeast, put it in warm water and it will start to swell. This procedure is called proofing the yeast—i.e., the yeast proves it is alive by swelling. The most important point to remember is that very hot liquid (over 120°F) will kill yeast. It is a good idea to use liquid that is just warm enough for you to stick your finger in and hold it there comfortably.

◆

◆

Here Comes Dessert

◆

INTRODUCTION

FOR THIS CHAPTER I have selected some fine examples of home baking. You will be learning all the basic steps of baking: how to cream butter and sugar for a cake batter, or how to rub shortening and flour together to make a pie crust. You will see the magical transformation of a few plain ingredients—flour, sugar, eggs—into a light, airy cake.

Part of the fun of learning to cook is to be able to make something that is a luxury. It is such a treat to sit down to a homemade dessert. But if the idea of frosting a cake is too daunting or time-consuming, try the Lemon Pudding Cake; you'll learn how to separate eggs and produce an enticing dessert with a custardlike base and a spongy cakelike top. There are also a number of good baked-fruit desserts here. However, if you don't even want to light the oven, try making one of the fresh-fruit desserts at the end of the chapter.

RECIPES

———

BASIC WHITE CAKE WITH CHOCOLATE FROSTING

CHOCOLATE FROSTING

PINEAPPLE UPSIDE-DOWN CAKE

ALMOND BUTTER CAKE

SOUR CREAM GINGERBREAD

KONA INN BANANA MUFFINS

LEMON PUDDING CAKE

BREAD AND BUTTER PUDDING

CHOCOLATE PUDDING

PECAN PIE

AMERICAN APPLE PIE

CRUSTLESS COCONUT CUSTARD PIE

CRISP AND CREAMY CHOCOLATE SQUARES

CHOCOLATE CHIP COOKIES

SNAPPY GINGERSNAPS

THE BEST OATMEAL COOKIES

CINNAMON TOAST

BAKED PLUMS AND APRICOTS WITH ALMONDS

SEATTLE CRISP

BAKED APPLES

BAKED BANANAS

GRAPES WITH SOUR CREAM AND BROWN SUGAR

A DESSERT OF FRESH FRUIT

FRUIT CHART

Basic White Cake with Chocolate Frosting

THIS RECIPE IS a good lesson in basic cake making. The crucial step in making a successful cake is to mix the ingredients together thoroughly. The butter is "creamed" or smoothly blended with the sugar and vanilla, and the water added. The dry ingredients are mixed, and then added to the butter mixture. The eggs go in last, and the batter is beaten to a smooth, even consistency. The result is a tender, flavorful cake just waiting for chocolate frosting.

TWO 8- OR 9-INCH ROUND LAYERS

1 tablespoon soft butter or nonstick cooking spray (for preparing the cake pans)

2 tablespoons all-purpose flour

½ cup butter (1 stick), softened to room temperature

1½ cups sugar

1 teaspoon vanilla

1 cup minus 1 tablespoon cold water

2½ cups cake flour

1 tablespoon baking powder

½ teaspoon salt

3 eggs

Chocolate Frosting (recipe follows)

Preheat oven to 375°F.

Preparing the Cake Pans

◆ Spread butter or nonstick cooking spray all around the bottom and sides of 2 8-inch round cake pans. Put about 1 tablespoon of flour in each pan. Shake the pan and tilt it to distribute the flour evenly over the bottom and sides. Now invert the pans over the wastebasket, and tap the bottoms to shake out any excess flour.

Mixing the Cake Batter

◆ Put the butter, sugar, and vanilla in a medium-size bowl and beat with an electric mixer or a large spoon until well blended.

◆ Add the water and continue to mix for another minute or so. This batter will look curdled, but it will smooth out when you add the flour.

◆ Mix together the flour, baking powder, and salt in a separate, smaller bowl. Add to the butter-and-sugar mixture and beat until smooth and blended.

◆ Crack one egg at a time right into the batter, beating well after each egg has been added, until the batter is smooth.

◆ When all the eggs have been added, beat one final time just until the batter is creamy and uniform in color and texture.

◆

CAKE FLOUR

Cake flour is made from soft wheat and it makes a delicate, fine-textured cake. But all-purpose wheat flour makes a very good cake too, and you can substitute all-purpose flour for cake flour if necessary and still have a good cake. Don't buy self-rising flour, because it will not work in any of these recipes.

◆

Baking the Cake

♦ Pour half the batter into each cake pan (you don't have to be exact) and put them in the lower third of the oven. Set the timer for 20 minutes. While the cake is baking, make the frosting as described in the following recipe.

♦ After 20 minutes, insert a toothpick in the center of each cake. If it comes out clean, with no batter sticking to it, the cakes are done. If not, bake another 5 minutes and check again. (Some ovens are hotter on one side than the other, so it pays to check on both cakes.)

♦ Remove the cakes from the oven and cool them in the pans for 5 minutes on a heatproof surface. Run a knife around the inside rim of each pan and invert the pans onto cake racks or waxed paper. Let them cool completely, upside down.

Frosting the Cake

♦ Arrange strips of waxed paper around the rim of a serving cake platter (to catch the excess frosting).

♦ With a spatula, transfer one layer to the serving platter, still inverted. Using a spatula or a table knife, spread the top of the layer with ½ cup of the frosting.

♦ Put the other layer on top, bottom side down, and spread the top of the second layer with ½ cup frosting. Spread the sides with the remaining frosting.

♦ Remove the strips of waxed paper and serve.

Chocolate Frosting

ABOUT 2 CUPS

USING COCOA MAKES this frosting simple to prepare, yet the cocoa gives it a rich and chocolaty flavor. You don't have the fuss of dealing with melted chocolate.

10 tablespoons butter
(1¼ sticks), softened to
room temperature

¼ teaspoon salt

4 cups confectioners' sugar

⅓ cup unsweetened cocoa

¼ cup milk

1 teaspoon vanilla

◆ Mix the butter, salt, and confectioners' sugar in a small bowl with a large spoon, stirring until smooth. Add the cocoa powder, milk, and vanilla and stir briskly until creamy. If the frosting is too stiff to spread easily, add another tablespoon or two of milk and blend well.

■

LEFTOVER FROSTING

If you have any leftover frosting, cover and refrigerate it. Spread it on graham crackers when you need something sweet. The frosting will keep for weeks in a covered jar in the refrigerator.

■

◆ TIPS FOR A SUCCESSFUL CAKE ◆

1. Before you begin to mix the ingredients for the cake, turn the oven on to the temperature called for in the recipe. It takes about 10 minutes for an oven to reach the desired heat, and it is important to start baking the cake in a preheated oven.

2. Have your pans ready so the batter (the uncooked mixture of wet and dry ingredients) doesn't have to wait to bake. The pans must be greased and then lightly floured. That film of flour over the greased pans makes it easier to remove the finished cake.

3. Check the expiration date on your baking powder can. Baking powder loses its oomph or rising power if it gets too old. If it is within a month of expiration, I think it is worth replacing the baking powder.

4. It is important to measure your ingredients accurately. For dry ingredients, fill the metal measur-

ing cup generously to the top, then level off the excess with a knife. For liquid ingredients, use a glass measuring cup with a spout, set it on a solid surface, and pour the liquid in up to the required measure. Check the mark on the cup by bringing it to eye level. By the way, both liquid and dry measuring cups hold exactly the same amount.

5. In mixing the ingredients, remember that the goal is to stir or beat dry and liquid ingredients together until they become one smooth batter.

6. After you have filled the cake pans, smooth the top of the batter with a thin spatula and tap the pans lightly on the counter to distribute the batter evenly. Make sure the cake pans aren't touching when they are baking in the oven. The heat needs to be evenly distributed around the pans.

Pineapple Upside-Down Cake

ONE 10-INCH CAKE

FOR 75 YEARS this cake has pleased young and old. It is terrific! Serve it with unsweetened whipped cream, which balances the sweetness of the cake.

CARAMEL TOPPING

¼ cup butter (½ stick), cut into 4 pieces	¼ cup heavy cream
¾ cup light-brown sugar	7 whole slices canned pineapple
	7 Maraschino cherries

THE CAKE BATTER

⅓ cup vegetable shortening	1½ cups all-purpose white flour
¾ cup sugar	2¼ teaspoons baking powder
2 eggs	1 teaspoon salt
2 teaspoons vanilla	1 cup milk

Preheat oven to 350°F.

Choosing a Pan

◆ You need to use a 10-inch skillet, 2 inches deep, or a cake pan with a 2-quart capacity. If you have only a skillet with a handle that's not ovenproof, wrap the handle in a double thickness of aluminum foil so it won't burn when it's in the oven. It's also a good idea to put a baking sheet under the pan or skillet that you bake in, so if the juices bubble over the edge of the pan the baking sheet will catch them.

Making the Topping

◆ Put the butter, brown sugar, and heavy cream in the skillet, and set the skillet over low heat.

◆ Stir the mixture until it is smooth and the butter has melted completely; this only takes 1 or 2 minutes. Remove from the heat and let the sauce cool a little.

◆ Arrange the slices of pineapple in the sauce, placing one in the center and the rest circling around.

◆ Place a cherry in the center of each pineapple ring. Set the pan aside.

Making the Cake Batter

◆ Put the vegetable shortening in a large mixing bowl. Add the sugar and use a hand-held electric mixer or a large spoon to mix the shortening and sugar together until smooth. Add the eggs and vanilla and vigorously stir the mixture—or mix with a hand-held electric mixer—until it becomes creamy and well blended.

◆ Add the flour, baking powder, and salt to the shortening mixture. Stir until the dry ingredients are mixed with the shortening and sugar. Don't worry if the mixture is rather dry and clumpy.

◆ Add the milk all at once and stir until the batter becomes smooth and blended.

Adding the Batter to the Pan

◆ Using a spatula, spread the batter evenly over the pineapple topping. This recipe makes just enough for a thin layer of batter, so spread it gently, trying not to mix it into the pineapple sauce, and easing it to the edges of the skillet. Remember, when you finish baking the cake and turn it upside down, the pineapple that's now on the bottom will be on top of the cake.

◆ Put the skillet or pan in the oven and set the timer for 30 minutes. When it rings, check the cake; it should look golden on top, but test by inserting a toothpick into the center of the cake. If it comes out clean, the cake is done; if not, bake for another 5 minutes and test again.

◆ Take the cake out of the oven and let cool for 5 minutes.

Serving the Cake

◆ To remove the cake from the pan, first run a knife around the edge of the pan. Put a plate that is larger than the cake over the pan. Holding the pan and the plate firmly, quickly turn the pan upside down, so the cake lands on the plate with the pineapple slices on top.

◆ Serve with unsweetened or slightly sweetened whipped cream.

Almond Butter Cake

ONE 9-INCH ROUND CAKE

ALMOND BUTTER CAKE IS NOT to be taken lightly just because you can stir it together in about 3 minutes, pop it in the oven to bake, and serve it within an hour. It's truly a unique cake, because it doesn't rise very high and it comes out moist, sticky, and chewy, like a cookie. It also keeps twice as long as any conventional cake.

THE CAKE BATTER

¾ cup butter (1½ sticks)

1½ cups sugar

2 large eggs

½ teaspoon salt

1½ teaspoons almond extract

1 teaspoon vanilla extract

1½ cups all-purpose white flour

2 teaspoons soft butter or nonstick cooking spray (for greasing the cake pan)

TOPPING

1 tablespoon sugar

4 ounces sliced almonds (¾ cup)

Preheat oven to 350°F.

Measuring and Mixing the Ingredients

◆ Melt the butter in a small saucepan over medium-low heat, stirring regularly. Pour the melted butter and 1½ cups of sugar into a large bowl and stir until smooth.

◆ Crack the eggs right into the same bowl and mix until the batter is creamy and all one color. Add the salt, almond extract, vanilla extract, and flour and stir briskly until the batter is smooth.

The Last Step Before Baking

◆ Grease the bottom and sides of a 9-inch round cake pan with butter or nonstick cooking spray. Using a rubber spatula, scrape the batter from the bowl into the greased cake pan. Spread it evenly in the pan. Sprinkle the tablespoon of sugar, then the sliced almonds, over the top of the batter.

Baking and Serving the Cake

◆ Put the pan on the middle rack of the oven and set the timer for 35 minutes. When it rings, check to see if the cake is done. It should be light brown on top, and when you insert a toothpick in the center, it should have a few sticky crumbs adhering to it. If the cake is not browned enough and the toothpick comes out too wet, put the cake back in the oven and check it again in another 10 minutes.

When the cake is done, remove it from the oven and let it cool on a heatproof counter for at least 30 minutes.

◆ Cut the cake into small wedges and serve with fresh fruit. This cake will stay fresh for about a week and will freeze indefinitely. Wrap it tightly in foil, or in a plastic bag you can seal with a zip or a tie.

◆

STORING NUTS

Whenever you have leftover nuts, freeze them in a plastic bag closed tightly. They will keep indefinitely in the freezer.

◆

Sour Cream Gingerbread

ONE 8-INCH CAKE

IT SEEMS THAT most people have forgotten about gingerbread, but it should be revived. A light, tender gingerbread is wonderful and spicy with ham, pork, beans, or salad, or it can be a fine dessert topped with whipped cream. If you use the ½ cup of sugar, the gingerbread will be more breadlike. If you use the full cup, it will be a sweet cake. So decide how much to add depending on how you plan to serve the gingerbread. It is always at its best served warm.

½ cup butter (1 stick), softened 1 hour at room temperature	1 teaspoon baking powder
	½ teaspoon baking soda
	½ teaspoon salt
½ to 1 cup sugar	1 tablespoon ground ginger
½ cup dark molasses	2 teaspoons soft butter or
½ cup sour cream	nonstick cooking spray
2 eggs	(for greasing the cake pan)
1½ cups all-purpose white flour	1 cup heavy cream for whipping (see box, opposite)

Preheat oven to 350°F.

Mixing the Wet Ingredients

• Put the butter in a large bowl, and, using a big spoon, vigorously stir and scrape and smash it against the side and bottom of the bowl until it is smooth and creamy. You can do this in an electric mixer if you have one. Add the sugar and continue to stir until it is all uniformly blended into the butter. Remember, use ½ cup of sugar if you plan to serve this as a bread, and 1 cup if it is to be for dessert.

• Add the molasses and sour cream and stir until the batter is all one color. Crack the eggs into the bowl and again stir briskly. You have mixed enough when the batter is very smooth and uniform in color.

Adding the Dry Ingredients

• Put the flour, baking powder, baking soda, salt, and ginger into a medium-size bowl. Use a fork to stir the ingredients around 5 or 6 times until well mixed.

• Dump about a third of the flour mixture into the bowl of wet ingredients. Mix the batter until it becomes one color and texture, then add another third of the flour and continue to stir. Finish up with the final third of the flour, and mix just until it is smooth. Don't overmix.

Baking the Gingerbread

◆ Grease an 8-inch square or round baking pan with butter or non-stick cooking spray.

◆ Pour the batter into the baking pan, then use a spoon to spread it evenly in the pan and smooth over the top.

◆ Put the pan on the center rack of the oven and set the timer for 30 minutes.

◆ When 30 minutes are up, test the gingerbread by inserting a toothpick or a small paring knife into the center of the bread. If the toothpick comes out clean, with no wet batter adhering, it is done. If the center is still moist, set the timer for another 5 minutes and test again. Remove the gingerbread from the oven and let it cool for 10 minutes.

◆ To serve the gingerbread, either cut pieces directly in the pan and remove them one by one with a spatula, or run a knife around the edge of the pan and carefully invert the gingerbread onto a serving plate.

◆ If you are having this gingerbread as a bread, serve it warm with plenty of butter. If you've made the sweeter version for dessert, serve with whipped cream.

■

HOW TO WHIP CREAM

Pour 1 cup of heavy whipping cream into a bowl. You can use an electric mixer, a hand-held mixer, a hand rotary beater, or a wire whisk. I use my hand rotary beater and it will quickly whip up a cup of cream. If you are adding sugar and vanilla to the whipped cream, add it after the cream has started to look a little fluffy from beating. Test by lifting the beater or whisk out of the cream—you will see that it barely manages to hold its shape.

If you are using an electric beater, watch carefully so as not to overbeat, or the whipped cream will turn to butter. Stop beating as soon as the cream is stiff enough to hold a peak when you pull the beaters out of the cream.

You can whip the cream ahead of time. Just cover it well and refrigerate until you need it. If it separates a little, just whip it again for a minute and it will be perfect.

Kona Inn Banana Muffins

TENDER, MOIST, AND RICH with banana flavor, these can be someone's birthday cake, or any-day cake, muffins, or cupcakes. Because of the unusual amount of banana in the recipe, these muffins don't dry out like most baked cakes—they keep very well and freeze indefinitely. This is the best way to use up bananas that are ripening faster than you can eat them.

½ cup vegetable shortening, plus a small amount for greasing the pans

1 ¼ cups all-purpose white flour, plus a tablespoon for dusting the pans

About 5 very ripe medium-size bananas

½ teaspoon salt

1 teaspoon baking soda

2 eggs

1 cup sugar

½ cup chopped walnuts

Special Equipment: a 12-cup muffin pan

Preheat oven to 350°F.

Starting the Batter

◆ Smear the muffin pan with a little of the shortening, sprinkle in the flour, and shake the pan to distribute the flour. Turn the pan upside down over the wastebasket and shake out any excess.

◆ Peel the bananas, put them in a bowl, and beat them well with a hand-held electric mixer or in a standing electric mixer. The riper the bananas and the more you mash them, the more tender your muffins will be. Don't expect absolute smoothness, though, because there will always be a few lumps.

◆ Stir together the flour, salt, and baking soda in a small bowl.

◆ Crack the eggs into a small bowl and stir well with a fork.

Mixing the Batter

◆ In a large bowl, mix together the shortening, mashed bananas, eggs, sugar, and walnuts.

◆ Add the combined dry ingredients to the banana mixture and stir just until the batter is thoroughly blended.

Baking the Muffins

♦ Pour the batter into a large measuring cup with a spout, and use the cup to fill the muffin cups about ⅔ full.

♦ Place the muffin pan in the lower third of the oven. After 15 minutes, check them for doneness. A toothpick inserted in the middle of a muffin should come out clean. If not, continue to cook for another 5 minutes and test again. When the toothpick comes out clean, remove the muffins from the oven, and let cool in the pan for 5 minutes.

♦ Run a knife around the edge of each muffin, and transfer them to a platter.

♦ Serve warm.

♦

TURNING MUFFINS INTO A CAKE

Preheat the oven to 350°F. Grease 2 9-inch round cake pans with butter or nonstick cooking spray. Divide the batter between the 2 cake pans. Put them in the oven. Set the timer for 25 minutes. Test for doneness by inserting a toothpick into the center of one of the cakes. If the toothpick comes out clean, the cake is done. If it has wet or sticky crumbs sticking to the toothpick, bake another 5 minutes and test again.

Remove the cake pans from the oven, and let the cakes cool in the pan for 10 minutes. Loosen the edges by running a knife around the edge of the cake pans. Turn each layer upside down onto a serving platter. Put ⅓ cup of powdered sugar into a small strainer and shake it over the top of each cake to give it a nice finish. Whip 1 cup of heavy cream (see box, page 263) until the cream just barely holds its shape and add a spoonful next to each slice of cake when you serve it.

♦

Lemon Pudding Cake

SERVES SIX

THIS IS A FIRST-RATE DESSERT for two reasons. First, you will learn some good basic steps in baking, beating egg whites, and folding them into batter (it's a very forgiving recipe, so even if you don't do everything perfectly your dessert will be wonderful). Second, this dessert goes through a magic transformation: as it bakes, it creates a creamy lemon custard and a tender layer of cake. Amazing! It is particularly good as the ending to a meal of Baked Red Snapper with Vegetables (page 78) or Shrimp Curry (page 83). But I really can't think of when it wouldn't enhance a lunch or supper.

1 cup sugar
⅛ teaspoon salt
¼ cup all-purpose white flour
4 tablespoons butter (½ stick)
3 large eggs
2 or 3 lemons (to make ⅓ cup
  freshly squeezed juice)

Grated zest from 1 lemon (for
  details on grating zest, see
  box, page 141)
1½ cups milk
2 teaspoons soft butter or
  nonstick cooking spray
  (for greasing the pan)

Preheat oven to 350°F.

Mixing the Cake Batter

◆ Put ¾ cup of the sugar, the salt, and the flour in a mixing bowl and stir with a fork until mixed together.

◆ Put the butter in a small saucepan over medium-low heat and melt it. Add to the flour mixture and stir to mix.

◆ Separate the egg whites from the yolks (for full details, see box, page 270). Put the whites in a clean medium-size glass or metal bowl. Put the yolks in the flour mixture and beat with a whisk or beater.

◆ Juice the lemons, and add the lemon juice and zest to the flour.

◆ Add the milk to the flour mixture. Stir until all the ingredients are mixed together and the batter is one uniform color. *Note:* This batter is very thin and liquidy. It doesn't look like the cake batter you are used to seeing—but fear not, it will work.

Beating the Egg Whites and Folding Them In

◆ Beat the egg whites (for full details, see box, opposite), adding the remaining ¼ cup sugar until the color of the whites change from clear to white and the whites form soft peaks.

◆ Folding the whites into the batter is a gentle process. You want to combine batter and beaten egg whites without losing the air in the

1   2

whites. 1) Using a rubber spatula, scoop up the whites and put them on top of the batter. 2) Now, using the edge of the spatula, cut down to the bottom of the bowl and bring up some batter, so it is on top of the whites. Turn the bowl a quarter, cut down, bring some batter up over the egg whites again. You are gently making a circle or loop by going from the edge of the bowl along the bottom to the center of the bowl, bringing the spatula up, and folding some batter over the whites gently. Repeat this process just until the whites and batter become one. Don't fuss if you see a little streak of white here and there that has not been incorporated; as long as most of the batter and whites are blended, you've done it right.

Baking and Serving the Cake

• Grease an 8-inch square baking pan with butter or nonstick cooking spray and scrape the batter from the bowl into it. Set this pan in a large baking pan that you have placed on the middle shelf of the oven. Pour into the large pan enough warm water so that it reaches halfway up the sides of the cake pan (see box, page 269, for full details on baking in a water bath).

• Set the timer for 25 minutes.

• When the timer rings, check to see if the cake is done. It should be a golden color. Insert a toothpick into the center of the cake about ¼ deep (the layer of cake is about 1 inch thick and the pudding is underneath, so all you probe is the layer of cake). If it comes out clean, it is done; if it has a little wet batter on the tip, let the pudding cake bake another 5 minutes and test again.

• When the cake is done, remove it from the water bath—leave the water bath in the oven to cool.

• To serve, spoon a portion onto a nice dessert plate and add a scoop of whipped cream to each portion.

■

BEATING EGG WHITES

Wash and dry thoroughly a large glass or metal bowl—don't use a plastic bowl, which can retain a greasy film. The bowl has to be free of any oil or greasy film for the whites to beat properly. Put the egg whites in the bowl and use an electric mixer or an electric hand-held mixer to beat the whites. You can also do this by hand using a balloon whisk, but it takes quite a bit of brisk beating to reach the point where the egg whites are shiny and moist—not dry—and hold a peak. If you are using an electric standing mixer, attach the wire whisk and start beating the whites on low speed. As the whites become foamy, increase the speed, and when the whites look shiny and moist—not dry—take a rubber spatula and scoop up some of the whites, hold the spatula with the whites upward; if the peaks hold their shape, the whites have been beaten enough and are ready to be folded into the batter. "Stiff and moist" is the perfect point of doneness.

Bread and Butter Pudding

THIS SOUNDS LIKE a good old-fashioned farm pudding, but it is far from it. It's made with slices of French sandwich bread (not sourdough)—or any good white bread—along with the usual milk, eggs, and sugar. But this pudding has a delicacy that makes it the perfect dessert after a simple meal. Leftovers are good straight from the refrigerator, or you can warm a piece for breakfast.

7 or 8 slices French bread (not sourdough)	1 cup granulated sugar
	⅛ teaspoon salt
4 tablespoons butter (½ stick), room temperature	4 cups milk (1 quart)
	1 cup whipping cream
5 large eggs	1 tablespoon vanilla extract
4 egg yolks	

Preheat oven to 375°F.

Preparing the Bread

• Trim the crusts off the slices of bread and discard. Spread each slice of bread with the softened butter, and put buttered side up into a 9-by-13-by-2-inch pan or Pyrex dish as many slices as it takes to cover the bottom of the pan. Set the pan aside.

Mixing the Custard

• Crack 5 eggs into a large mixing bowl.

• Crack and separate 4 eggs (see page 270 for full details on separating eggs). Save the 4 egg whites in a container suitable for freezing for a future use. Put the 4 yolks in the large mixing bowl with the 5 whole eggs.

• Add the sugar and salt and stir with a large spoon until the ingredients are well blended.

• Pour the milk and cream into a saucepan and turn the heat to medium-high. Stand right there and don't let it boil. You just want to have it good and hot. Using a whisk or large spoon, add the hot milk and cream to the eggs, stirring rapidly as you pour so the eggs are immediately blended into the hot liquid. Continue to stir until the custard is smooth and well mixed. Stir in the vanilla.

Finishing the Pudding and Baking with a Water Bath

◆ Pour the custard through a fine wire-mesh strainer over the bread slices. The slices of bread will float to the top.

◆ The pudding is now ready to bake in a water bath in the oven (see box).

◆ Bake the pudding for 35 minutes, then test for doneness. The pudding at the edge of the baking dish should be firm, the center should still tremble a bit, and the top should be lightly golden. Take a wooden skewer or toothpick and insert it into the center of the pudding. If it comes out with wet pudding on it, cook for another 10 minutes and check again. The pudding usually takes about 35 to 40 minutes to bake. When done, remove it from the water bath—leaving the water bath in the oven to cool. Let the pudding set for a few minutes. Cut into squares, and serve warm with a little heavy cream poured over each serving.

◆ BAKING IN A WATER BATH ◆

A water bath is a pan of hot water into which you set a custard dish or cake pan to be baked. The water bath protects delicate baked dishes and keeps the edges and bottom from becoming too brown. The water acts as a shield, controlling the direct oven heat. Be sure to protect yourself too when carrying a shallow pan (I use my roasting pan) to the oven. Make sure there is plenty of room for the custard or cake pan in the larger one. The safest way of doing this is to put the larger pan in the oven empty and set the custard or cake in the large pan. Then pour very hot water ⅔ up the sides of the large pan.

When it is time to remove the cake or custard, using pot holders, first lift the cake or custard out of the water bath. Set it on a heatproof surface to cool. Either turn the oven off and let the pan of water cool down in the oven, or carefully carry the pan of hot water to the sink and dump it.

STORING OF EXTRA EGG YOLKS AND EGG WHITES

When you have leftover egg yolks or egg whites and you know you will use them within 2 days, just store them in a covered container in the refrigerator. If you don't plan to use them within 2 days, put the whites in a covered container and freeze them. They will keep indefinitely. Egg yolks don't freeze well, so it's not worth bothering. Use them in an omelet or make a fried-egg sandwich.

◆ HOW TO SEPARATE EGGS ◆

Separating egg whites from yolks is an important technique to master. If the whites get bits of yolks, which are fatty, in them, they simply won't beat properly. First, get out two small clean bowls. There are two ways to separate the eggs. Use whichever method seems easier for you.

USING YOUR HANDS: Crack the egg on the side of one of the bowls, put the raw egg in your hand and use your fingers as a strainer, allowing the egg white to fall into one bowl while the yolk remains in your hand. Put the yolk in the other bowl. If you do get a speck of yolk in the whites, dip a piece of eggshell in the white and scoop it out. The shell works like a magnet—attracting the yolk so you can remove it easily from the white.

USING THE SHELL: Holding the egg gently, give it a crack in the middle of the shell, on the side of a bowl. Carefully pull the halves apart. Your goal is to get most of the white into a bowl, keeping the yolk in one half of the shell. As you pull the shell apart, some of the white will fall into the bowl. Now tip the yolk to the edge of the shell and some more of the white will fall away into the bowl. Keep moving the yolk from one shell to the other, letting the white fall away. Usually if you do this two or three times you will have only a little white left on the yolk, which doesn't matter.

Chocolate Pudding

THIS IS A SMOOTH, CREAMY PUDDING with a gentle chocolate flavor. It is very easy to make, and is especially nice served warm and topped with a little sweetened cream. When you are cooking the ingredients, the trick is to stir constantly with a large spoon, sweeping the bottom and sides of the pan with a brisk motion. The pudding cooks in just a few minutes, so you can decide on the spur of the moment to have this for dessert. It's done in a jiffy.

3 tablespoons cornstarch	¼ teaspoon salt
¼ cup sugar	2 cups milk
2 tablespoons cocoa	1 teaspoon vanilla

Measuring and Mixing the Ingredients

• Put the cornstarch, sugar, cocoa, salt, and ½ cup of the milk into a 2-cup (1-pint) jar with a lid. Screw the lid on tightly, and shake the ingredients together vigorously for about 10 seconds, so everything is smooth.

Cooking the Pudding

• Pour the remaining 1½ cups of milk into a small saucepan (about 1-quart capacity—it doesn't have to be exact), set the pan on the stove, and turn the heat to medium high.

• As soon as the milk forms a ring of tiny bubbles around the edge of the pan, give the cornstarch mixture another good shake and pour it into the hot milk.

• Stir the mixture constantly in a circular motion, using your large spoon to scrape the bottom and sides of the pan as you stir. Within a minute—or two at the most—the pudding will have thickened. Take the pan off the stove and tilt it so you can see the bottom. The pudding at the bottom of the pan will have thickened the most, because it has been closest to the heat. Return the pan to the burner and continue to stir constantly for a few seconds longer, until the pudding all has the same thick, creamy texture.

• Remove the pan from the heat and stir in the vanilla.

• Pour the warm pudding into 4 small bowls and serve warm with a good spoonful of slightly sweetened whipped cream. If you'll be using the pudding later instead of immediately, pour it into a bowl, let cool, and refrigerate.

◆

CORNSTARCH

Cornstarch is used to thicken sauces and pie fillings. It is twice as powerful a thickener as flour; 1 tablespoon of cornstarch will do what 2 tablespoons of flour will do. Cornstarch creates a transparent sauce, unlike flour, which makes the finished sauce opaque. Remember when cooking a sauce with cornstarch that it must boil only for 1 minute. Boiled longer, it will lose its ability to thicken.

◆

Pecan Pie

ONE 9-INCH PIE

MOST BEGINNING COOKS I've encountered are uneasy about learning to make pie dough. Making pie dough is a lesson that will make you wonder what all the commotion is about. Even if your first pie crust is not quite as light and flaky as it will be after you've made a few more, your first attempt will surprise you. It may even remind you of making mud pies, a good memory for most of us. Just get your hands into the floury bowl, follow the instructions, and don't court failure by worrying. Once you have mastered the dough, you can make any kind of pie. Try the American Apple Pie that follows and then go on to other fruit and berry pies, following the sauce guidelines.

As for this Pecan Pie, it's the best I've ever eaten! You will be proud of yourself when you serve it.

THE PIE DOUGH

1 ¼ cups all-purpose white flour	⅓ cup vegetable shortening
¼ teaspoon salt	¼ cup cold water, or a little more

THE FILLING

¼ cup (½ stick) butter	½ teaspoon salt
3 eggs	1 cup dark corn syrup
½ cup plus 2 tablespoons granulated sugar	1 cup pecans

Preheat oven to 425°F.

Making the Pie Dough

• Put 1¼ cups of flour and ¼ teaspoon salt in a large mixing bowl, and stir them around to mix.

• Fill a ¼-cup measure with shortening. Scoop the shortening out of the cup with your fingers and put it in the bowl with the flour. Rub some flour on your hands, then roll the shortening around in the flour so the fat isn't too sticky to handle.

• Break the shortening into 4 or 5 smaller pieces and coat them all with the flour in the bowl. 1) Now lightly rub small pieces of the shortening and flour together with your fingers for about a minute, to make little lumps. If there is loose flour at the bottom of the bowl, scoop it up to the top with your fingers and rub shortening into it to make more lumps.

1

- Continue scooping up and rubbing, always working lightly, letting the bits of shortening fall back into the bowl. When most of the flour and shortening have been transformed into lots of little lumps and the dough looks like grated cheese, you have mixed enough.

Adding the Water

- 2) Sprinkle the cold water over the dough, and stir with a fork all around the sides and bottom of the bowl so no dry flour remains hidden. Stir until the water is mixed into the flour and has disappeared. Reach down to the very bottom of the bowl and gather up all the pieces of the dough. 3) Now pat and press the dough together until you have a ball of dough. If some of it is still so dry that pieces fall away, sprinkle that area with a little more water and gently press and pull the dough apart, sprinkling a little more water on it. Pat it into a ball again.

2

3

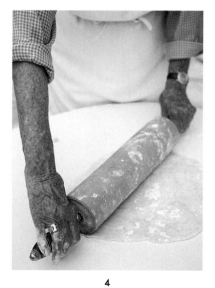

4

Rolling the Dough

- Sprinkle a large cutting board or a countertop lightly with a small handful of flour. Spread the flour into a circle bigger than your 9-inch pie pan.

- Put the dough in the center of the circle of flour. Flour the rolling part of a rolling pin. Flatten the dough a little with the rolling pin, 4) then begin rolling from the center of the dough out to the edges to make a circle. Don't roll back and forth. Move the dough now and then to make sure it isn't sticking to the surface.

- If it is sticking, slide a metal spatula in a wiggling motion under the dough to loosen it. Sprinkle more flour on the board underneath it, then continue to roll out the dough into a big circle, about 1½ inches larger all around than your pie pan.

5   6

7

◆ To make sure, put the pie pan upside down in the center of the dough and check that your circle is about the right size, then remove the pan and set to the side. The dough will be about as thin as a cracker.

◆ 5) Roll the dough around the rolling pin. Lift the pin up and center it over the pie pan, then unroll the dough into the pan, with the fold in the center of the pan. Now unfold the dough against the inside of the pan and pat the dough all around the inside edge to fit snugly into the pan.

◆ 6) Now fold the hanging dough back up onto the rim to make a double thickness of dough around the edge of the pan. Be careful not to tuck the dough *under* the edge of the pan, which would make it hard to dislodge after the crust is baked.

◆ 7) When you have neatly folded the dough all around the edges of the pie pan with your two forefingers, press indentations into the dough, squeezing the edges together, to make a scalloped edge.

Preparing the Filling

◆ Melt the butter in a small saucepan over medium-low heat.

◆ Break the eggs into a medium-size bowl. Add the sugar, salt, corn syrup, and the butter you have just melted. Mix with a large spoon until well blended. Stir in the pecans.

◆ Pour the filling into the unbaked pie shell.

Baking the Pie

◆ Bake on the middle shelf of the oven for 40 minutes, or just until the center of the pie feels almost firm to the touch. When the pie is done, remove from the oven and allow to cool.

◆ Serve with lightly whipped, unsweetened cream.

6 or 7 large tart, firm apples
(to make about 8 cups
sliced)
¾ cup sugar

½ teaspoon ground cinnamon
¼ teaspoon ground nutmeg
Dough from the preceding
recipe (Pecan Pie)

ONE 9-INCH PIE

Preheat oven to 425°F.

Preparing the Filling

• Peel the apples and cut away the core. Slice the apple pieces into ¼-inch slices and put them in a large mixing bowl. Measure the sugar, cinnamon, and nutmeg into a smaller bowl and stir to mix well. Sprinkle this sugar mixture over the apple slices. Use a big spoon or your hands to toss and mix so all the slices are coated.

Preparing the Dough and Filling the Bottom Crust

• Follow the directions for making the Pecan Pie crust, but double the amount of dough for this two-crust pie.

• When the dough has been mixed and patted into a ball, roll out one half of the dough, fold it in half, as described, and fit it into a 9-inch pie pan, leaving a 2-inch edge of dough all around the rim of the pan.

• Distribute the apple slices over the dough-lined pan, mounding them in the center.

Preparing the Top Crust and Baking

• Roll out the remaining half of dough and roll it up over the rolling pin. Unroll the dough over the apple-filled pan, leaving a 2-inch overhang. Trim the edges if necessary.

• Tuck the edges under so they are on top of the rim of the pie pan, as described in the previous recipe, except here you will be tucking under two layers of dough.

• Make a scalloped edge all around the pan as described. Cut several little slits in the center of the top of the pie dough to allow steam to escape while the pie bakes.

• Bake 30 minutes at 425°F. Turn the oven down to 350°F, and bake another 20 to 30 minutes.

• After 50 minutes test for doneness by piercing through the crust into the apples. If they feel soft, and the top crust is lightly golden, the pie is done. If not, bake another 10 minutes and test again.

• Remove the pie and let it cool a little before serving. Serve plain or with ice cream or whipped cream, or a wedge of cheddar cheese.

Crustless Coconut Custard Pie

ONE 10-INCH PIE

THE EASE, SPEED, AND SIMPLICITY of this pie make it worth the little effort it takes. And it's a bonus that its taste is much better than you'd think such plain ingredients could produce. Serve it with a wedge of papaya, mango, or pineapple . . . or just by itself.

2 cups milk
½ cup all-purpose white flour
1 teaspoon baking powder
¼ teaspoon salt
4 large eggs

1 cup sugar
1½ teaspoons vanilla
1 cup sweetened packaged
    coconut

Special Equipment: food processor

Preheat oven to 350°F.

Preparing the Batter

◆ Put the milk, flour, baking powder, salt, sugar, and vanilla in the bowl of a food processor fitted with a metal blade. Crack the eggs, one by one, right into the food processor bowl. Process for 3 minutes.

◆ Add the coconut and process for 2 or 3 more seconds.

◆ If you don't have a food processor, you can make this batter in a large mixing bowl using an electric mixer, or by beating vigorously with a wire whisk.

Baking the Pie

◆ Pour the batter into an ungreased 10-inch pie pan, using a rubber spatula to scrape up any batter that clings to the sides of the bowl. Put in the oven and set the timer for 30 minutes.

◆ After 30 minutes, check to see if the custard is done. It should be golden brown with a fairly firm center. Insert a small sharp knife into the center of the pie. If it comes out clean, it is done. If it is not done, bake another 5 minutes and check again.

Serving the Pie

◆ Serve this pie warm or cold, cut into wedges.

Crisp and Creamy Chocolate Squares

EVERY HOME COOK NEEDS several good chocolate desserts to count on. This is definitely a pleaser—creamy, with a crisp top and a deep chocolaty taste.

4 large eggs

2 cups sugar

½ cup all-purpose white flour

½ cup unsweetened cocoa

¾ cup walnuts

1 cup butter (2 sticks)

2 teaspoons vanilla

2 teaspoons soft butter or
nonstick cooking spray
(for greasing the pan)

Preheat oven to 325°F.

Mixing the Ingredients in a Big Bowl

- Crack the eggs into a large mixing bowl. Add the sugar and stir with a large spoon or whisk until thick and all one color.
- Add the flour and cocoa and mix until smooth.
- Chop the walnuts into pieces the size of peanuts. Add to the bowl along with the butter and vanilla, and mix until blended.

Baking the Squares

- Grease a 7-by-11-inch baking dish with butter or nonstick cooking spray.
- Using a spatula, scrape the batter from the bowl into the greased baking pan. Run the spatula over the top of the batter so it is level.
- Put the pan on the center rack of the oven and bake for 50 minutes.
- Check for doneness by inserting a knife ½ inch from the edge of the pan. If the knife comes out clean, it is done; remove from the oven. The center will still be quite moist. If the knife has wet batter sticking to it, bake another 5 minutes and check again.
- Cut into squares and serve warm with whipped cream (see box, page 263) or vanilla ice cream. They also taste good cold, and will keep well if wrapped tightly and stored in the freezer.

◆

SUPER SAUCE

Choose a good-quality vanilla ice cream. Scoop a serving or two into a bowl. Let it melt. You now have a delicious vanilla cream sauce. You can do the same with other flavors of ice cream, such as strawberry or chocolate.

◆

Chocolate Chip Cookies

ABOUT 50 COOKIES

THESE ARE ALL-AMERICAN COOKIES that satisfy chocolate lovers, and they also appeal to the plain old cookie lover. Serve with a glass of cold milk.

1½ tablespoons soft butter or shortening or nonstick cooking spray (for greasing the cookie sheets)	1 egg
	¾ teaspoon vanilla
	1¼ cups flour
	½ teaspoon salt
½ cup (1 stick) butter, softened to room temperature	½ teaspoon baking soda
	1 cup (6 ounces) semisweet chocolate chips
½ cup dark-brown sugar	½ cup chopped walnuts
½ cup sugar	(optional)

Preheat oven to 375°F. Grease 2 cookie sheets with nonstick cooking spray, shortening, or butter.

Mixing the Batter

• Using an electric beater or a big spoon, cream the butter in a mixing bowl until smooth. Add the brown and white sugar and continue to beat until creamy and light. Crack the egg into the bowl, add the vanilla, and mix again until smooth. You can also do this by hand, with a wooden spoon and a strong hand.

• In a separate bowl, combine the flour, salt, and baking soda and stir with a fork. Add to the butter-sugar mixture and blend until smooth.

• Pour the chocolate chips and chopped nuts, if you are using them, into the bowl and stir well, until evenly distributed throughout the dough. Do not use an electric beater for this step.

Baking the Cookies

• Scoop up a rounded teaspoonful of dough and place near a corner of one of the baking sheets, about 2 inches from the edges. Place a second teaspoonful of dough about 1 inch away from the first. Continue to arrange the cookies in this way until you've filled the baking sheets.

• Put the cookies in the oven and set the timer for 8 minutes. While the cookies are baking, fill the second baking sheet with rounded teaspoonfuls of cookie dough. It's best to bake one sheet of cookies at a time.

- After 8 minutes, check to see if the cookies are done. If they are slightly brown around the edges, remove from the oven; if not, bake another minute or two and check again.

- When the cookies have been removed from the oven, let them cool for a few minutes. Using a spatula, lift them off the baking sheet and put them on a plate to serve.

Storage

- If you can't eat up all the cookies within a few days, they can be frozen in plastic baggies. But sometimes baked cookies take on an old flavor from the freezer, so I prefer to bake only the number of cookies I'll use up and refrigerate or freeze the remaining dough to bake later (see box).

■ STORING COOKIE DOUGH ■

If you don't want to bake all your cookie dough, you can refrigerate or freeze it and bake it into cookies later. 1) Shape the leftover dough into logs about 1½ inches in diameter, and wrap them airtight in waxed paper or plastic wrap. The dough will keep in the refrigerator about 2 weeks, and in the freezer indefinitely. 2) When you want to bake, leave the dough out at room temperature for a few hours, then slice it into ¼-inch-thick coins and bake as described. You will not need to press the rounds of dough with the palms of your hands, because cutting the chilled dough will give you neat, thin slices.

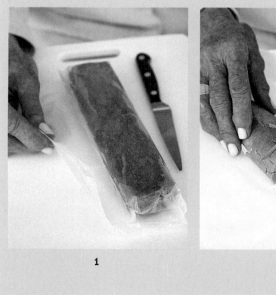

1   2

Snappy Gingersnaps

ABOUT 40 1½-INCH ROUND COOKIES

THESE ARE THE BEST gingersnap cookies I've ever eaten. They have just the right amount of spicy, peppery taste, and they are crisp but not hard. They also have that classic crackle top (see illustration).

¾ cup shortening (Crisco is
    my choice)
1 cup sugar
1 egg
¼ cup dark molasses
2 cups all-purpose white flour

2 teaspoons baking soda
½ teaspoon salt
1 tablespoon ground ginger
1 teaspoon cinnamon
⅓ cup sugar (to roll the cookie
    dough in)

Preheat oven to 350°F.

Mixing the Cookie Dough

◆ Put the shortening, 1 cup sugar, the egg, and the molasses in a large mixing bowl. Using a large spoon, beat the mixture until it is smooth and blended.

◆ In a small bowl, mix the flour, baking soda, salt, ginger, and cinnamon with a fork.

◆ Add the dry ingredients to the shortening mixture. Stir vigorously until everything is smooth and blended.

Finishing the Cookies

◆ Spread a 12-inch-long piece of waxed paper on the counter. Put the ¼ cup sugar on the waxed paper and spread it out a little.

◆ Scoop up a rounded teaspoonful of dough and roll it into a ball between the palms of your hands. Roll the ball in sugar, and place this first ball near a corner of an ungreased baking sheet, about 2 inches from the edges. Continue rolling the dough into balls, and placing them in rows 2 inches apart until you've filled up the baking sheet. You want to give the cookies plenty of room to spread out. Don't flatten the dough or the cookies won't crackle. Repeat with a second cookie sheet.

◆ Put an oven rack in the center position of the oven and bake one sheet of cookies at a time. The cookies will bake more evenly this way.

Baking the Cookies

◆ Set the timer for 10 minutes. When it rings, check to see if the cookies have flattened out and started to develop cracked tops. Test for doneness by sticking a toothpick into the center of a cookie. If it comes out clean, the cookies are done. If there is some sticky dough on the toothpick, let the snaps bake another 2 or 3 minutes.

◆ When the cookies are done, remove from the oven and let them cool for 10 minutes. Meanwhile bake the second sheet of cookies.

◆ After 10 minutes, using a spatula, lift the cookies off the baking sheets and put them on a plate to serve. If they aren't all snapped up right away, put some in plastic baggies and secure with a tie. These gingersnaps freeze very well.

◆

GINGERSNAP DESSERT

You can turn these cookies into a dessert by putting three or four cookies on a plate and topping each one with sweetened whipped cream.

◆

The Best Oatmeal Cookies

ABOUT 48 COOKIES

THIS IS NOT YOUR run-of-the-mill oatmeal cookie. It has won the taste contest in my kitchen because it has all the virtues of a true oatmeal cookie without the usual "klutzy" coarseness. The fact that this Best Oatmeal Cookie is homey doesn't mean it can't be refined.

1 cup butter (2 sticks),
   softened to room
   temperature
1 cup sugar
1 cup all-purpose white flour
2 cups quick-cooking,
   1-minute oats

1 teaspoon baking soda
½ teaspoon salt
¼ teaspoon ground nutmeg
1 teaspoon vanilla

Preheat oven to 350°F.

Mixing the Batter

• Be sure the butter is soft, then put it along with the sugar in a large bowl. Using the back of a spoon, vigorously mash and scrape the butter against the sides and bottom of the bowl, gradually mixing it into the sugar until it becomes smooth and pale yellow. You can also do this with an electric mixer.

• Add the flour, oatmeal, baking soda, salt, nutmeg, and vanilla to the bowl. Using your hands (a sturdy spoon or electric mixer will also work), blend the dry ingredients into the butter by pressing and squeezing the dough between your fingers until it becomes one solid mass with no loose flour or oats in the bowl.

Baking the Cookies

• Grease 2 cookie sheets with butter or nonstick cooking spray.

• Using a small spoon, scoop up 1 rounded teaspoon of dough, then gently roll it between the palms of your hands to form a small ball. Place the dough ball on a corner of the greased cookie sheet, about 1 inch from the sides. Form another ball of dough and put it on the cookie sheet about 2 inches from the first one. Continue until you have filled up 2 cookie sheets, with 12 evenly spaced balls of dough on each.

♦ Using the palm of your hand, press lightly on each ball to flatten it to a ¼-inch-thick round.

♦ Put an oven rack in the center of the oven. Put one cookie sheet in the oven at a time—this lets the cookies bake more evenly. Set the timer for 10 minutes.

♦ When it rings, check the cookies. If you can see just a little golden-brown color on the outside edges of the cookies, they are done; remove the pan from the oven. If not, bake for another 2 minutes and check again.

♦ Put the second sheet in the oven and repeat the baking directions.

♦ Set the cookie sheets on a heatproof counter or stovetop and let cool for about 10 minutes. Use a spatula to remove them to a flat surface.

♦ Grease the cookie sheets again, and continue to make cookies until you've used up the dough.

Cinnamon Toast

Serves one, two, or four

IN MY HOUSE, cinnamon toast was a daily after-school indulgence. It is a perfect sweet pacifier, easy to make, and nothing in the world is quite like it. Mix 1 cup of sugar with 1 tablespoon plus 1 teaspoon of ground cinnamon. Stir to mix well, and store it in a plastic bag, having it ready so you can make cinnamon toast in a minute.

4 slices fresh white bread

4 tablespoons butter

4 tablespoons sugar

1 teaspoon ground cinnamon

Preparing the Cinnamon Toast

◆ Toast the bread. Spread each slice of bread generously with butter, about 1 tablespoon.

◆ Mix the sugar and cinnamon in a small bowl until the mixture looks tan-colored. Using a spoon, sprinkle the toast from edge to edge, so each slice is completely covered with the sugar mixture.

◆ Put the toasts in a single layer on a baking sheet.

Broiling the Toast

◆ Put the oven rack about 3 inches below the broiling element.

◆ As soon as the broiler element heats and turns red, slide the baking sheet under the broiler. Stand right there and keep an eye on the toasts. It will take a minute or two for the sugar to melt and begin to bubble a little. When the sugar bubbles, remove the toasts and eat immediately.

Baked Plums and Apricots with Almonds

T HIS DISH IS SIMPLE to prepare and is good hot or cold. Just before you sit down at the table, put it in the oven to bake, and it will be bubbling hot for dessert. Serve in bowls with heavy cream or ice cream.

SERVES SIX

8 large apricots (about
      2 pounds)
6 large plums (about 1 pound)
⅔ cup plus 6 tablespoons sugar

⅔ cup water
1¾ cups whole unblanched
   almonds*

Preheat oven to 350°F.

Preparing the Fruit
- Wash the plums and apricots. Cut the fruit in half, remove and discard the pits, and put the fruit in a sauté pan.
- Put the ⅔ cup sugar in a small bowl and add the ⅔ cup water to it. Stir until well mixed and pour over the fruit in the pan.

Cooking the Fruit
- Set the pan on the stove, put a lid on it, and turn the heat to low. Cook for 5 to 7 minutes, just until the fruit is tender when pierced with a fork. Check after 5 minutes, and remove from the heat as soon as the fruit is tender but still holding its shape. You don't want it mushy.

Preparing the Almonds
- If you have a mini–food processor, process the almonds with the remaining 6 tablespoons of sugar until very fine—dry like sand but not gummy. If you don't have a processor, chop the almonds very fine and mix with the 6 tablespoons sugar.

Finishing the Dish
- Spread the almond mixture evenly over the bottom of a 9-by-13-by-2-inch rectangular baking dish. Place the plums and apricots, cut side down, on top, then pour ⅔ cup of the fruit juices remaining in the sauté pan over the fruit. Bake for 1 hour. Use a spoon to taste a bit of the fruit and the juices; if it tastes too tart, sprinkle on a little sugar. (The sugar will melt, because the dish is still hot.)
- Serve warm with heavy cream or ice cream.

* Unblanched almonds are raw almonds with their brown skins left on.

Seattle Crisp

A CRISP IS A TRADITIONAL, homey American dessert, with sweetened fruit on the bottom of a baking dish, and a mixture of flour, sugar, and butter on top. As it cooks, the fruit becomes soft and the topping turns golden brown and crunchy. This crisp can be made with practically any fruit you like, and it's the best version I've ever eaten.

THE FRUIT:

5 to 6 medium-size apples (Granny Smith and Macintosh apples work well)	½ to ¾ cup sugar
	2 tablespoons all-purpose white flour

THE TOPPING:

1 cup all-purpose white flour	½ teaspoon salt
¾ cup sugar	1 large egg
1 teaspoon baking powder	½ cup butter (1 stick)

Preheat oven to 375°F.

Preparing the Fruit

• Peel and core the apples and cut into ¼-inch-thick slices—a little thicker than a cracker. Measure out 6 cups of cut apples, give or take a little.

• Put the apples and ½ cup of sugar in a large bowl and stir around until the sugar evenly coats the fruit. The amount of sugar you use depends on how sweet the apples are. Taste an apple slice to see if it seems sweet enough. If not, add the remaining ¼ cup of sugar and stir again.

• Add 2 tablespoons of flour to the bowl and mix until it is evenly distributed on the fruit.

• Put the apples in an 8-inch square or a round 1½-quart baking dish. Don't bother to butter the dish.

Making the Topping

• Mix together 1 cup flour, ¾ cup sugar, the baking powder, and the salt.

• Crack the egg into a small dish, beat with a fork until it is all one color, and add to the flour-and-sugar mixture.

◆ Using your hands or a fork, gently mix the egg into the flour-and-sugar mixture until the egg evenly moistens the dry ingredients. Be sure not to press the dough into one solid mass. The topping should be loose and crumbly so that it can be sprinkled over the fruit.

Putting the Crisp Together

◆ Sprinkle the crisp topping evenly over the top of the apples.

◆ Melt the butter in a small saucepan over medium-low heat, stirring regularly.

◆ Spoon the melted butter over the top of the crisp so that it is evenly coated with butter.

◆ Put the crisp on the center rack of the oven and bake for 30 minutes.

◆ When 30 minutes are up, check to see if it's done. If the top of the crisp is a deep golden brown, and the fruit is bubbling, it is done. Remove it from the oven. If not, bake another 5 or 10 minutes and check again.

◆ Cut the crisp into squares and lift from the pan with a small spatula onto individual serving plates. Serve warm with whipped cream or vanilla ice cream.

■

USING OTHER FRUITS

This crisp can be made with any fresh fruit you like, but the type of fruit you use will dictate how you prepare it.

If using fruit with a peel and a pit such as peaches or apricots, peel, cut in half, and remove the pit. Cut each half into ¼-inch-thick slices. If using plums, there's no need to peel them. Pears you would treat the same as apples.

If using berries, simply remove the stems. Berries produce a lot of juice when cooked, which means your crisp will have a lot of liquid.

If using rhubarb, cut each stalk crosswise into ¼-to-½-inch-thick pieces. Since rhubarb is so tart, you will need to increase the sugar to 1¾ cups.

Once the fruit is prepared, measure out the 6 cups (give or take a little) you'll need for the recipe.

■

Baked Apples

SERVES FOUR

THE HUMBLE, homey baked apple, done properly, is equal to if not better than the fanciest pastry. Bake more than you need for one meal. They keep well in the refrigerator for 3 or 4 days, and are easy to reheat and serve warm.

4 firm apples	½ cup water
1 lemon	⅛ teaspoon salt
⅓ cup sugar	

Preheat oven to 350°F.

Preparing the Apples

♦ Using a vegetable peeler or sharp paring knife, remove the peel from the top third of the apples and discard.

♦ Carefully cut the core out of each apple, being sure not to break the apple apart. You can do this either by using an apple corer or boring a small sharp knife down the center of the apple and turning it (like screwing in a screw) until the tough core is removed.

♦ Set the apples upright in a deep baking dish.

Making the Syrup

♦ Remove the zest from the lemon and cut into large strips (see box, page 141).

♦ Put the lemon zest, sugar, water, and salt in a small pan, stir, and bring to a boil over high heat. Once it boils, stir again and remove from heat.

♦ Pour the syrup over the tops of the apples. Cover the baking dish with a tightly fitting lid or aluminum foil.

Baking and Serving the Apples

♦ Put the baking dish in the oven and set the timer for 30 minutes.

♦ When the timer rings, check for doneness by piercing an apple with the tip of a knife. If it pierces easily and is tender, it is done.

♦ Set the apples on individual dessert plates and serve with slightly sweetened whipped cream (for full details, see box, page 263).

Baked Bananas

SERVES FOUR

BANANAS ARE ONE FRUIT we can count on finding in the market all year. Baking them this simple way turns an everyday fruit into a really special dessert.

4 tablespoons butter	4 tablespoons light- or dark-
1 tablespoon fresh lemon juice	brown sugar
4 firm bananas	½ cup heavy cream

Use an 8-by-8-by-2-inch baking dish or pan, or a dish that is large enough to hold the bananas. Preheat the oven to 350°F.

Preparing the Bananas and Sauce

• Put the butter and lemon juice in the baking dish and place it in the oven for 2 or 3 minutes, just long enough to melt the butter.

• Remove the dish from the oven and stir the butter and lemon juice together.

• Peel the bananas and put them into the baking dish, turning them over so they are coated with the butter mixture. Sprinkle a tablespoon of brown sugar over each banana.

• Bake the bananas for 15 minutes.

Serving the Bananas

• Take the bananas out of the oven and put each banana on a dessert plate. Spoon the sauce from the baking dish evenly over each banana and then pour 2 tablespoons of heavy cream over the top of each serving. Serve warm.

Grapes with Sour Cream and Brown Sugar

SERVES FOUR

I LOOKED THROUGH many of my very old cookbooks for this recipe, but found not a one. That probably shouldn't have surprised me, because it's not really a recipe. It's simply a matter of assembling three humble ingredients, which makes this dessert ideal after a meal that has been a bit demanding to prepare.

1½ lbs Thompson seedless grapes
½ cup sour cream (light sour cream is okay)

½ cup light-brown sugar, plus a little extra

Preparing and Chilling the Grapes

- Wash the grapes and pat them dry with a paper towel.
- Remove the stems and put the grapes in a medium-size bowl. Cover with plastic wrap and refrigerate. They should be good and cold before serving.

Just Before Serving

- Put the sour cream and ½ cup brown sugar in a small bowl. Using a fork, stir the ingredients together until smooth. There should be no grainy chunks of brown sugar remaining.
- Add the sour cream and brown sugar to the grapes and stir until all the grapes are evenly coated.
- Spoon the grapes into individual serving bowls. Sprinkle about 1 teaspoon of brown sugar on top of each serving and serve right away.

A Dessert of Fresh Fruit

HERE ARE SOME DESSERTS that are as simple as a smile. If you are short of time or confidence about making dessert, these combinations will provide some no-fail answers. Europeans have long understood how satisfying fresh fruits can be at the end of a meal. And for some reason we have overlooked the virtues of fresh seasonal fruit that can be made appealing with just a touch or two. Check the Fruit Chart for directions on how to choose ripe fruit.

Persimmons
- Ripe Fuyu persimmons are delicious chilled, sliced, topped with light-brown sugar stirred and mixed into plain yogurt. A spoonful or two will be ample for each serving.

Grapes
- Try the Italian way of serving bunches of grapes—green, red, or purple, or a combination—in a pretty glass bowl with pieces of ice and water; accompany with a soft cheese, such as Camembert or Brie, and crackers.

Dates
- For 4 people, use about ½ pound of Medjool dates. Run a paring knife along one side of each date and remove pit. Stuff each date with a little cream cheese and a piece of walnut.

Figs
- The two varieties that are briefly in the market are the black Mission fig and the more luxurious green Calimyrna. The softer and riper they are, the better. They are wonderful simply eaten plain; if you must "gild the lily," serve the figs sliced in a glass dish and pour a little heavy cream over them.

Papaya
- Cut the papaya in half lengthwise and remove the seeds. Save about 1 tablespoon of the seeds (rinse them off under cold water). Squeeze the juice of half a lemon or lime over both halves of papaya. Sprinkle a rounded teaspoon of seed over each half (they are crunchy and good with the soft fruit). Check the Fruit Chart for guidance in choosing ripe papayas.

◆

IS IT RIPE?

Fruits that do not ripen after they are picked: blackberries, cherries, grapes, lemons, oranges, grapefruit, pineapples, raspberries, strawberries.

Fruits that change in color, texture, and juiciness but do not change in sweetness or flavor after they are picked: apricots, blueberries, melons (except watermelon), figs, peaches, persimmons, and plums.

Fruits that do get sweeter after they are picked: apples, mangoes, papayas, and pears.

The fruit that ripens only after it is picked: avocado.

◆

Strawberries

◆ When strawberries are sweet and ripe, try serving them with their stems on with a bowl of sour cream and one of brown sugar, so you can dip them into the cream and sugar, then pop them right into your mouth.

Oranges

◆ Peel 4 or 5 oranges and separate into individual sections. Cut the sections crosswise in 4 or 5 pieces. Put the pieces of orange in a bowl and stir in about ⅔ cup of orange marmalade. Stir to mix and coat the orange pieces with the marmalade. Cover the bowl and chill. Serve in pretty stemmed glasses.

Peaches or Nectarines

◆ Use only ripe, sweet peaches or nectarines; see Fruit Chart for directions on how to choose ripe fruit. Peel the fruit and, using a paring knife, cut large pieces of fruit from the pit. Sometimes you can gently twist and separate the fruit in half and then easily pry the pit out. If this doesn't work, cut large chunks of fruit from the pit. Cut the fruit into bite-size pieces and put in a bowl. Depending on the size of the fruit, each serving should be equal to about 1 cup of cut-up fruit. If the fruit isn't very sweet, sprinkle a few spoonfuls of sugar over and toss the fruit so the sugar coats all of it. Let sit for about 15 minutes so the sugar dissolves and melts over the fruit. Add about ½ teaspoon of balsamic vinegar for each whole fruit that you cut up. Balsamic is amazingly good on peaches and nectarines. The acid and sweetness balance and intensify the fruit flavor. You can find balsamic vinegar in the supermarket, usually with the vinegars and oils.

Fruit Chart

Limited to Fruits Called For in This Book

Fruit	Look For	Storage	Will Keep
Apples	Firm apples, stems intact, not bruised or discolored.	At room temperature or refrigerate in a plastic bag in crisper.	7–10 days at room temperature, several months refrigerated.
Apricots	Reasonably firm when squeezed gently. Outside surface colored golden yellow, perhaps with a red blush. Avoid hard and greenish-yellow fruit.	Ripen at room temperature 2–3 days. If fruit becomes softer, taste it; if it tastes good, use it or refrigerate in a plastic bag. If it is still hard, let it stand 1 or 2 days more.	Use soon after ripening. May keep 1–2 days refrigerated in a plastic bag.
Bananas	Plump, well-filled, firm, bright-yellow bananas. Avoid bruised ones.	Ripen at room temperature 2–3 days. When ripe, brown specks will appear. Refrigerate on a plate uncovered.	After ripening, refrigerate 3–5 days. They will turn black on the outside but will still taste good
Blackberries	Firm, plump, blue-black berries. Berries not stuck together. Turn berry container over; underside should be dry and free of berry stain.	Sort and remove squashed or soft berries. Store good berries in the container in which they came if it is dry. If wet from berry juice, put a folded paper towel on the bottom and fill it with the remaining berries; refrigerate.	Use as soon as possible. May keep a few days.
Blueberries	Firm, plump, uniformly sized purple-silvery blue berries. Turn berry container over; underside should be dry and free of berry stain.	Same as blackberries.	Use as soon as possible. May keep 3–7 days.
Cranberries	Firm, plump, scarlet berries, not shriveled or discolored.	Refrigerate in bag they came in or freeze in sealed plastic bag.	2 months refrigerated. Up to a year frozen.
Figs	Firm to fairly soft fruit, may even be shriveled and wrinkled by sun—if so they are ripe. Avoid sour-smelling ones, a sign that a fig is too ripe.	Let unripe figs ripen at room temperature 3–4 days. Taste them when they get soft: if they are sweet, they are ripe. Refrigerate when ripe.	2–3 days in refrigerator after ripening.

Fruit	Look For	Storage	Will Keep
Grapes	Firm, full-colored, plump fruit, firmly attached to their stems.	Refrigerate in a plastic bag, unwashed.	1–2 weeks.
Lemons	Firm fruit, heavy for size, greenish yellow.	Refrigerate, *not* in a plastic bag. The ideal place in the refrigerator is the crisper or another drawer.	Up to a month.
Mangoes	Firm, smooth-skinned mangoes that have begun to color from greenish to golden orange. Hold mango between the palms of both hands and squeeze gently—it's mature if it yields just slightly.	Ripen at room temperature. Ripe when softer and fragrant. Refrigerate when ripe in a loosely closed plastic bag.	2–3 days when ripened.
Oranges and Grapefruits	Firm fruit, heavy for its size and free of soft spots.	Refrigerate, *not* in a plastic bag. The ideal place in the refrigerator is the crisper or another drawer.	Up to a month.
Papayas	Smooth, unblemished, greenish golden-yellow. Stem end (smaller part of fruit) yields slightly when squeezed gently.	Ripen at room temperature—ripe when fruit yields slightly when squeezed gently.	Ripens in 2–3 days. After ripening, refrigerate 1–2 days.
Peaches	Fragrant fruit that gives just slightly when squeezed gently. Look for yellowish or creamy outside color—sometimes will have crimson to pink tints. If hard, store in paper bag a few days and, if needed, add sugar when serving.	Room temperature until ripe, usually 2–3 days. If it is ripe, it will yield slightly when squeezed gently and be fragrant. Put in a plastic bag and refrigerate when ripe.	5–10 days after ripening, if refrigerated and stored in a plastic bag.
Pears	Unblemished and unbruised fruit. Should be hard to firm when squeezed gently. Avoid soft spots.	Ripen 2–3 days at room temperature. Should yield slightly when squeezed gently. Bosc pears will remain very firm, but will get sweeter. Should be crisp like an apple.	Refrigerate when ripe.

Fruit	Look For	Storage	Will Keep
Persimmons (Hachiya)	Hachiya variety is shaped like an acorn—about the size of a peach. Look for hard or soft, plump, bright red-orange fruit.	If not soft when purchased, ripen at room temperature, which can take 5–10 days. This persimmon will ripen to a firmness suitable for slicing or it may be left to ripen to the point of being soft enough to eat with a spoon.	Refrigerate when ripe. Should keep 5–10 days after ripening. If Hachiya persimmons are very ripe and soft, store on a plate covered with plastic wrap until ready to use. They may also be frozen.
Persimmons (Fuyu)	Fuyu variety is round but slightly flat, about the size of a small tomato. Look for bright-orange color. Buy hard to firm fruit—it can be ripe when very firm.	Ripen at room temperature. Difficult to tell if ripe without cutting and tasting. Ripe fruit will be firm to the touch, crisp to the bite, mild and sweet.	Refrigerate on a plate (not in a plastic bag) when ripe. Will keep 3–5 days or more after ripening. May also be frozen.
Pineapples	Large, heavy fruit with an outside that is colored yellow to golden orange. Avoid discolored leaves, soft spots. Will not get better if purchased unripe.	Refrigerate—*not* in a plastic bag.	3–5 days refrigerated.
Plums	Plump well-colored fruit that yields slightly when squeezed gently. Avoid soft spots, splits, and discolorations.	If hard, ripen 2–3 days at room temperature. Refrigerate ripe fruit in a plastic bag.	3–5 days refrigerated after ripening.
Raspberries	Firm, plump, bright berries. Turn berry container over; underside should be dry and free of berry stain and any mold.	Same as blackberries.	Use as soon as possible. May keep refrigerated a few days.
Rhubarb	Crisp, firm, and fairly thick stalks, bright pink or pale red or cherry red.	Refrigerate in a plastic bag.	2–3 days.
Strawberries	Brightly colored, plump berries with green stem cap attached. Avoid shriveled ones.	Same as blackberries.	2–3 days refrigerated.

Index

A NOTE ABOUT THE AUTHOR

Marion Cunningham was born in Southern California and now lives in Walnut Creek. She was responsible for the complete revision of *The Fannie Farmer Cookbook* and is the author of *The Fannie Farmer Baking Book, The Breakfast Book, The Supper Book,* and *Cooking with Children.* She travels frequently throughout the country giving cooking demonstrations, has contributed articles to *Bon Appétit, Food & Wine,* and *Gourmet,* and writes a column for the *San Francisco Chronicle* and the *Los Angeles Times.* She has also been a consultant to a number of well-known West Coast restaurants.

A NOTE ON THE TYPE

This book was set in Minion, a typeface produced by the Adobe Corporation specifically for the Macintosh personal computer, and released in 1990. Designed by Robert Slimbach, Minion combines the classic characteristics of old style faces with the full complement of weights required for modern typesetting.

Composed by North Market Street Graphics,
Lancaster, Pennsylvania

Printed and bound by R. R. Donnelley & Sons,
Willard, Ohio

Designed by Cassandra J. Pappas

Other Useful Equivalents

bread crumbs, 4 sandwich slices
     fresh . . . . 4 ounces = 2 cups, loosely packed
     dry . . . . 4 ounces = ¾ cup
brown sugar . . . . 1 pound = 2⅓ cups
confectioners' sugar . . . . . . 1 pound = 4 cups
egg whites, U.S. large . . . . . 1 = 2 tablespoons
                          8 = 1 cup
egg yolks, U.S. large . . . . . . 1 = 1 tablespoon
                       16 = 1 cup

Fruits, Nuts, and Vegetables

fruits, dried and pitted
     plumped . . . . 1 pound = 2⅔ cups
     cooked and puréed . . . . 1 pound = 2⅓ cups
fruits, fresh, such as apples and pears (3 medium-small)
     raw and sliced . . . . 1 pound = 3 cups
     cooked and chopped . . . . 1 pound = 1⅔ cups
     puréed . . . . 1 pound = 1¼ cups
nuts
     chopped . . . . 4 ounces = ¾ cup
     ground . . . . 4 ounces = 1 cup, loosely packed
carrots and other root vegetables (6 medium)
     sliced . . . . 1 pound = 3 cups
     puréed . . . . 1 pound = 1⅓ cups
onions (3 medium)
     sliced or chopped . . . . 1 pound = 3 cups
potatoes (3 small-medium)
     raw, sliced, or chopped . . . . . 1 pound = 3 cups
spinach and other leafy greens (destemmed)
     cooked and chopped . . . . 1 pound = 1½ cups

Butter, Shortening, Cheese, and Other Solid Fats

Spoons and cups	Sticks	Ounces
1 tablespoon	⅛ stick	½ ounce
2 tablespoons	¼ stick	1 ounce
4 tablespoons (¼ cup)	½ stick	2 ounces
8 tablespoons (½ cup)	1 stick	4 ounces (¼ pound)
16 tablespoons (1 cup)	2 sticks	8 ounces (½ pound)
32 tablespoons (2 cups)	4 sticks	16 ounces (1 pound)